Blessed Souls

The Teachings of Sri Karunamayi

Volume Three

Bhagavati Sri Sri Sri Vijayeswari Devi

Sri Matrudevi Visvashanti Ashram Trust, Inc.
(SMVA Trust, Inc.)
New York, U.S.A.

Published under the auspices of:

SRI MATRUDEVI VISVASHANTI ASHRAM TRUST ®
Penusilakshetram, Nellore Dt., Andhra Pradesh 524342, India.

KARUNAMAYI SHANTI DHAMA ®
14/5, 6th Cross, Ashok Nagar, Banashankari lst Stage,
Bangalore 560050, India. Ph: 650-9588 Fax: 660-0518

SRI MATRUDEVI VISVASHANTI ASHRAM TRUST, INC.®
New York, NY 11372, U.S.A.
Ph: 718 898-2841 Fax: 718 458-8583

KARUNAMAYI VISWASHANTHI FOUNDATION ®
London, England, U.K.
Ph: 181 941-5054 Fax: 181 941-5668

1st Edition: 1000 copies

Printed by: California Wholesale Printers,
San Gabriel, CA 91776
(626) 571-7543

Sri Karunamayi, Bhagavati Sri Sri Sri Vijayeswari Devi is revered as the incarnation of Divine Mother. She was born on Vijaya Dashami in Gudur, Nellore District, Andhra Pradesh, India. Vijaya Dashami is the culmination of the sacred nine day Navaratri celebration honoring the Divine Mother, and commemorates Her victory over the negative forces of the universe. Hence Sri Vijayeswari's name—Goddess of Victory. She is also known as Karunamayi, the Compassionate Mother, or simply and more intimately as Amma, our own beloved mother.

The purpose of Sri Karunamayi's mission is universal peace and the spiritual upliftment of humanity. She offers to lead everyone to higher levels of consciousness through the regular practice of meditation.

ACKNOWLEDGEMENTS

The editors are grateful to Bob Mataloni, without whose tireless efforts to record Amma's talks, these books would not have beeen possible, and to all the transcribers across the length and breadth of the United States who converted these precious recordings into words on paper.

TABLE OF CONTENTS

Forward vii
Introduction viii

Divine Discourses

The Path to Salvation 1
Being Near Mother is True Happiness 21
Purity is the Best Jewel of a Devotee 34
Spread the Fragrance of Peace 74
Drink the Elixir of Rama's Name 103
Come to Mother with Empty Hands 110
Oneness is the Essence of Spirituality 116
God Dwells in the Temple of the Heart 128
Meditation Reshapes Man from Mortality
to Divinity 142
Dharma is the Jewel 170
All Devatas are Within Divine Mother 187
Mother is the Ever-Blooming Flower of
Consciousness 200
Sri Rama's Sacrifice 220
Utilize Your Energy in a Positive Way 233
The Power of the Mantra 250
The Greatness of the Saraswati and
Mrityunjaya Mantras 271
You are the Essence of Brahman! 295

TABLE OF CONTENTS

Divine Mother Lives in Your Heart 299
The Bhagavad Gita—All Paths Lead to the Same Destiny 312
Mother Helps You up the Ladder of Dharma . . . 324
Be Always in Eternal Dharma 332

Appendices

Pronunciation Key 361
Stotra, Sloka and Kirtana 362

FORWARD

Words spoken by the Divine are automatically recorded in the cosmos for eternity. It is said that these words can be heard at any later date by one who rises to the same level of Divinity—that is, a Self-Realized soul can hear them:

Bramhavid Bramhaiva bhavati
"One who knows Brahman becomes Brahman."

It is equally true that everyone cannot rise to that level, but they have the desire to read those divine words or hear that divine voice. For this they have to rely on books or audio and video cassettes. Some devotees have worked with dedication to provide the former for the benefit of all readers, and have approached me for this forward because of my proximity to Sri Karunamayi Amma.

All Amma's children who have heard Her discourses have been inspired with enthusiasm towards greater spiritual endeavors. May this book help everyone who reads it become worthy of Amma's expectations by making them exemplary in their behavior in cultured society, leading to universal peace and plenty.

Lokāḥ Samastāḥ Sukhino Bhavantu

Jai Karunamayi!

Vijayeswarananda

Swami Vijayeswarananda
Bangalore, March 14, 2001

INTRODUCTION

Jai Karunamayi! This is Book 3 in a series of discourses given in the United States by Bhagavati Sri Sri Sri Vijayeswari Devi, known as "Karunamayi," or the Compassionate One. In the spring and summer of 1997, Amma or "Mother," as She is known to Her devotees, spent over two months traveling the length and breadth of the country in order to bring love, acceptance, comfort and enlightenment to many thousands of Her "children." Since Amma spoke on fifty-five different occasions, Her 1997 talks have been divided into multiple volumes, of which this is the first.

The beauty of Amma's discourses lies in their universal appeal. They are a wonderful mix of simple wisdom and profound philosophy. We can get what we need at a given moment from these pages, only to find on returning to them later that there are deeper levels to be absorbed. Amma guides us on our individual journeys through Her unconditional love, compassion, personal example and divine message.

Woven throughout this volume are Amma's teachings on such topics as the importance of righteousness, sincere devotion, truth, mental detachment, cosmic love, and meditation. At the request of many of Her children who wish to understand the *Lalita Sahasranama*, the Thousand Names of Lalita Devi, Amma has given several talks on this beautiful hymn of praise, describing its true inner spiritual meaning. She touches on the essence of such texts as the *Bhagavad Gita* and the *Ramayana*. All topics are explained in simple, clear terms with examples from holy persons and scriptures of the world.

Amma continues to spread Her message of universal peace and brotherhood. "The entire cosmos belongs to you," She often repeats. She exhorts us to be open-minded about all religions and holy persons—to receive their blessings and show respect for them. She gently suggests that we give up the "I," "me," and "mine" and enjoy instead the rewards of mental detachment and selfless service within our daily life: "Where there is less self, there only is service, children."

Amma motivates us to strive for purity in thought, word and deed. We should give up the "show devotion," She says. One moment of genuine sincerity and true devotion is all that is needed—not hours of chanting and worship with a dry mind and heart. Amma wants us to elevate ourselves. "Do not walk on the muddy path of worldliness, always walk on the path of rose petals," She tells us gently.

How can we reach these goals in this lifetime? By going on an inward journey through meditation to find the Self. Seekers at all stages of the spiritual journey can find many practical suggestions on how to improve and enhance their lives. Amma emphasizes that we can find truth only through inner experience—knowledge derived from the practice of meditation, which cannot be found in books and talks.

We can learn much from Amma's personal example. She gives us hope and self-confidence, always emphasizing only the positive while explaining with great love and compassion that harboring negativities or indulging in wrong actions is damaging to us. "If you make one thousand mistakes also, Divine Mother will forgive you," She often says tenderly. "Divine Mother is tender—beyond tender—softer than butter."

Amma is the embodiment of unconditional love. She makes us aware of how deeply She cares for us, and yet leaves us free to think for ourselves and use our own judgement in all matters. "You have wisdom," She tells us. Now, we know that often we act in unwise ways, but She instills in us the confidence to think for ourselves. Amma can see the purity of our heart buried deep under the dust of our *samskaras*, deeds from previous births. She wants us to realize our true selves: "You yourself are truth, you yourself are wisdom, you yourself are knowledge." When we make mistakes in our day-to-day lives, as is only human, Amma's words give us the positive reinforcement to realize our mistakes and try once again.

Being on this journey with Amma has been like peeling the layers of the onion—every year we come to a deeper, more subtle level of understanding within. We, along with all Her children, are indeed blessed beyond words to have been chosen by Amma as Her very own "babies," infants surrendered to the Divine Mother so that She may lead us onward in this exciting quest for the Self. We hope and pray that the wisdom, knowledge and solace within these pages, given to all freely, gently and most lovingly by Amma with no strings attached, will help you, as it has helped us, on the path to peace, love and Liberation.

We surrender ourselves totally at the lotus feet of that Divine Mother, without whose wish neither an ant nor Brahma can stir,

Geeta

On behalf of all of Amma's blessed children who had the honor and Grace to work on this project.

The Teachings of Sri Karunamayi

DIVINE DISCOURSES

Blessed Souls - Volume 3

ॐ

THE PATH TO SALVATION

Ātmā tvam Girijā matiḥ sahacarāḥ
Prāṇāḥ śarīram gṛham
Pūjā te viṣayopa bhoga racanā
Nidrā samādhi sthitiḥ
Sañcāraḥ padayoḥ pradakṣiṇā vidhiḥ
Stotrāṇi sarvā giro
Yadyat karma karōmi
Tat tad akhilam
Śambho tavārādhanam

Blessed Divine Souls!

Amma conveys Her love to you as your very own birth mother. Today I wish to talk about the *Lalita Sahasranama*. Even Adisesha, the divine serpent with two thousand tongues, cannot describe the names in the *Lalita Sahasranama*. The four-faced Brahma does not know about the *Lalita Sahasranama*, and the five-faced Parameshwara also cannot describe this divine *stotra*. It is only Lalita Devi Herself who can understand the *Lalita Sahasranama*. It is very difficult for anyone to understand this extraordinary Truth, which is beyond the *Vedas*.

Therefore, let us pray to Divine Mother with great devotion, because Divine Mother is Bhakti vashya—She who is captured by pure devotion—and ask Her to illuminate the throne of our heart. Let us make this body Her shrine and pray that all the flowers bloom within so that we may attain the wealth of the exquisite knowledge of the Self. Mother is described as Chaitanya kusumaradhya —She who loves to be worshipped with the flowers of

Divine Consciousness. She is Chaitanya kusuma priya —She who is pleased by the offering of the *atma*, our own soul, as the flower of worship. Let us pray to Her to make the flower of *atma jnana,* that unique knowledge of the soul, bloom in our hearts, and let us begin our discussion of the *Lalita Sahasranama.*

Sudhā sindhor madhye sura viṭapi vāṭī parivṛte
Maṇidwīpe nīpopavana vati cintāmaṇi gṛhe
Śivākāre mañce Parama Śiva paryanka nilayām
Bhajanti tvām dhanyāḥ katicana cidānanda laharīm

Devi resides in Manidwipa which is surrounded by the *kshira sagara,* the ocean of milk. She is lying on a couch that is really Lord Parameshwara. She is the Mother of the Trinity—Brahma, Vishnu and Maheshwara. It is said in one song,

Brahmānanda maya Maṇidwipa vāsinī
Bindu trikoṇa Sri Cakra sancāriṇī
Brahma dhyāna sukham dehi dehi Manonmanī

Devi resides in Manidwipa which is full of the bliss of Brahman. Starting from the *trikona bindu sthana*, the dot in the center of the innermost triangle of the *Sri Chakra,* She travels through every level of the *Sri Chakra.* She is Antarmukha samaradhya and also Bahir mukha sudurlabha. She can be understood easily when one becomes inward and prays to Her internally. It is difficult to understand Her solely by performing external worship. Whoever turns his mind inward and worships Devi sincerely will be graced with *Brahma dhyana sukham,* the bliss of meditation. This is the blessing of Divine Mother, who resides in the *bindu sthana* in the center of the *Sri Chakra.* This is not ordinary happiness but supreme bliss, *Brahma jnana sukham,* which is attained through the permanent knowledge of *Brahman.* The chanting of *Sri Lalita Sahasranama*, as well as meditation, *mantra japa* and *puja,* are the various paths leading to the achievement of such bliss.

Let me pose a question to you here: How is Lalita Devi seated on the throne? All of you present here, meditate on Lalita Devi. What is the significance of Her posture? Why is Her left leg folded while the right one rests on the floor? Every God and Goddess is shown seated in a particular posture that has much significance. For example, Ayyappa Swami is in one posture, Narasimha Swami is in another, while Lakshmi Devi is always shown in *padmasana,* and so on. What is the significance of the posture in which Lalita Devi is portrayed? Her posture is entirely different from those of other Goddesses. As we are entering into the kingdom of *Sri Lalita Sahasranama*, we must first understand the significance of the posture of Lalita Parameshwari. It is also mentioned in the *Vedas* that there is no need for Mother to give Her blessings with the *abhaya mudra.* Simply praying to Her lotus feet is enough.

Swamiji: One of the main differences that we find between Lalita Parameshwari and other Goddesses is that when we see the Goddesses Lakshmi, Saraswati, Gayatri, or any other form of female divinity, we find that the left leg rests on the ground, and the right one is folded. That is their posture. However, when we observe Lalita Parameshwari, we clearly see the right leg resting on the floor, with the left leg folded. When we look at pictures, though, we find some artists making mistakes. Many artists just look at the position in which Lakshmi Devi is seated and mistakenly portray the same for Lalita Parameshwari. Amma has explained this recently in the *ashram* in India also. If you observe Lord Siva when depicted in human form, He is shown with the right foot on the floor and the left leg folded. Likewise, we see the same in portrayals of Maha Vishnu and other Gods.

However, among the female deities it is only Lalita Parameshwari who has this posture. Actually, when we observe ordinary families, we find that men are often more dominating than women. The *shastras* have praised Lalita Parameshwari as

Brahmādi pipilakanta Jananī

"She is the Mother of the Creator, Brahma, as well as the tiny ant." In other words, She is the Universal Empress who controls the whole universe. She is the primal basic Energy of the entire cosmos. That is why She alone can sit in that posture, with the right foot down and the left leg folded. That is the main difference between the posture of Lalita Devi and those of other Goddesses.

Amma:

Dhyāyet padmāsanasthām vikasita vadanām
Padma patrāyat ākṣīm

Dhyayet—meditate! And how do you meditate? Open the lotus of your heart with devotion, fill your heart with that extraordinary Divine Consciousness, and meditate in the lotus posture.

Hemābhām pīta vastrām karakalita lasad
Hema padmām varāngīm
Sarvālankāra yuktām satatam abhayadām
Bhaktanamrām Bhavānīm

Let us take the word, "*pitavastram*" here.

Lakṣmīm hiraṇya varṇām hariṇīm
Suvarṇa rajata srajām

Divine Mother's true form is pure Consciousness filled with the brilliance of extraordinary golden rays. Mother Divine does not need the ordinary earthly clothes that we wear—She wears divine raiment. Anyone who meditates on the form of Mother, who wears divine garments, and who illuminates millions of universes, will have a face glowing with joy and bliss. A face that blooms like a beautiful flower shows the presence of *Brahmananda sukham*—the blissful state of *Brahmic* Consciousness. We smile when we are at peace. When we are worried, it shows on our face. There is no peace, and the face wilts. When there are waves of peace, contentment, equanimity, and *atma jnana* resulting from meditation, the face of the *sadhaka* blooms and glows more brightly than a lotus, even brighter than the sun, with the bliss of *Brahmananda.* Therefore, in the opening prayer of the *Lalita Sahasranama*, you see this word, *dhyayet,* which means, "meditate!"

The literal meaning of this prayer is that Divine Mother is seated in *padmasana* in meditation. She has a radiant face and She gives *Brahmananda* to Her devotees. However, considered from a yogic viewpoint, the whole meaning changes. This prayer tells the meditator how to meditate: "Be seated in *padmasana* and meditate." What happens when you sit in the lotus posture? All the seventy-two thousand *nadis* in the subtle body are stimulated. The seven main *chakras,* the centers of conscious energies, blossom. The energy in the *chakras*, which are aligned in the subtle *yogic* body, will become concentrated and will no longer be scattered. Eventually, the meditator will attain *Brahmananda* and will have a glowing, radiant face. The literal meaning describes Jagat Janani as very beautiful with a smiling countenance. Spiritually, it means that you, the meditator, are getting that *vikasita vadana,* a glowing face, as a result of experiencing *Brahmananda* and attaining a state of peace. This is how we open the gates of *Sri Lalita Sahasranama.* Why is Mother sitting like this, and why are we praying in this manner?

Sindūrāruṇa vigrahām trinayanām
Māṇikya maulī sphurat
Tārānāyaka śekharām smita mukhīm
Āpīna vakṣoruhām
Pāṇibhyām alipūrṇa ratna caṣakam
Raktotpalam bibhratīm
Saumyām ratna ghaṭastha rakta caraṇām
Dhyāyet Parām Ambikām

The *devatas*, Brahma, Vishnu and Maheshwara have meditated on that Divine Mother who is without any bondages, who belongs to *Paraloka*, the supreme world, who illuminates the entire universe by the brilliance of Her lotus feet. She is the Mother of the *Vedas*, of Brahma, as well as all the three billion *devatas*. She is the Mother of everyone. That is why the devotee, with great humility, prays to those divine lotus feet, surrenders himself and asks, "Mother grant me the wealth of *atma jnana,* true knowledge. Remove the darkness of ignorance in me."

It is only as a consequence of meritorious *samskaras* accumulated through innumerable births that one meditates on the *Lalita Sahasranama*. That is why we first say, "I am meditating on the Divine Mother who abides in Manidwipa, shines gloriously in the middle of the ocean of nectar, and whose throne is Parameshwara. Meditation on the Divine Mother will destroy the darkness of ignorance which has surrounded me through innumerable births, and thus I am blessed."

Bhajanti tvām dhanyāḥ

"The one whose merits from innumerable births have borne fruit and who meditates on You is blessed, Mother. There is nobody more blessed than he." Therefore, the devotee praises Her thus:

Hé Iśwarī brahmāṇḍa Bhāṇḍodarī
Kānti dhūta japāvalī
Akhilaṇḍa koṭi brahmāṇḍa nāyakī
Koṭi koṭi yoginī gaṇa sevitā

Mother is Stotra priya. When we recite Mother's *stotras,* hymns praising Mother, She becomes very happy.

Nāma sāhasra pāṭhaś ca yathā carama janmani
Tathaiva viralo loke Srī Vidyācāra vedinaḥ

"The one for whom the present birth is the last and who is not going to get further entangled in the wheel of birth and death, such a one alone will be able to meditate on Devi." This is a true statement from the *Vedas*. Devi is:

Janana maraṇa bhava nāśinī

"She destroys birth, death, and *bhava,* worldly life." She is

Janma mṛtyu jarā tapta jana viśranti sthāna

"She removes the fear of birth, death, disease, and old age and takes one to a restful state of higher consciousness."

So we are able to chant this sacred *stotra,* the *Lalita Sahasranama,* only as the fruit of the merits accumulated from performing worship in millions of births. When we meditate on Divine Mother, She bestows on us *Brahma vidya,* the complete, pure knowledge of *Brahman* and *atman,* as a fruit of our meditation, and fills the vessel of our heart with *Brahmananda.*

If you were to ask, "What will I get if I pray to Lalita Devi," the answer would be, "Praying to Lakshmi brings you wealth. Chanting the *Mrityunjaya mantra* removes ill health and confers good health. Meditating on Saraswati Devi blesses you with a good education and knowledge.

What do you get by meditating on Lalita Devi? She grants *moksha*, salvation or liberation."

Devi is seated on Her glorious divine throne in Manidwipa. There are innumerable universes in the millions of galaxies. In each *brahmanda* or universe there is a Brahma, Vishnu and Ishwara. Thus, Devi is Pancha kritya parayana. She is eternally performing the five activities—*srishti* (creation), *sthiti* (maintenance), *laya* (re-absorption), *nigraha* (casting of illusion) and *anugraha* (grace)—in millions of *brahmandas,* or universes.

One day when all the *devas*, multitudes of *rishis* like Valmiki, and *siddhas* like Kapila were seated together, along with millions of humans, Jagat Janani, creator of the world, wanted to give them *darshan.* Eight *devatas* were instantly born from Jagat Janani, four to Her left and four to Her right. They were the *Vagdevatas*, Goddesses of Speech, such as Vasini, and others. These *Vagdevatas,* who surpassed even Saraswati Devi in wealth of speech, had inward minds, and shone brilliantly with a unique luminescence. They came and sat at Mother's lotus feet with their eyes closed and palms folded. Mother then transmitted *shakti* to them. With that *shakti* they recited a small *stotra* extemporaneously, which contained the essence of all the *Vedas*, *Upanishads* and all religions!

Take the example of the *Vishnu Sahasranama*. You all know that Pitamah Bhishmacharya recited the *Vishnu Sahasranama* on the battlefield of Kurukshetra. This was a *prasada* given by Lord Krishna to Bhishma, which we heard through his voice. In this way, we have obtained each *Sahasranama* from some individual. But when we ask from whom the *Lalita Sahasranama* came, it can be stated that it did not come from this Earth. Valmiki did not write it, nor did Vyasa Maharshi. They are not the composers of this *Sahasranama*, nor is Parameshwara. By giving this extraordinary *shakti* to the divine energies born from Her own form, Jagat Janani gave them the power of *ashu kavitvam,* extempore poetry, through the different aspects of speech —*para vak*, *pashyanti*, *madhyama* and *vaikhari*.

If you were to say to Mother, "I do not know anything, Mother," by Her mere touch She could transmit energy to you, and then you too would be able to recite extempore poetry, and chant the *Vedas*. However, it would not be you chanting, but Mother, in the *rupa,* form, of *para vak, pashyanti, madhyama* and *vaikhari.* Is it possible to remember everything that I have said and repeat it as it is? I am speaking continuously without any breaks—have you noticed? My son here is translating. However, Amma is sitting in him and talking to you through him. That is wonderful! That is the power of Mother and Her play. That is why, by transferring that extraordinary *shakti* of Hers to the *Vasinyadi Vagdevatas*, She has revealed the secrets of *yoga* in the form of the *Lalita Sahasranama* and sent it down to us as a blessing from Manidwipa.

When Ravana kidnapped Sita and was flying in the *pushpaka vimana,* Sita removed Her jewels and threw them on the ground from the sky for the *vanaras*. Similarly, a large bag full of jewels and diamonds has descended for you from Manidwipa. From that bag of treasure you have taken one jewel, and looked in wonder and amazement at its beauty. That jewel is the *Lalita Sahasranama*. Adorn yourself with that priceless gem of devotion. Open the bag, examine all the other gems as well, realize their value, and adorn yourself with them.

The first *nama* from *Sri Lalita Sahasranama* that we are going to discuss today is Sri Mata. In Sanskrit the word *mata* means, "mother." In Telugu it is *thalli*. The true meaning of *mata* or its equivalent is "the first one." In Sanskrit, they call it *Adi* or *Arya*. *Adi* is the beginning. That means it is the first one. She is the Arya Devi. In Telugu it is *mula thalli. Mula* means the eternal beginning or origin, the root. This means that She is the Mother of all the *devatas* and lesser *devatas*—the Mother of all beings. Lalita Devi is also the Mother of the three Mothers:

Gāyatrī Vāṇī Saraswatī sannutāyai namo namaḥ

Gayatri Devi Herself prays to Lalita Devi. So, does Lalita Devi have a Mother? No, there is no mother for Lalita Devi. However, Lalita Devi is the mother of everyone. So,

Vāṇi Ramā sevitā
Vande Mātaram Ambikā Bhagavatīm
Vāṇi Ramā sevitā

"When all mankind is meditating on Vani and Rama, Saraswati and Lakshmi, they are meditating on Ambika Bhagavati." So it gets confusing here. Who is this Ambika? Is She the wife of Ishwara? No, She is not. It is said that She is the mother of Ishwara. But isn't Parvati the mother of Ishwara? We also say that Parvati is Ishwara's wife. However, Ambika is the mother of even Parvati Devi, Lakshmi, Saraswati and Gayatri.

Kataksha kinkari bhuta kamala koti sevita: *Kamala koti* means that Divine Mother, who is the embodiment of compassion, is worshipped by millions of Lakshmis. This appears to be puzzling, but this is not a question being posed just today. This question has been troubling even the *rishis* since the beginning of creation. When the *rishis* were meditating in the Naimisharanya Forest one evening, all of those who were gathered there posed a question to one of the *rishis*, "Whom do you worship?"

The *rishi* replied, "I do *upasana* or worship to the Sun God."

"Oh, is that so? Are you meditating on him for good health?"

Worshipping the Sun God is very good and beneficial to health, and also confers *jnana*, knowledge. The Sun is the secret behind the power of Gayatri, who is worshipped as Bala Gayatri at dawn, as the great *Shakti* Maheshwari at noon, and as Vaishnavi at dusk. *Aditya Hridayam* is a *stotra* in praise of the Sun God. Chanting the *Aditya Hridayam* bestows unique power on one who chants it.

The *rishi* had a doubt whether the worship that he was performing was right, and whether he was on the correct path. For some say that Ishwara should be meditated upon, and others say that Kameshwara is Brahma *Vidya swarupa,* the embodiment of true Knowledge, but we know that there is a power even beyond Kameshwara, and therefore the doubt arises.

Brahmādi pipīlakānta Jananī

Then again some say that if we worship Brahma, all our desires will be fulfilled. Well, there is a power even beyond Brahma and that is the Mother of Brahma. Maybe we should worship Narayana, but Karanguli nakhotpanna Narayana dashakritih. In all the *yugas,* the *dashavataras,* or the ten incarnations of Narayana, have come from the fingernails of Devi.

So what should we do? To whom should we surrender? Should we worship Kartikeya or Adideva Ganesha? The *rishis* continued to question. Finally, they concluded that the One who rules the entire universe, the Creator of all the universes, the lovely Arya Devi, the embodiment of exquisite beauty, who is playful and sportive, with a gentle heart softer than butter, extremely loving and of the form of *amrita,* nectar, is the Divine Mother. She is the Truth hidden behind the eye of ignorance, in the third eye of every *jiva* or being. The final conclusion reached by the *rishis* was that the sooner one realizes that it is the destiny of every *jiva* in this creation to realize this Truth, the quicker will one attain salvation.

No matter whom we worship, that particular deity has an office or position, so to speak. In any office, there are several people with different posts. Brahma has the post of creator, Vishnu, of preserver, and Maheshwara, of destroyer. Agni and fire perform their own functions. There is a nuclear power that controls the *pancha krityas—srishti* (creation), *sthiti* (maintenance), *laya* (re-absorption), *nigraha* (casting of illusion) and *anugraha* (grace). That power is called Arya Devi, *tholi thalli,* the first Mother in Telugu, and *Adi Maha Shakti,* the Great Primal Energy.

What is the form of this great primal Energy? It is the root of all the energies present in this world. As an example, imagine an enormous ball of blazing fire, from which are splattering countless diamond-like sparks. These sparks are millions of suns, moons, stars, and planets such as Venus, Earth, Jupiter and Pluto. Rahu and Ketu are sub-planets that move in a different way. Trillions of suns are emitted from this immense ball of fire like diamonds. Imagine the source of such Energy! Do you understand this point? If you understand it, you have understood Lalita Devi, who is the source of love, the source of nectar, the source of all the energies in the universe.

Millions of universes are nothing but sparks flying about like dust particles from that source of great Energy. When we think of this Maha Shakti as the Mother, this *nirakara* or formless Shakti becomes *sakara*, with form. When did She take form? On *Vijayadashami,* the tenth day following *Navaratri,* Devi manifested from the *agni kunda,* the fire-pit, with *tri netra,* three eyes, and four arms holding the *pasha, ankusha, ikshu kodanda*, and *pancha banas*—the noose, goad, sugarcane bow and five arrows. She appeared from the *Sri Chakra* that manifested from the *homa* fire. Thus, Divine Mother's appearance was witnessed by all the *rishis* and *devatas* and they exclaimed, "Sri Mata!"

The word *Sri* means auspicious and therefore, all the *rishis* addressed Her as Sri Mata, Amma, Devi, and so on. When you feel hungry, whom do you approach? You go to your Mother and say, "Amma, please give me food, I am hungry." A child plays all kinds of games with his mother and even sulks at her. A mother tolerates all these games—after all, she has borne the child in her womb for nine months, given her flesh and blood, and protected her child. Therefore, we say, Kataksha kinkari bhuta Kamala koti sevita. For She gives birth to countless *jagats,* worlds. Just as a mother bears a child for nine months and then gives birth, Brahmanda Janani gives birth to millions of universes from Her womb. She is also called:

Dīna hṛdaya sandāyinī

Here the word *dina* does not mean a poor person, or an orphan. It refers to the Mother as One who alleviates the pain of all those who feel pain in their hearts. Since She relieves their suffering, She is called "Mother." She creates and gives birth, feeds those who are hungry, loves, tolerates, plays with Her children and blesses them. Not only does She do all this, She also gives *moksha*, salvation.

Whose Mother is She?

Brahmādi pipīlakānta Jananī

"She is the Mother of Brahma, as well as the Mother of the tiny ant." She is not partial, and does not discriminate between the two. She is the same to both. She is also the Mother of Siva, Keshava and others. She is the Mother of everyone, but there is no Mother for Her. Such a Devi is called Arya Devi, Sri Mata, and Lalita Bhagavati by the *Vedas* and *Dharma Sutra.* She is Vedatita, beyond the *Vedas*. The *Shrutis, Agama, Nigama* and *Dharma Shastras* have extolled Her as Vedatita, Sarvatita, Jnanatita, Gunatita, Uhatita and Lokatita. That is to say, She is beyond imagination and cannot be understood through knowledge, but only through experience. She is beyond this world and cannot be grasped by the *Vedas*. She is beyond everything, She is without attributes, She is Jagat Janani, and is therefore praised as Sri Mata. How can we possibly comprehend Her?

There are sixteen divisions in *Sri Lalita Sahasranama.* It is only after we have matured through many births—in our minds, intellect, inclinations and tendencies—that we understand why we are reading the *Lalita Sahasranama.* In the first division, starting with Sri Mata, Sri Maharajni, Srimat Simhasaneshwari, She is described from Her toes to the crown of Her head as an inexpressibly beautiful form of Mother. We can see the whole cosmos in Her form. Once you have the vision of Her lotus face, there is no need to worship the nine planets. When you meditate on Mother, you will find all the nine planets in Her face.

She is Siva Shaktaikya svarupini. She has the *surya netram, chandra netram,* and the *agni netram*—the sun, moon and fire—as Her eyes. Then you have air. Brahma and the other *devatas* are all in Mother's throat. In the glowing mark of *kumkum* that Mother has adorned Her forehead, Brahma is present somewhere as a tiny, subtle atom.

Her hair is decorated with the *Vedas*. She is called Vamakeshi. When She loosens Her braid and shakes Her hair, all the four *Vedas* can be heard, for the *Vedas* decorate Her braid like stars. Millions of *brahmandas*, universes, are revolving under Mother's lotus feet. Her divine form resides in a state of liberation beyond these millions of universes in indivisible silence. When one meditates on such a form, one matures tremendously.

As an example, let me talk about my daughter in Vijayawada who is extremely good-natured. She used to perform a lot of worship. However, she also had a great deal of anger. She told Mother that she was worshipping Devi, and also that she had a lot of anger inside. She would shout, and everybody, including her husband, would be afraid of her bad temper. I observed her for a long time, and finally one day when nobody was around, I told her that one who worships Divine Mother should never get angry. I informed her that she was treating her husband in a very demeaning manner in front of everybody, which was reducing his self respect. If she did not respect her husband, no one else would. Whenever she raised her voice in anger, he would think that Devi had come on her. Also, she would wear a large *bindi*, the dot on the forehead, which made her look even more fiercc.

In the *Lalita Sahasranama*, one of the names of Devi is Krodhakar ankushojjvala—Devi controls the anger in the one who meditates on Her. She uses Her weapon called the *ankusha,* which is symbolic of *jnana*, knowledge. It is a pointed instrument used by the elephant-keeper to control the animal. When the keeper pricks the elephant with his goad, the huge and mighty elephant comes under his control. The weapons are held in Devi's hands for a reason. The ego in us that we have carried from many births is like a huge elephant, which is controlled by Her *ankusha*. Therefore, even after meditating for so many years, if you vent your temper at your own family members, how can others respect them? When I told her this, she understood my point very well. She gradually reduced her temper and attained a peaceful countenance after some time.

This example is not a laughing matter, since many of us behave in this crazy manner thinking that Devi has come on us. When we behave in this way, we demean those on whom we vent our anger, and weaken their character. To respect a human being and see divinity in everyone is the foundation of Indian culture. Our culture teaches us to see divinity in humans, in animals, in mud, in air, and in all the five elements. When all these five elements are present in the human body, it is not good to lower the status of human beings by not seeing divinity in them.

When I observed her weakness, I could not talk to her about it in front of other people, because we are all sentimental and very sensitive. It was only after many days when I got an opportunity to find her alone, that I told her personally, "Your husband is very nice." And she said, "Yes, he is very nice." Then I told her, "See how you are lowering his self esteem in front of everybody by behaving as if Devi has come on you? Wearing that huge dot on your forehead only makes you look ugly." A husband is your companion, bestowed on you by God because you cannot walk alone. Similarly, a wife is a companion bestowed on the husband by God because he cannot walk alone. You are both each other's strength. There is a great difference between traveling a path alone and traveling with a companion. God has provided the institution of marriage because you cannot travel alone on the spiritual path. If you could, you would be celibate like Vivekananda or Shankaracharya. Therefore you should not insult your companion. God gives you a husband, God gives you a wife, and God gives you children. If you insult them and speak to them indecently in the name of spirituality, like this lady, it is disgraceful. That is why I told her, "You need to cultivate peace in your personality. You must first of all learn to be calm."

Dhyāyet padmāsanasthām
Vikasita vadanām padma patrāyatākṣīm
Hemābhām pīta vastrām karakalita lasad
Hemapadmām varāngīm
Sarvālankāra yuktām satatam abhayadām
Bhakta namrām Bhavānīm

This *mantra* tells us that Devi becomes a *dasi* to Her *bhaktas,* a serving-maid to Her devotees, and exhibits extreme humility. She is submissive to the love of Her devotees. Like a maidservant who works in your house sincerely, She resides in the heart full of pure devotion. And if you were to fall sick and your family members were asleep, Janani would Herself come and press your feet and take care of you. Such is the Divine Mother whom we call Lalita Devi. Therefore, consider everything you get in this world as Mother's *prasada.* You should feel that your mother, your wife, your children and your friends are all Mother's *prasada.* You should always feel that She has given you very good *prasada.* Instead, although we are devotees, we wrong ourselves.

In the second division, the slaying of Bhandasura is described. The ego called Bhandasura has been ostentatiously displayed in us since millions of births. Sleep, hunger, *tamas* and *rajas* are the qualities of Bhandasura, who has been making millions of *jivas,* souls, fall from dignity and virtue in millions of births. On the day when the devotee meditates on the lotus feet of Divine Mother, who is of the form of *Omkara,* She comes silently into the heart of the meditator: Bhandasura vadhoyukta shakti sena samanvita. With Her *ankusham,* She slays the Bhandasura who resides within. She drives him out permanently with all his qualities of anger, lust, greed and other negativities, and bestows on Her devotee the qualities that lead to *atma jnana.*

The devotee then develops the positive qualities such as *viveka* and *jnana*. She burns his ignorance to ashes and completely destroys his ego. She develops in him a sense of discrimination and awakens knowledge, leading him to liberation. Therefore, when you meditate on Lalita Devi, the ego called Bhandasura is totally destroyed. Mother Herself comes and battles with the demon inside the meditator's heart.

Lalita Devi gave her vision to all the *devatas*, celestial beings, on *Vijayadashami* day. She is born from the *chidagni kunda—agni kunda* is the *homa* fire pit, and *chid* is the brilliant luminescent radiance of Devi—in Her divine form, with four arms, bearing divine weapons. In Her soft, lotus hands She carries the *ankusham* and *pasham*. The *pasham* is a symbol of *anuragam,* which means love, attachment and affection. She throws the weapon of *pasham* and pulls the *jiva* close to Her. She loves all *jivas* and draws them close. If She did not love, how would anyone be able to come close to Her? It is She who pulls us close to Herself with Her love. She shoots the sweet arrows of Her *pancha vanas*, and is the support of the *jiva* in all the joys and sorrows of life. Therefore it is said that salvation comes easily to one who meditates on such an extraordinary Janani, who is the Creator and ruler of millions of universes.

Where *Omkara* took birth, that is Devi. Considering it in numerical order, She is: 1) Omkara svarupini, 2) Ardha narishwara svarupini, Siva Shakti mayi, 3) Trimurti janani, 4) Chaturveda svarupini, Chaturveda mayi, 5) Pancha bhuta mayi—in the five elements, 6) Shad chakra mayi—present in all the six *chakras,* 7) Sapta loka mayi—present in the seven *lokas* and shining in the seven *chakras,* 8) Ashta Lakshmi mayi—one who removes the eight kinds of poverty and bestows *jnana aishwaryam*, *shanti aishwaryam*, *prem aishwaryam*, *bhakti aishwaryam,* and other forms of wealth. She is the one who bestows the state of *atma kaivalyam*, the state of being one with the Absolute, the Supreme Self. 9) Such a Divine Mother is Nava shakti mayi, Nava chakra mayi, Nava bija mayi, Nava raga mayi, Navanita mayi. Therefore, after meditating on such a Mother, who is seated on a throne studded with the nine precious gems in Manidwipa, in the *bindu sthana* in the innermost *trikona,* triangle, in the center of the extraordinary *Sri Chakra,* can one get anger instead of *moksha*, *nanna?*

One uses anger only to scare people. We lower ourselves when we become angry, we lower our *bhakti*. Since we are in *Kali yuga,* we do not have *bhakti* of good quality. We have only one percent devotion. During the time of Thyagaraja, people had ninety-nine percent devotion when songs such as "*Tera tiyaga rada,*" "Remove the curtains of darkness," were composed. They may not have had enough food to eat, but all they craved for was God. These were not songs but their dialogues with God. When Thyagaraja was asked, "What do you want?" He simply queried in reply:

Nidhi chālā sukhamā Rāma
Ni sannidhi sukhamā

"Does wealth give one happiness or does Rama's nearness give true happiness?" This is one hundred percent high quality *bhakti,* full of radiance.

In this day and age, we have only one percent *bhakti* and ninety-nine point nine percent materialism. We think this is good, but truly speaking we have not developed good qualities. It is only the *Lalita Sahasranama stotra, puja* and meditation on the divine lotus feet of Devi that will develop true *bhakti* in us.

Upon meditating on Divine Mother, She could grant *moksha* to Brahma Himself. She is the Mother who can fill our hearts with light, and drive the demon called Bhandasura from every dark nook and corner of our hearts—drive him out completely and permanently from our lives. We do not need anger, lust, greed, arrogance, ignorance and ego. The Divine Mother, Janani Lalita Devi, who is Omkara rupini, can destroy all these negative qualities and fill our hearts with radiant *atma jnana.* She can bestow on us extraordinary inner freedom, spirituality, true devotion, *Maha vidya*, *Brahma vidya* and *Brahmananda sukham.*

Hari Om Tat Sat

Dallas *7 April 1997*

ॐ

BEING NEAR MOTHER IS TRUE HAPPINESS

[The following discourse has been translated from Telugu.]

Embodiments of Divine Souls, Amma's Most Beloved Children,

Divine Mother is *Om. Om* is the primal sound and the all-encompassing syllable. How else can we describe Her? She is the Chaturveda, the four *Vedas*. She is Pancha bhuta mayi, the five elements. She is Shat chakra mayi, the six *chakras*. She is also in the *sapta rishis*, the seven *rishis*. She is Ashta aishvarya mayi. *Aishvarya* is wealth—not only material wealth, but also spiritual wealth. She gives us both. *Mayi* means pervading. That is the best way to describe Her. She is Nava shakti mayi, the nine *shaktis*. She is also Nava bija mayi. *Bija* means seed.

So, when will She give bliss and *atma jnana?* When we have a hundred percent devotion. And that devotion must have absolute purity. This being the *Kali yuga,* we probably have about one percent true devotion; we are missing ninety-nine percent, barring a few exceptions. Amma gave the example of Thyagaraja yesterday. He wrote a beautiful lyric in Telugu which says: "Remove all these curtains." *Tera* is the curtain. "Please remove this whole drama." This is the literal meaning. He first asks: *"Nidhi sukhama?" Nidhi* is material wealth. "Does material wealth give happiness?" Then he answers: *"Sannidhi sukhama." Sannidhi* means nearness, being near You. "Being near You is true happiness." This is hard to translate because one has to understand and appreciate Telugu.

Thyagaraja is a very good example of pure devotion. We must develop that kind of devotion, although we are living in *Kali yuga.* Lalita Maha Devi gave salvation to Brahma, so She can definitely give us all salvation. And when we pray to Her, She will bestow *Brahmananda,* supreme bliss, on all of us.

The fourth division of the *Lalita Sahasranama Stotra* is about the *Sri Chakra.* As many of you know, the *Sri Chakra* is the diagrammatic representation of the Supreme One, and is described in this division. In the *Sri Chakra varnana, Brahma vidya* is described. *Vidya* is knowledge and *Brahma Vidya* is the attainment of the knowledge of the Supreme *Brahman,* and *trikala jnana. Tri* is three, *kala* is time—the present, past and future. It gives us the knowledge of all three.

Amma gives us a beautiful example of how great the *Lalita Maha Devi Stotra* is. At one time Vyasa Maharshi, or Sage Vyasa, was meditating in the Himalayas after he had written some of the greatest of all the holy texts. He wrote the *ashta dasha Puranas,* the eighteen *Puranas.* Not only did he write the *Puranas,* which are great volumes, but he also wrote the *Upapuranas,* or minor *Puranas.* Amma is asking us: "The *Mahabharata* is a great classic. Do you remember how many verses there are in the *Mahabharata?* Can anyone guess?"

["One hundred thousand" is one answer.]

The *Mahabharata* has one hundred thousand, a little over a hundred thousand verses. The reason it is called the *Mahabharata* is that it is the greatest text. *Maha* means supreme or great. Of course, Vyasa also wrote the *Bhagavad Gita,* as many of us know, and he wrote the *bhashya* or commentary on the *Brahma Sutras.* The *Gita* is a part of the *Mahabharata.*

But having achieved all these wonderful things, Vyasa Mahamuni was still not quite content, as he was not at peace with himself. So while he was thinking about it, and while Lord Ganesha, who was his helper, was with him, Sage Narada walks up to him. And Vyasa Mahamuni asks Narada, "Why do I lack peace of mind, having written all these books? What is the matter?"

Sage Narada meditates for a while and he tells Vyasa Mahamuni, "Please pray to Divine Mother, who is the ultimate *Brahman,* and ask Her how you can remove your restlessness and be peaceful within." So when he prays to the Supreme Divine Mother, Mother appears before him. In what form? In the greatest of all forms—the illuminated *Sri Chakra!* And you must have seen the triangle or *trikona* in the *Sri Chakra. Tri* is three, and *kona* means angle. In this *trikona,* Lalita Maha Devi is sitting, *asina,* in a beautiful posture, and She blesses Vyasa Mahamuni, telling him to write the *Devi Bhagavatam.* It is a very famous classic.

Amma also said something very interesting at the end of Her Telugu discourse. The epic *Ramayana* is about the *kutumba* or family. It teaches us how to keep the family together and make it prosper and grow in *dharma.* It illustrates ideal relationships between husband and wife, father and son, between brothers, and the perfect attitude of the servant towards his master, so beautifully depicted in the character of Hanumana. It is an incredible story about family life. When you read the *Ramayana,* you can learn everything about ideal family relationships.

Amma says that the *Mahabharata* talks about *samaja* or *sangha dharma.* In other words, correct attitudes and behavior in social life. How should we live in society? What are the conflicts that generally occur? The *Mahabharata* is a classic, because in it we see every kind of situation. In Andhra, whenever there is a small fight in the house, we say, "A *Mahabharata* is going on." [Laughter] We can see almost every human frailty of society in the *Mahabharata,* and how it is resolved. It is amazing how Lord Krishna, in one sense, as Amma explained the other day, seems to be helping one person, and appears to be hurting another, as though playing a game of chess. Actually we can see every one of the things He does happen in our daily life. So the *Mahabharata* is about *samaja dharma* or *sangha dharma.*

If we look at all the great *maha rishis,* who gave us the scriptures and other holy writings, we can basically categorize them into two types. They are all wonderful children of the same Divine Mother, but we can see a distinct pattern. Some, like Vyasa Mahamuni, are more father-loving, with a tendency to be drawn towards the male way of thinking. We can observe this in the *Mahabharata.* As you know, some children, when they can't get something from their father, go to their mother. And usually the mother gives them what they want, whereas the father does not.

Then there are the mother-loving ones, such as Valmiki, as we see in the *Ramayana.* So are Gautama, who did the greatest meditation on Gayatri, Vishwamitra and Kanva. Amma told us a story yesterday which is absolutely wonderful.

Valmiki prayed and prayed to the Divine Mother for a very long time, and Sitamma [respectful name for Sita] spent fourteen years with Valmiki. The usual interpretation is that, due to public censure, Sita had to go to the forest. But before Sita came to his *ashram*, Valmiki found out that Sita Devi was in the forest, and he apparently came to Her and said, "Please come and live in my *ashram.*"

Sitamma told him, "Your reputation may be spoiled."

But Valmiki answered, "I have been praying to You for billions and billions of years, so please come and stay with me."

Amma says that those of you who have read the *Valmiki Ramayana* will know that Valmiki's most beautiful descriptions, poetic or devotional, are about Sita Devi. Those of us with male tendencies sometimes get more drawn by the pure righteousness of Sri Rama, and somehow miss the delicate feeling of Mother's love. If you study the *Ramayana,* you can see this clearly. The *Mahabharata* has a masculine quality, whereas in the *Ramayana,* there is *mridutva,* or soft tenderness, the feminine quality.

In the *shlokas* in which Lalita Maha Devi is described, all the way from the *Sri pada,* Her lotus feet, to the *Sri Chakra,* at the crown of the head, She is described as Marali manda gamana. The literal meaning of Marali manda gamana: *marali* is a *raja hamsa,* a royal female swan; *manda* means slow and graceful, *gamana* is walking. So *marali manda gamana* means that She moves very gently and gracefully. There is a wonderful spiritual meaning in these words. This *marali manda gamana* is our life. We should lead this life like a *raja hamsa,* a royal swan, not like a crow. When we observe the life of a crow, we know that is not the kind of life we should lead. So when we say *manda gamana,* it indicates the kind of life we should lead.

Śuddha paramahamsa āśram gītam

Amma is quoting from a very famous *kirtana* that some of us know—*Pibare Rama rasam. Rasa* means drink. *Rama rasam*—there is no greater drink than singing the praise of Lord Rama. Amma compares *manava gitam*, the song of life, to the life we should lead, to *shuddha paramahamsa ashram gitam. Shuddha* means absolute purity.

Paramahamsa is the highest of swans, the Self-Realized soul. *Ashram gitam* is *manava gitam,* our life. That is how we must lead our life.

Maha Lalita Devi doesn't always sit on one of these *kamalas,* lotuses. She goes from one *kamala* to another. She goes beyond the *shat kamalas,* the six *chakras.* As these *shat chakras,* such as the heart *chakra,* the *vishuddha chakra,* and others are opened, we eventually realize, "I and my Mother are one." That is the essence of the opening of all the *chakras.* Of course, as many of you know, that is also the essence of *advaitic* philosophy. Some Hindus consider it to be the highest level. It is difficult to reach that level, but it is the ultimate. At the end of the *Lalita Sahasranama Stotra,* many of the descriptive names of Divine Mother are the words of *advaitic* philosophy, in which the thought, "I and my Mother are one," is expressed.

Amma also told us something else that we did not know. In the *Vishnu Sahasranama,* several names are repeated, and in fact, in several other *sahasranamas,* the same thing happens. Those of you who do the *Ganesha Chaturthi puja* may have noticed this in the *Ganesha Sahasranama.* In the *Lalita Sahasranama,* there is no repetition, because Devi is so great, so wonderful and supreme.

Parayana is the repeating of a text every day in a disciplined fashion. Similarly, there can be a monthly *parayana.* Brahma, Vishnu and Maheshwara do the *parayana* of the *Lalita Sahasranama Stotra.* Why? Because it gives great energy. Of course, as we understood earlier from Amma's teaching, this energy is the supreme energy. It sustains your life, it sustains life beyond, and it opens your third eye and gives you *Brahmananda.*

What Amma is telling us now is incredible! I've never heard this before. It's so wonderful, I can't describe it. We are so blessed! Amma says that the repeated chanting or *parayana* of the *Lalita Sahasranama Stotra* will lessen your *krodha* or anger. Not only *krodha,* but all your *malinyas. Malinyas* are all your impurities or negative qualities, such as anger, egoism, lust or passion. All of them will be gradually reduced and eventually eliminated. However, to get to that stage, you must have *ekagra bhakti. Bhakti* is pure devotion. *Ekagra* means one-pointed, with the mind totally concentrated on one object and with one purpose. Amma said earlier that you must be like Thyagaraja in your devotion. You must forget to eat, you must forget to drink, you must forget to sleep, you must only pray to the Divine Mother. Amma is saying that your prayer must be *antaranga,* internal. *Antaranga* means, as you know, that it should come from the bottom of your heart, not simply from the lips.

Amma gives a beautiful example. There were many great sages, such as Gautama Rishi and Vishvamitra, who did the *parayana* of the *Lalita Sahasranama Stotra.* Kanva Maharshi was one such sage. Once, Kanva Maharshi, who was unmarried, prayed to Devi to be his daughter, so She came to him as a little child. As you know from the *Puranas*, many devotees, like Daksha, prayed that Devi would be born as their daughter. The story of Daksha is also well known. There are several such examples.

Kanva being a bachelor obviously could not have a daughter. Yet he prayed to Devi. So She came, because Devi always comes to Her children when they call. It always happens, there are no exceptions. So when Devi came as a little girl, Amma says, the whole universe came to a standstill, because She is described as *Akhilanda koti brahmanda nayaki.* So all the Gods came running to Kanva, and they begged him, "Please release this baby, She is the Supreme Lord of everything. Without Her, nothing will happen in this universe." Finally Kanva gave Her up.

As a follow up to the Kanva Mahamuni story, Amma says that earlier we talked about a trillion suns coming out of the sun. Astronomically, scientifically, we know today that the whole planetary system came out of the sun. So if the sun was one big mass of fire, all these small planets came out of it as small balls of fire. Right? And from one of these billions and trillions of fireballs came this tiny, tiny speck called the Earth. And Kanva Mahamuni captured the Supreme Sovereign of the whole universe, Maha Devi, in his lap and held Her! Why? Because he had *ekagra bhakti,* the purest, single minded devotion. Lalita Maha Devi is Bhakti vashya. *Bhakti* is devotion, and *vashya* means bound or controlled by.

She is bound by the devotee who loves Her with his whole heart. She is Amrita Svarupini. *Amrita* means the nectar of absolute salvation. There is no *mrityu* or death for such a devotee. She is the embodiment of the Eternal. So Amma is encouraging all of us to pray to the Divine Mother, Lalita Maha Devi, with *shuddha bhakti,* pure, pure devotion and nothing else.

Now, this is a beautiful interpretation. The *Lalita Sahasranama* was originally called a *rahasya,* a secret. Other *sahasranamas* were not necessarily called secrets. A simple interpretation would be, "O, we should keep it away from people who don't have a need to know." This question came up a couple of days ago on another sensitive subject—"We shouldn't teach it to women, we shouldn't teach it to these people, or to those people." Well, Amma says that the reason it was called a *rahasya sahasranama* has not been correctly explained. The *Lalita Sahasranama* was said to be a secret because it contained *yoga vidya.* It had superb knowledge of the Absolute embedded in it. You know what that means? The knowledge is in there, but only those with spiritual insight can see it.

So, the reason they called it a *rahasya* was, they wanted us to go to a true *Guru,* or Self-Realized one, who had inner understanding. That *Guru* would teach us the *vidya* or knowledge concealed in the *Lalita Sahasranama,* so that we would understand it, and not just repeat it mechanically. So Amma is saying, go to your own *guru,* whomever that *guru* may be, and learn the wonderful *yoga vidya* in the *Lalita Sahasranama Stotra.* Do the *parayana* repeatedly, and you will most certainly attain salvation.

As we go through the *Lalita Sahasranama,* we find beautiful descriptions of the *Sri Chakra, Sri Vidya*, and *kundalini shakti.* All these have been described with a *yogic* or a spiritual viewpoint, that is why it is called secret. And we were encouraged, and we should be encouraged, to go to *gurus* to learn this secret and ask them to explain it to us. What kind of *gurus* are these? Amma says they should be *antara mukha jnanis.* A *jnani* is a knower of the Self. *Antara mukha* means one who is inward and has eternal knowledge. We should learn these secrets from such a *guru.* And Amma says this knowledge is for everyone, it is not meant to be a secret or to be hidden from anyone. We say, *"abala gopala." Abala gopala* means "from small children to shepherd boys." Everybody can share it, everybody can learn it. They can go to the appropriate *guru* and understand it.

Lalita Maha Devi is Tattvadhika Svarupini. *Tattva* is the Supreme Knowledge. It also indicates *"Tat tvam"* or *"Tat tvam asi,"* "Thou art That." This is one of the basic tenets of Hinduism. She is above the *tattvas* and She is also Tattva Svarupini, the embodiment of the essence. What kind of *tattva* is that? *Siva tattva.* Only those who have experienced the *Siva tattva* must be your *gurus.* It is not enough to say it, or repeat it, or meditate on it. You must experience it! Amma has been saying this many, many times. You must go to those people who have experienced it. Once you experience it yourself, you will be liberated. You will be freed from all the poisons, the *malinyas,* the negativities. You will be prevented from making mistakes. As Amma said yesterday, if you take poison, whether you intend to or not, you are going to die. It's just like standing in the rain and saying, "I am not going to get drenched or wet." You are going to get wet.

So the repeated *parayana* of the *Lalita Sahasranama Stotra* gives you an infinite understanding of cosmic love and protects you from all calamities. At the beginning of the *Kali yuga,* it had to be decided who would go to Earth first. Many of the pious people said, "We do not really want to go to Earth in the *Kali yuga."* But now that we are in *Kali yuga,* we must remember the story of Vyasa that Amma told us last night, where having written all the beautiful scriptures and commentaries and doing so much work, he was unable to attain inner peace.

And Narada Muni told him to go to the Mother. Vyasa performed penance for five thousand years, and then for another five thousand. And he prayed to Amba and, we know now, that Amba Maha Devi asked him to write the *Devi Bhagavatam.*

Amma is saying that She gives you what you pray for. Vyasa was a writer, so She asked him to write the *Devi Bhagavatam.* Shivaji was a great king, and according to our history, when he prayed to Bhavani, the Divine Mother gave him a sword, because She knew that he wanted to defeat his enemies. So Amma grants your desires. She is the instrument, not you, but you have to pray for the right thing.

The *Devi Bhagavatam* clears many questions that arise in our minds from reading the *itihasas* and *Puranas*. The *itihasas* are histories, and the *Puranas,* epics. And sometimes many questions also arise from the study of other sacred texts. The *Lalita Sahasranama* provides the answers to many of these questions. Amma said this yesterday, and I'd like to repeat it.

In the *Ramayana,* the Rama-Ravana war was not a war between two kings, or a king and a demon. It was the war of *dharma,* or righteousness, the right path, versus *adharma,* the wrong path. The same applies to the *Mahabharata.* It was not a war between the Kauravas and the Pandavas because, as Amma told us yesterday, the battlefield of Kurushektra should have been a splendid, lush basil garden. Instead, thousands of people were killed, and blood flowed everywhere. Why? Because the egos of a few people came into conflict and created a war. That is the lesson to be learned from it.

There was a beautiful incident which occurred at about one o'clock this afternoon, and some of us who were here saw and heard it. A devotee brought some lovely flowers, and Amma looked at them. She always observes everything, I can assure you, whether She appears to do so or not. She said, "There are fourteen flowers, beautiful flowers. How long will this bouquet of flowers last? Maybe fourteen days. But see how much beauty it has, and how much pleasure it has given! How much enchantment and peace of mind it has given!"

Some of us have spent fifty years, some, ninety years, but do we have *viveka,* discrimination, or *vijnana,* true knowledge? Hopefully we will look back and realize that so much time has gone by. But don't worry about what has gone. Start a fresh chapter, and recite the *Lalita Sahasranama Stotra* because, as Amma has explained, every one of us humans has a cosmic tree inside. In the *Bhagavad Gita* it is called the *ashvattha vriksha.* Amma told us this at one o'clock this afternoon. That tree is magnificent, it is unlimited. It can keep growing anywhere. Well, in many of us, this tree does not grow, because we are limiting it. The reason the tree does not grow is, we have four small weeds within that limit its growth. What are those four weeds? They are *kama, krodha, moha* and *lobha—kama,* desire; *krodha,* anger; *moha,* attachment and illusion, and *lobha,* greed. They are limiting our growth. Each of them is a small weed choking the cosmic tree. Just see what small weeds can do. By praying to Mother, with Her help we can pull out all these weeds and let the cosmic tree grow and blossom.

Amma is giving an example: A devotee comes to Amma in the middle of night and says, "Please come and see my child who has just undergone surgery." And of course Amma never says no, but on the other hand, the physical world has all kinds of rules. The hospital won't let you in because the visiting hours are over. There is no transportation, because there is no car. But Amma says stubbornly that She must go!

So in the middle of the night, to answer the devotee's call, Amma goes and sees the child. Amma always does. This shows that Mother's love is so pure. She answers all prayers, some seen, others unseen. We are under the delusion that what we see is all there is. It is not so. In fact, I sincerely believe that what we don't see is much more than what we do see and all our prayers are always answered.

So Lalita Maha Devi is *Shakti*, She is the infinite Spirit. Pray to the infinite Spirit. Remember what that infinite Spirit did for Vyasa. He had a passion for incorporating the male qualities in his writings. Instead, the repetition of the

Lalita Sahasranama Stotra gave him *mridutva,* a sweet softness, and his heart became very tender. So when he wrote the *Devi Bhagavatam*, it was full of tenderness, like the *Ramayana.* And the feminine feeling, the motherly love of *Shakti*, took over. Amma says love is divine, it is unconstrained, don't limit it. Have pity, have compassion, and have a tender heart full of *mridutvam.*

In the *Lalita Sahasranama Stotra,* the spiritual meaning is different from the literal meaning. That is why it is called a *rahasya stotra,* not for any other reason. It is not to be kept secret or hidden from anybody. Lalita Maha Devi is Antara mukha samaradhya. We are advised to go to *gurus* who are *antara mukha jnanis,* and learn from them. After this, when we pray to Mother with *antara mukha samaradhana* or *archana,* She will certainly give us everything we want. She will bless us with something wonderful: *sampurna satya. Sampurna* is absolute and complete fullness. *Satya* is eternal truth. This *sampurna satya* will be more satisfying than a good *bhojana* or meal. Many of us call a good meal *shad rasa upaita*, that is, having six *rasas* or tastes such as sweet, sour, bitter, etc. *Rasa* is the essence of food. We enjoy food which has many *rasas* in it. How good will Mother's meal be? It will have not six, but a hundred and one *rasas* in it! So Lalita Maha Devi will give us such a wonderful meal, we will be completely satisfied and fulfilled.

Amma says: Having come to this stage of life, be motivated, do the *Lalita Sahasranama parayana,* liberate yourself, don't be bound, don't be limited. The *Lalita Sahasranama* is not secret. Go to your *guru,* learn it from *antara mukha jnanis*, and attain salvation!

Hari Om Tat Sat

Dallas *7 April 1997*

ॐ

PURITY IS THE BEST JEWEL OF A DEVOTEE

Translator: *Jai Karunamayi!*

A person of good deeds and pleasant, sweet speech has no enemy. Purity leads to wisdom and immortality. Purity is of two kinds: firstly, internal or mental and secondly, external or physical. Internal purity, that is, cheerfulness of mind, one-pointed concentration, and the conquest of both mind and body, make a seeker fit for Self-Realization.

Purity is the best jewel of a man. It is the best and greatest treasure of a sage. It is the best wealth of a devotee. Practice of compassion, charitable acts, and loving service purifies and softens the heart. It turns the heart lotus upwards, preparing the aspirant for the reception of divine light.

Japa, the repetition of a particular name you believe in, *kirtana,* singing the praise of the Lord or whoever else you believe in, devotion, charity, *pranayama*, breath control, and meditation can burn all sins and purify the heart.

Truth is the highest wisdom. Truth alone stands even if there is no other support. Truth is eternal. Truth is supreme. Those who are truthful, honest and pure do not die. Those who are untruthful and lustful are as though already dead. If you want to realize the Self, you must have a pure mind. Unless the mind is free from all worries, desires and cravings, as well as pride, delusion, lust, anger, attachment, likes and dislikes, it cannot enter into the state of supreme peace.

Speaking the truth is the most important qualification of a seeker. Speaking the truth, one is freed from worries and restored to peace and strength. If truth and thousands and thousands of good deeds are weighed in a balance, truth will be heavier. Mother is Truth. Mother can be realized by observing truth in thought, word and deed. By speaking the truth always, in all circumstances, a meditator acquires *vak siddhi. Vak* is speech; *siddhi* is the highest level of attainment. Whatever you think or speak comes true. You can do anything by mere thought.

This *atman* or soul is realized by the strict observance of truth. It is the emphatic declaration of the *Vedas* and holy books the world over that there is nothing greater than truth.

Be honest, children. Honesty, integrity, freedom from fraud, frankness, fair dealings are the only virtues upon which individual life can rest safely. Society can only endure when it is cemented with the mortar of honesty, justice, and righteousness. There is one immutable law—honesty. Honesty in the office, in politics, in business, on the highway, in the courts of justice, and in all assemblies, that is what we need. Honesty is not only the best policy—it is the best virtue, the highest wisdom. Honesty means conforming to justice and moral rectitude. The basis of high thinking is perfect honesty.

Openness, genuineness or sincerity characterizes an honest man. He is faithful, sincere, straightforward, true, trustworthy and upright. He always acts with careful regard for the rights of others, especially in matters of business or property. He scrupulously observes the dictates of a personal honor that is higher than any demands of mercantile law or public opinion, and will do nothing unworthy of his own inherent nobility of soul. He does not steal, cheat or defraud. He will not take unfair advantage under any circumstance. He who is honest in the highest and fullest sense is scrupulously correct, even in his thoughts. Deceitfulness, dishonesty, faithlessness, treachery, falsehood and hypocrisy are the opposites of honesty. Without honesty, there can be no progress in *yoga* or spirituality. *Hari Om Tat Sat. Jai Karunamayi!*

Amma's Discourse:

Embodiments of Divine Souls!

Amma conveys Her wholehearted and unconditional motherly love to you all. Today we will talk about the extraordinary *mantras* in the *Lalita Sahasranama.* The *Lalita Sahasranama* is not of this Earth, it is cosmic, given to us from above.

In this great *stotra,* Divine Mother is called Antar mukha samaradhya—only one who has inner vision will be able to understand this entire universe. If our vision is always external, we can never attain God-Realization in this birth. If our view is confined to the physical, we can never achieve divinity. Due to lack of regular *sadhana*, we have poverty in devotion, poverty in peace, poverty in wisdom, and in so many other aspects. But we have hope. Thousands and millions of Amma's hands are in front of you. Close your eyes and open your third eye, see Her, enjoy Her in bliss only. Go beyond the body, mind and intellect cages. Enjoy divinity in yourself and everywhere. This is possible, because Mother is Antara mukha sama aradhya.

Translator: Divine Mother is called Para mantra vibhedini. We must have the correct attitude and great enthusiasm to be on the spiritual path. As many of you know, *mantra* is the *sukshma svarupa*, the subtle and condensed form of a very noble phrase or thought. For example, *Om* is very short, but there is so much meaning in it. Para mantra vibhedini: The meaning of this name of Mother Jagat Janani on whom we meditate is very subtle. When we meditate on a *mantra* of subtle consciousness, the *mantra* cuts through the limited individual consciousness or *chaitanya* and transforms it into a vast, strong and concentrated consciousness.

Vibhedini—Amma gives a beautiful explanation: *bheda* means splitting, but this is not a small split, it is like a nuclear explosion. *Para,* (as we discussed the other day), means *para loka*, the higher spiritual sphere. It is like a seed that explodes and creates a whole new world, growing into new life. As it blossoms it gives indescribable, infinite illumination, which removes the darkness of ignorance and the clouds inside our heart.

This name has an extremely beautiful meaning, which should be an example to us. Nature teaches us many extraordinary lessons, but we do not have the heart to learn them. If we open our hearts, we can learn many wonderful lessons in every second. Take the example of a seed. When we sow it in the earth and water it, the seed perishes and gives rise to new life. From that seed, a new life, a new sprout takes birth—the seed is transformed. Similarly in this instance, what is it that the meditator is ending in himself? Earlier we talked about honesty. For many births, we have not been honest. Truthfulness, tranquility, peace, and divine knowledge—we lack all these. When we attain all these extraordinary qualities, Mother grants us the state of *kaivalyam*, eternal emancipation or union with the Supreme, for She is Kaivalya pada dayini. Everything is made clear in the *Lalita Sahasranama.*

If you ask, "What will I get if I do this?" The answer is: Mother will establish you in *kaivalya pada*. Mother takes the aspirant to a state where there is no doubt or uncertainty, and establishes the seeker in *purnatva* or wholeness. Similarly, just as a seed destroys itself in order to sprout, when a *jivi,* an individual, destroys his ego, an uncommon knowledge and pure intelligence awakens in him or her. What happens when this consciousness is awakened? He witnesses the *para tattva,* the essential principle of transcendence, and his heart is illuminated.

That is why Divine Mother is called Prajnana ghana rupini. People with ignorance and pride cannot understand this principle even a little bit. *Ghana* is Supreme; *rupini*, She is the form; *prajnana—pra* in Sanskrit always means "of a higher level," *jnana* is spiritual knowledge. So, Prajnana ghana rupini means She is of the form of Supreme Knowledge. Amma repeatedly says that where truth shines, purity resides and *antah sveccha* not only evolves but endures. *Antah sveccha* means inner liberation. Once you get liberated, you don't have to worry about any problems.

This *Bhagavat Chaitanya—Chaitanya* means Supreme Consciousness, and *Bhagavat* means Divinity—must be seen everywhere. Whether you go to a church, a temple, a synagogue or a mosque, you must see it everywhere. That is what Jesus did, that is what Rama did, that is what Buddha did. When you chant the *Lalita Sahasranama Stotra,* you will not have any *ajnana*, you will have *paripurna sveccha—pari* means boundless, *purna* means complete, *sveccha* means freedom. This Mother, Lalita Devi, is the Soul of all souls. She is the Ultimate.

When children are small, they learn arithmetic and algebra. They think they can solve problems, but during examinations, they make mistakes and fail. Similarly, when we study and recite the scriptures, such as the *Bhagavad Gita*, it appears as if we understand everything. However, when it comes to actual practice, we are not truthful. We do not have wisdom. The wonderful flower of knowledge does not bloom in our heart because our heart is closed. The doors of liberation open when that extraordinary Truth shines. Where there is sanctity, only there will be inner freedom. Where there is inner freedom, only there is revelation of Truth, of *Atma*. This is the essence of all religious paths.

The *Lalita Sahasranama* teaches us that by reciting these names, contemplating the meaning of the *mantras*, and living accordingly, our lives can be immersed in *yoga*. The meaning of the name Para mantra vibhedini is that in order to achieve the state of transcendence, *para*, just as a seed perishes to give birth to new life, the seeker whose ego perishes will be illumined by the wonderful *para chaitanya,* transcendental consciousness.

Devi's name, Prajnana ghana rupini means that just as candy tastes sweet inside and outside, all the way through—it is not bitter outside or pungent inside—in the same way, one should see God Consciousness in everything. Seeing God in the church or temple, in our homes and in holy people is good. It is devotion of the first or initial stage. Having the feeling that God is in all living beings is even better. It is the second stage. Seeing God in good and bad and in everything is the highest stage. So, Prajnana ghana rupini means "She who contains the greatest and most superb knowledge about all living creatures."

Just as only a diamond merchant knows the true value of a diamond, only the seeker who has attained divine knowledge truly knows the Divine Mother, who is of the form of Knowledge. We cannot know the Divine Mother when we are in a state of ignorance. That is why She is said to be Prajnana ghana, the condensed form of Knowledge. Just as candy is sweet all through and salt is salty in and out, this *Shakti*, this God Consciousness, pervades all living beings from ant to Brahma.

That is why the *Lalita Sahasranama* is not the history of a person on Earth. It is not the history of Rama, Krishna, Jesus or Mohammed, but it talks about the cosmos. That is why it is known as *rahasya*, or secret. If we want to know about the cosmos, we have to go to those who have meditated upon these secrets and received divine knowledge. That is what this *mantra* tells us. So, Prajnana ghana rupini means, "of the form of superb Knowledge." Those with any ignorance or pride do not know Mother. Mother shines only in the heart of complete inner freedom, and radiates as purity and liberation. She is the Light of all lights and the Soul of all souls. Many countless universes have exploded into existence like countless sparks from a huge fire. This Earth is a very small planet in the universe. The *Lalita Sahasranama* does not talk about happenings in this miniscule Earth.

Mahiyasi is one of the names of Divine Mother. *Mahi* means earth. From the formless state, the Supreme Consciousness of *Brahman,* Divine Mother manifests on this Earth with form. Why? Because millions of humans have taken birth on this Earth. It is with Her remarkable *sankalpam* or will that She created all these beings, and by giving them the wonderful knowledge to realize Her, She directs a play. We say this is a long play. So, one who has *vijnana* lives on this world stage as a spectator. Being immersed in this play, indulging in excessive laughter and crying at the experience of joy and sorrow is being immature. One whose understanding is mature is neither excited in great joy, nor agitated in sorrow. Even if great sorrow comes to him, he will be steadfast.

How is one stable minded, even when one receives a tremendous blow? How is one so balanced? It is because one is in *samatvam*, equanimity. The *mantra* Sama gana priya means, "She loves *samatvam,*" equal vision, which leads to equanimity. People usually translate the *mantra* Sama gana priya as "the Mother who loves *Sama gana,* the chanting of the *Sama Veda.*" The melodious chanting of the *Sama Veda* by *pundits* is truly magnificent, and Divine Mother enjoys it. However, Amma gives us a beautiful spiritual meaning: *Sama* stands for equal vision, a balanced view. In other words, seeing all living beings—from the tiny ant, the *pipilaka,* to Brahma, the Creator—as divine. Lalita Mata, Divine Mother, enjoys the *gana* or chanting of oneness—it is a very beautiful meaning. And when we see God in all, everywhere, we will reach the fourth state, the *turiya* state, the state of supreme bliss.

Those who are balanced in life, they have *samipya,* or closeness, to Mother. When one is close to *agni*, fire, there is no cold. When one is close to tranquility, there is no agitation; when one is close to light, there is no darkness. When close to Mother, we have everything. There is nothing amiss.

So, in the *mantra,* Sama gana priya, when the *sadhaka* with the aid of the *para mantra* cuts asunder the little ego, Knowledge is attained and the aspirant witnesses God Consciousness within. Then he sees divinity in everything at all times. It is not amazing to see God only in holy people. When you can see divinity in poor and even wicked people, and love and serve them, you become a great seeker. Experiencing your self as *Brahman,* seeing that same *Brahman* in everyone and everywhere, this is the wonderful *turiya* state. There are many great states. That is why She is referred to as Prajnana ghana rupini. But this knowledge cannot be attained if there is even one percent pride and ignorance in the heart.

Which flowers does Mother like? We always do physical worship by offering flowers and fruits to God. The *Gita* says:

Patram puṣpam phalam toyam
Yo me bhaktyā prayacchati

"Whosoever offers me a leaf, flower, fruit or water is my devotee." That is good, however, is there not a greater worship that you can perform?

Bhavet pūjā pūjā tava
Caraṇayor yā viracitām

Brahma, Vishnu and Maheshwara place their crowns on Mother's lotus feet when they bow to Her in salutation. The jewels in their crowns shine brightly like an *arati*. She is the Mother of Siva, Vishnu and all the other Gods. Vishnu maya vilasini, Govinda rupini, are the names by which She is praised. During creation, She is in the form of Brahma; while performing the role of maintaining the universe, She is in the form of Govinda; and during dissolution, She is in the form of Rudra. She is called Pancha kritya parayana as She performs all the five actions—creation, maintenance, re-absorption, *nigraha* and *anugraha*.

Mother, as Kaivalya pada dayini is the One who gives *kaivalya pada,* the state of liberation, to living beings. Therefore, to meditate on the Divine Mother who is Prajnana ghana rupini, it is necessary to give up the ego, because people with pride and ignorance cannot attain liberation. Those who have destroyed their inner enemies and are clear minded, whose lives are filled with love, are *Brahma jnanis.* They are very sacred.

Even seekers who have destroyed their ego and pride receive God's grace with great difficulty. To receive and experience divine grace, they have to do *sadhana* for forty or fifty years. It is not something that will easily fall into your lap. We have accumulated a lot of weeds, like anger, jealousy, and greed over a number of births, which have grown huge like the *guruvinda* plant, which grows wild with a profusion of flowers. Those flowers are worldly desires. When we are in the intoxication of these material desires, our eyes do not open. When the eye of Self-Realization is opened, man's life moves forward with great speed toward the marvelous Light.

So, Vishnu Himself in the form of Hayagriva tells Agastya Muni that a human attains salvation by chanting these *mantras*. Agastya Maharshi, who taught the *Aditya Hridayam* to Sri Rama, came to Hayagriva's *ashram*, took care of the cows for eighteen years and did a lot of *seva* for the *Guru*. It was only then that Hayagriva taught him the *Lalita Sahasranama*. So sacred and holy is this *Yoga vidya*. Agastya Muni was no ordinary person. He was born of the essence of Rudra. Lord Shankara Himself incarnated as Agastya. Even such a person had to serve the *Guru* for eighteen years to receive this sacred knowledge of the Supreme Consciousness!

See how valuable this *Lalita Sahasranama* is? Therefore, I cannot tell you to read or not to read this *Sahasranama*. Your own *samskaras* from your previous births will guide you. One cannot be coerced into reading it. Only one for whom this is the last birth will hold the Divine Mother's hands. One who has more births is still trying to come closer to Mother. It is not that one has sinned and cannot come close to Mother. Even one who has sinned is not far away, and will one day reach Mother and hold Her hands.

If one reflects on these *mantras*, one will go beyond this world, and beyond the constellations of the sun and moon, to the very source of *Akhanda Shakti*, Supreme Indivisible

Energy. Mother is called Mula Shakti, Primordial Energy. When one goes to that Mula Shakti and understands the *mula,* root, then there are no more of these insignificant stories to tell. The stories relating to the world of man are not relevant in that state. One will go beyond all these worldly stories, powers, and energies, and will be indifferent to intellectual things, even the *Vedas*.

There was once a devotee. Mother appeared to him and asked him what he wanted. He said he did not want *Brahmatvam*, claiming it was too small a position. He said, "Mother, I don't want *Vishnutvam* at all." Neither did he want *Rudratvam*. The devotee threw away the elevated states of Brahma, Vishnu and Rudra like a blade of grass. In the *crores* of *brahmandas*, there is *Brahmananda sukham* only in proximity to Mother, sitting near the feet of Mother. If that is obtained even for a second, what else is there to desire? We have asked for the fulfillment of many desires in innumerable births. Seeing Mother, the devotee had only one desire—to be with Mother only. He did not want anything else. For a *Brahma jnani*, even the states of Brahma, Vishnu and Maheshwara are trifles compared to proximity to Mother. So he prayed, "Mother, please let me always meditate upon Your divine lotus feet." The devotee asks Mother only for closeness to Her. This is very elevating.

The *Lalita Sahasranama* does not limit one's mind by small stories. It is very elevating, and that is its specialty.

When we read the *Lalita Sahasranama*, the *gunas* melt. This is not our doing. Vishvamitra and others, after doing *tapas* for thousands of years, with great difficulty, reduced their *gunas*. Mother comes and reduces our load of *karma*, and takes us to a high state in a second—just as Ganesha took Avayyar. So, it is not in our hands to destroy the *samskaras* of many births. Divine Mother is Karma bandha vimochani. She will destroy all bondage.

We have many bondages. Our hands, legs and bodies are tied up with big iron chains. The creeper called attachment binds our legs. We are constantly interested in and thinking only of "my family." We are not interested in the families of others. The only thing that concerns us is whether our own son or daughter, brother or grandson is coming. We do not even care to take the names of others. That is how we have become. Therefore, when our own dear ones come, our heart leaps. *Yogis, Brahma jnanis* and true devotees of Mother feel that everyone in the world is Divine Mother. She takes them to that state. Where then is the state of "me" and "mine?" Even the *Vedas* do not amount to anything there.

How great are the *Vedas?* Bharadwaja Muni meditated on the *Vedas,* and after a very long period of meditation, had the vision of Brahma. He asked Brahma to measure the wisdom of the *Vedas*—the wisdom of the *Rig Veda*. He wanted to drink up all the knowledge of the *Vedas*. Brahma said, "O, is that so? Will you see the *Vedas*?" Bharadwaja said, "Yes." When he saw the *Vedas*, the *Rig Veda* alone was as high as a *crore* of Meru Mountains! Imagine how high all the four *Vedas* would be!

Compared to the *Lalita Sahasranama*, the *Vedas* are small, like a penlight. The *Rig Veda* that is as high as a *crore* of Meru mountains as shown by Brahma, and the light of all the *Vedas,* is like a small flashlight, like a doctor's thin flashlight, when compared to the light of *Sri Lalita Sahasranama*. Mother is Vedatita. As She is beyond them, the *Vedas* cannot understand Mother.

In India, many *pundits* of the *Vedas* are stagnant in their paths. They themselves say this, not I. They say, "Amma, I am stuck in the path as I still have some pride." There was this great *pundit* in whom I did not see any pride, but he told me he had pride. He said he felt jealous if anyone else recited the *Vedas* better than he did. When asked, "Why, child?" he was open before Mother, and confessed his jealousy. So, even after studying the *Vedas*, pollution has not gone from our minds, and inner beauty is not shining. The reason, Amma says, is that it is not enough simply to recite the *Vedas* or read the *Bible* or any other holy scripture. That will bring you some spirituality, but you need to elevate yourself to the highest peak of spiritual attainment, that is very, very important.

You must remove all your negative qualities and cultivate spirituality. Already a long time has gone by in life, yet you have not reduced your passion and anger, nor have you cultivated purity of soul. But it is not too late, you must begin now. So Amma encourages all of us to get rid of the bondages of anger and passion, and be ready with an open door—the door of the heart.

Selfless service, honesty and admitting our mistakes—all these are very important for spiritual life. We must first admit that we have a problem before we can solve it. When you go to a doctor, you first have to explain your problem to the doctor. So don't get trapped, be happy; be at peace with yourself. We are poor in devotion, not poor in the material sense, but when we pray to the great Mother Lalita, we should do it happily, very happily.

Mother is described in the *Lalita Sahasranama*, but truly Her beauty is indescribable. Mother is *Karunyam,* compassion. Man has *nava rasas,* nine emotions. If only one emotion, like anger, is present all the time, how will it be? We cannot tolerate even five minutes of another's anger. Imagine how it will be if he is always in the emotion of anger. Similarly, the aggressive feeling of a sword-wielding warrior is not nice to have all the time. Some emotions like fear, anger, *shringara* or romance, aggression, and others are not beautiful for a very long duration. *Karunya rasa*, however, will always give joy. Even when it is time for one to sleep, one will get up and work. At a time when others are impatient and emotional, one will forgive and love with compassion. Such compassion is always sweet. Even during extremely difficult circumstances, when one is steadfast, the radiance of the *atma* of a compassionate nature is most beautiful.

Of all the nine emotions, compassion is the only emotion we can always keep in the heart. That unique compassion gives us a wonderful diamond-like radiance. At the end of the *Sahasranama,* Mother Divine is described as Avyaja Karunamurti, the essence of unconditional compassion. When a seed sprouts and becomes a big tree, it flowers and bears fruit, and the essence of the ripe fruit is obtained and consumed.

Similarly in the beginning of the *Sahasranama*, Mother is compassion, *yoga, Sri Chakra,* Sarvananda maya bindu rupini—all the *ananda,* the bliss in life, is contained in Her. *Sarva* means all, *ananda* is bliss, *maya* means She is everywhere, *rupini* means of the form of: She is in all beings everywhere as bliss, the soul of all. In other words She is the very essence of all life.

You must have seen the design of the *Sri Chakra*. All the triangles that are one inside the other look very confusing. However, in the central triangle is a distinct *bindu,* a dot, that does not touch anything. That is the *Sarvananda maya bindu,* the concentration of all joy and bliss. The aim of life is to gain knowledge of the Self and experience that joy and bliss. One who has not gained the knowledge of the Self will be scattered here and there in darkness, and will remain stagnant in the negative qualities of selfishness, pride, and the egoism of "me" and "mine." If even *vedic pundits* are stuck in this mire, you can imagine the state of ordinary people.

You probably know the story of Jambavana. In our *Puranas,* he is a huge bear and a very great, enlightened soul. He was alive during all the ten *avataras* of Vishnu. Once the demons and the gods took the great snake Vasuki and used it as a rope for the *Kshira Sagara manthana,* the churning of the Ocean of Milk. Jambavanta, being a great *jnani,* was the one who brought Vasuki there. He was present during the *Kshira sagara manthana,* the churning of the Ocean of Milk. As he was very strong, the Gods told him to bring all the herbal medicines and put them in the ocean, and he did so. He saw the *manthana* and the emergence of Lakshmi Devi from the ocean.

The beauty of the story is, Jambavanta was alive during the time of *Rama avatara*. He was very close to Rama and helped the Lord in many ways. And he was also living during the time of the *Vamana avatara*, when Vishnu appeared as a dwarf and subdued Bali, the demon king, by taking three steps—two of which covered heaven and Earth. In other words he was very closely associated with all the *avataras*. At the time of *Krishna avatara*, Jambavanta had a daughter named Jambavanti, and Krishna was attracted to her. (It is a long story; we will not go into all the details).

Jambavanta did not recognize Krishna as Vishnu even though he was so close to God so many times. So he fought with Krishna for twenty one days, and in the end he was defeated. Then he prayed to Lord Rama. Finally Krishna revealed Himself as Rama and said, "Look, I am the same One." The moral of the story is that no matter how close you think you are to God, the same thing can happen to you. So you must open your mind and have purity all the time. And another point beautifully brought out by Mother is that you must be able to see the Lord in everybody, no matter who or what they are. Even if they hate you, you must reach the state in which you see the Lord in them also.

During the *Ramayana* period, Jambavana was in the company of Sri Rama for a long time. He was a good person with clarity of mind. During the *Krishna avatara*, when the same Rama came as Krishna, Jambavana was unable to recognize Him as God. Jambavana was present before the appearance of Lakshmi Devi. He was the one who brought all the medicines for the *samudra manthana*, who circumambulated the *Vamana avatara* three times, and who roamed in the forests with Sri Rama for a long time. Yet he could not recognize Krishna as the Supreme Lord!

God keeps coming closer and closer in each era. In the *Rama avatara*, Rama was reserved and did not speak much. Even when He met Anjaneya for the first time, He said, "Lakshmana, this person looks like a *vedic scholar*. Ask him about Sugriva." He did not speak directly to Hanumana. Instead, he told Lakshmana what to say. Hanumana did not feel hurt that Sri Rama did not speak to him directly. He was satisfied with whatever he got, because he knew Sri Rama was God, and he did not have any expectations. Whatever was God's will was fine with him.

So, Rama was reserved. But when the *yuga* changed, God came closer. The essence being the same, it just came closer. Jambavana could not realize this. This is what we call *moudyam*, cloudiness. A veil forms in front of the eyes like a cloud, and due to that cloud, we are unable to realize the Truth. Therefore, when God came close to Jambavana, he fought a battle with Him. He wrestled with Krishna for a very long time and was defeated. He had this pride and ego that he was the great Jambavana, who did three perambulations of the Lord in the *Vamana avatara*, and had roamed in the forests with Sri Rama in the *Rama avatara*. He felt that he was no ordinary person! He wondered who this victorious Yadava was. He cried to Rama, "This ordinary man is fighting with me and defeating me. If I am Your true and faithful devotee, please be gracious and help me defeat this man." Then Krishna appeared to him as Rama and said, "Oh foolish one! God is standing before you. See how your vision is blinded? See how much blindness is in the heart? You fought with me!" From this story we learn the lesson that *ahamkara* comes with us from many *yugas*. It does not matter which *avatara* you are with, if you have not destroyed the ego.

The *Lalita Sahasranama* takes us from this level to a very exalted state. It does not let us stay stagnant. Stand with your arms raised in surrender. Then you will have the opportunity of your hand being held. If you sit all the time with curled up hands, who can reach out to you? Be with arms raised, with an open heart, full of faith, removing the clouds covering the heart. This *Atma vidya, Maha vidya, Sri Vidya* is the knowledge that gives the auspicious *Brahma svarupam,* becoming one with the essence of Brahma. It is inexhaustible. You can gaze at it forever and still not be satisfied.

Amma:

Yeshṭeshṭu nodidaru sāladammā
Yeshtardha gala kudava drushtānta rahityā
Yeshṭeshṭu nodidaru yeshṭeshṭu
Pāditaru yeshṭeshṭu pogidataru sāladammā

Translator: However much we can see or sing it is not enough. *Jnanis* with great discipline worship Mother. They are not like the ordinary people bound by the *arishadvargas* who mediate upon Her. They have attained the knowledge of the *Atma.* Devi has twelve such devotees. The first devotee is Lord Shankara. The second is Vishnu, the third, Brahma, the fourth, Ishwara. The sun, Kubera, Durvasa, Lopamudra—women are also part of this group—extraordinary beings like these are Mother's devotees. Manmatha, God of Love, is also one of them.

The devotee prays, "Along with all illustrious souls who are Self-Realized, who are dispassionate, who have destroyed the ignorance in their heart, who have transcended the time scale of past, present and future and have attained *Brahma jnana,* I am also singing your names, Amma! I only desire the knowledge of *Brahman* which You can bestow on me by removing the ignorance and sins accumulated over many births. I want to be always in *Brahmananda,* the inner bliss. Please destroy my impurities, kindle the light of knowledge within and destroy the curtains of ignorance of many births." Thus, the devotee sits in solitude and weeps and prays to Mother. This prayer becomes a daily ritual. It is a prayer for liberation, and with this prayer, the seed of *ahamkara* perishes.

Mother is Para mantra vibhedini. Going beyond the *mantra,* She takes the devotee to the wonderful state of transcendental consciousness. As we said yesterday, a small plant with a short life span of only forty-five days bears so many flowers, and freely gives away the essence of its life to the world. We have lived in this world for forty, sixty, seventy years now, but have any flowers blossomed in our hearts? In these seventy years, our anger is not reduced, my attachment, pride, egoism has not decreased. We have not attained any knowledge of the *Atma!*

Some of us have been born in the *karma bhumi,* the *Veda bhumi* of India, which has given marvelous wisdom, a unique culture, and *vijnana,* the highest knowledge of Truth, to this world. Yet our ignorance has not been removed at all. We are not able to sever our bonds, life is always filled with gloom, the *arishadvargas* are roaming in the heart with abandon. Getting old, and closer to the grave day by day, when will we realize Mother? Our age is now sixty or seventy. What meditation can we do now? What *puja* or *japa* can we perform now? How many times do we reflect on Mother? To attain this wonderful knowledge, if we had started to lead a spiritual life from childhood, we could have gained some understanding.

Okay, is there any way out of this? The *Lalita Sahasranama* says, "Yes!" It shows us the way out of this mire. If these names are sung or listened to with devotion, man gets liberation.

Nishṭayol bhajisuvā

"Jnanis have worshipped You with great resolve." I do not have much discipline or resolve, or even great devotion. Amma, I am just trying. No clouds have been lifted from my heart. I can't even sing the song

Terā tiyaga rādā....

"Won't you remove the curtains of ignorance? Mother, will You abandon your child in this darkness?"

It has been said, "There may be a bad son, but there can never be a bad Mother." Wonderful! See what beautiful prayers the *Vedas* have given us! They elevate man to a very exalted state. However, these prayers should not be repeated mechanically, but said with feeling. One should not feel dry even in the performance of small tasks. There should be a tender feeling behind every task. There should be tenderness in the heart. Then only will we understand the *Lalita Sahasranama*. We should not be harsh. If we are impatient, we can never understand the *Lalita Sahasranama*. If the disease is advanced, even medicines do not work. The medicine is simply thrown out of the system. That is how it will become.

So make the heart tender and tranquil, with deep and one-pointed devotion. Cry out, lamenting, to Mother. Develop insight—will *sadhana* without *jnana drishti,* insight, be successful? Man should have an understanding of his actions. This does not apply only to meditation. Meditation is not a small thing; it is a great task. It is a task for *rishis* and Ishwara, not for men. Let us put meditation aside for now.

Amma: When we sing this *Lalita Sahasranama Stotra*, it is beautiful, right from the start. Towards the end, it says:

Ajā Kśaya vinirmuktā Mugdhā Kśipra prasādini
Antarmukha samāradhyā Bahir mukha sudurlabhā
Trayi trivarga nilayā Tristḥā Tripuramālini
Nirāmayā Nirālamba Svātmārāmā Sudhā sṛtiḥ
Samsāra panka nirmagna samuddharaṇa punḍitā

Translator: We see *pundits,* learned scholars, of the human level, adorned with shawls. *Lalita Sahasranama* talks of only one *pundit*, the great *pundit*—Samsara panka nirmagna samuddharana pundita. A scholar is one who gets educated in a college and becomes a lecturer or professor. But to learn this *Brahma jnana vidya, vedic* scholarship is useless. To realize the Universal Mother, who is Vedatita, beyond the *Vedas,* what is needed is inner purity. A heart as pure as crystal is necessary.

There is a lady in New York who is like a crystal. Really wonderful! I was amazed at her. Even we Hindus don't have devotion like her. I don't see that kind of humility. I see less humility in Indians. We are very rash. She sits by herself, with eyes closed, with great humility. She recites the *Lalita Sahasranama.* She is married to an

Indian. I congratulated him saying that he must have taken a thousand births to get married to a *sadhvi,* a very chaste lady, like her. She is a *maha sadhvi*. That lady's *samskaras* brought her this merit.

Purity, like a clear crystal without any pollution or imperfection whatsoever, has to come to man before he can attain *Brahma jnana*. That is wonderful. Even the mother who gives you birth cannot give you such *samskaras*. You have to elevate yourselves.

So, blessed souls, why do you still retain anger in yourselves? We do not want any more anger, any more bonds. Samsara panka nirmagna—we have fallen into the mire of *samsara*. Mother will take pity and come to you one day. If you do not extend your hand at that time, you will miss the opportunity. We may go out of the house, leaving it in the care of a guard. When we return and find the guard sleeping on the job, how will we feel? That is what we are doing.

We are sleeping in every birth. We have been doing the same thing in every birth for millions of births. Even then Mother forgives and loves us and brings us closer to Her. So remember that this body is a house for Mother. In that house, remain as a *sharanagata,* and watch for Mother's coming, watch for the light of wisdom. Be ready with the doors open. It is said in the *Bible* also: "When I knock on the door, you will have to open it. When I knock on the door of wisdom, you should be ready to welcome me."

Yes, that is what the *Lalita Sahasranama* also conveys —that you should all reach that *sarvananda maya bindu sthana*, the place of the all-blissful *bindu* in the *Sri Chakra*. You should not be in sorrow or in the total darkness of ignorance. Never shed tears from your eyes. Be happy, contented and peaceful. Peace is the wealth we are lacking, and that is why we are in a state of poverty. There is poverty in devotion, in knowledge and many other aspects of life. We are only craving for material wealth and that is where we are wrong. Divine Mother can give us all the *ashta aishvaryas* such as truth, peace, knowledge, love, service, humanity, divinity and godliness. All these are available from Divine Mother.

Mokṣa dvāra kavāṭa pāṭanakari

"Unless Mother opens the door of *moksha*, liberation, one cannot do anything." Even Ishwara cannot move.

Śiva Śaktyā yukto yadi bhavati
Śaktaḥ prabhavitum
Na ca Devo Devam
Na khalu kuśulaḥ spanditumapi

She is Vishnu maya vilasini. By Her *maya* She can make anyone dance. When you surrender yourself at the feet of the Mother who possesses the great power of *maya*, She will protect you like the cat that protects her kittens who surrender to her completely.

Let us take the example of Durvasa Muni, who was a great *jnani*. He had performed great *tapas*. When talking of great souls we should not talk of their negative qualities and say such things as, "He was an angry person." It is not right to talk of them like that. He went to Manidwipa, but they closed the doors on him. He got angry. He was a great man but he got angry because nobody paid any attention to him. He looked at the people of Manidwipa and said, "Wait and see what I am going to do to you all." But they were not at all afraid at Manidwipa. They replied, "Nobody can do anything to us because we chant a *mantra* of *Para Shakti* that is very powerful. We are under the wings of Divine Mother, *Para Shakti,* whose eyelid protects us like a soft blanket. Even Brahma, Vishnu and Maheshwara—the

Trinity—cannot do anything to us with the *trishula* or any other weapon, because we are surrounded by Mother's love. We have *Shakti* with us, we have Her compassion and protection. She always protects us—Her love protects us on all sides."

A true devotee of Devi will decline even the greatest position of power over all the millions of galaxies, even *Brahmatvam, Vishnutvam* and *Rudratvam.* All these positions appear to be very insignificant to him. If you ask a true devotee, "What do you want?" His answer will be "Only Divine Mother!" In the *Vedas* it is said that motherly affection is the greatest love in all the universes. Even Vyasa has described it beautifully in the *Vedas*. Divinity is Vedatīta, beyond the *Vedas*. Its beauty spreads like the rays of the sun. What is the distance between the sun and earth? Whether you like it or not, whether you want it or not, the sun's rays descend and illuminate the whole Earth.

In a similar manner, the love of the Divine Mother illuminates the whole heart. However, if you close your doors and remain in a dark room, you cannot experience the sunshine. But when you open the doors and come out, that is, when you remove the curtain of ego, you will experience the Inner Light and freedom.

Therefore, we see that Durvasa Mahamuni was not yet spiritually mature, and that is why he got angry. Consequently, when he angrily cursed the people of Manidwipa, his *tapas* was wasted. He was not allowed to enter Manidwipa. It did not matter how great he was, or that he had performed a hundred thousand years of *tapas,* or that he had read all the *Vedas*. What was required of him was purity. He was not permitted to enter because instead of purity he had anger.

Then he was told, "Leave your anger, pride and ego at the door. Go empty handed as a destitute to Divine Mother.

Leave all your sense of doership and egoistic feelings and go empty handed to Mother. Then She will fill you hands with all you need. Forget about how many years you did *tapas*. Take some water in your hands and wash off all these feelings of ego and arrogance. Fold your hands in reverence, cry out, 'The 'I' in me is dead!' and then come in. Then we will let you in."

He went back and did another hundred thousand years of penance. When he returned a second time, again they denied him entry. Once again he got angry, and was again asked to leave. In order to come to Divine Mother one needs a lot of purity and peace and tenderness. *Tapas* is not required. Just as we are checked for the correct visa when we cross from one country to another, and are sent back if we do not have the correct visa, he was being denied entry and sent back. In this way, no matter how hard he tried, he was unable to get the visa to enter Manidwipa.

No matter how long he did *tapas*, even for two hundred thousand years, the papers reflecting his qualifications were not in order! So he went back and did *tapas* for another hundred thousand years. This time he came back full of pride, because now he had done three hundred thousand years of *tapas!* One should not have such pride. He was yet again denied entry, because he now had the ego of being a great *tapasvi*. Again he went back and did *tapas* for another hundred thousand years. On his return he asked. "How long can I go on doing *tapas* like this? What else do I need to do? Please let me enter."

It was then, after so many attempts, that he matured, and let go of his ego. There and then he entered Manidwipa very peacefully. Divine Mother was seated in the middle of the ocean of nectar in the *Sri Chakra bindu sthana,* shining brilliantly with the luminosity of sixty four thousand lights, and smiling at him lovingly and peacefully. She blessed him and purified him and sent him back.

Divine Mother desires nothing from us—neither *ashtottaras* nor *ashtakams*. We do these only to purify ourselves. Whatever donations we may make in temples or charities, to organizations or individuals, are for our own purification. You may take pride in all the wealth that you own, but for Divine Mother all the wealth of all the universes in all the galaxies is equal to a speck of dust at Her feet. Whatever good deed we do—meditation, devotion or selfless service—it is for our own purification, for enhancing our inner beauty.

However, Amma's question to you now is that in spite of doing all these things, if you do not develop further, what is the use of all these actions? You have been meditating for sixty years, chanting the *Lalita Sahasranama* for seventy years, and you are eighty years old, but your anger is not reduced, your attachment to your family is not reduced and your arrogance is not reduced. Then what have you done so far? What is the use of all your *sadhana* so far? This is the significance of the story of Durvasa. Amma does not like your arrogance of *tapas*. Man has to become humble. Therefore, when the purity of soul begins to shine in a human, all the divine qualities of the soul shine through brightly. Instead, we are only exhibiting sub-human qualities. Even ordinary human qualities are not present in us, and our behavior is less than human.

If you are walking peacefully in the forest and a tiger crosses your path, the tiger will not harm you. But if you go with the intent to kill, it will take care of you! We get angry so many times in a single day. The tiger of anger is inside you, and you have to control it. You must have *viveka,* discriminating faith. One hundred percent, not ninety-nine percent. Faith and discrimination are *divya lakshanas,* divine qualities. Do everything in a humble spirit.

Samskara is more than culture—culture is a close word but does not quite convey its true meaning. All the debates that the *pundits* go through about who is greater, are useless—and we have some of these in the churches in this country also. You don't need debates for salvation—all religions take you to the same destination.

But we get angry so many times in a single day. You can see the traits of snakes and tigers in humans. We can also see the traits of rabbits, deer, parrots, peacocks, tortoises, foxes, eagles, and other animals in our natures. Thus we find the natures of all the animals in the villages and forests, in the entire universe mingled in Divine Mother and that is the inner meaning of the Gayatri *mantra*.

The word *bhargah* in the *Gayatri mantra* means to illumine the intellect, and to give us the awareness and the knowledge of the all-pervading *Brahman*. The *Gayatri mantra* talks about the cosmos. Therefore it is good to have ordinary faith, but we need to develop a hundred percent discriminating faith, that is, faith coupled with discrimination. Not ninety-nine point nine percent, but one hundred percent faith. For if we have even ninety-nine point nine percent faith, it will be shaken by the smallest disturbance, and we will fall down.

Suppose you have climbed a high mountain, and you are appreciating the beauty all around. As you are standing there, if one small, loose stone moves under your foot, you will fall all the way down! But if you have the firm foundation of discriminating faith, you will not fall. If you have indiscriminate, blind faith, you will definitely fall. That is why Amma insists that you should have not ninety-nine point nine percent, but one hundred percent fully discriminative faith. Knowledge of the Self, compassion, equanimity, pure devotion, inner faith, complete divine love, are the qualities that illumine the heart. That is why these names are called *atma nama,* names of the soul. This knowledge is referred to as *Atma vidya, Brahma vidya* and *Maha vidya.*

The *Lalita Sahasranama* is not just a *stotra,* but the embodiment of *Brahma vidya.* No matter how many schools we have attended, we have failed in our studies, because our ego problem has not diminished. If we study in the school of Divine Mother, our ego problem will decrease and we will develop humility and culture with the help of the *Lalita Sahasranama*

You may ask, "What will we gain by studying the *Lalita Sahasranama*?" It will give you the state of *kaivalya,* and will take you to *Maha Kailasa.* By *Kailasa* we do not mean the snow-capped mountains of this Earth. It is the vision of the cosmos from the *sahasrara* lotus. By the opening of the lotus blossom of the *sahasrara,* one experiences the whole cosmos as oneself, and does not get entangled in narrow religious conflicts.

One should not indulge in arguments and debates on the *Vedas,* as some *vedic pundits* do with heated emotion. If one becomes very emotional in the process of arguing, one cannot really experience the Truth. Take the example of the formation of a pearl in the oyster. The oyster remains closed in the ocean, but inside, the pearl is forming. One has to be silent like the lady in New York I told you about. There is no question of religion or caste in the spiritual quest. A devotee has no race and is beyond all limitations and restrictions, with no boundaries. Once you have become a devotee of the Divine Mother, everyone in this universe belongs to you.

When there are no limitations, one has attained liberation and is free from all bondages. With the *khadgamala,* Her shining sword, Mother severs the bonds of anger and *moha, lobha, irsha, ahamkara* and *ajnana.* She releases the individual from his cage of limitations, grants liberation from all bondages and opens the eye of knowledge. When the *jnana netra* is opened, the seeker exclaims:

Yeshṭeshṭu nodidaru salādammā

"Amma! Wherever I look I see You only! There is no place where I do not see You. No matter how long I look, I am not satisfied. I see You in all of creation, yet no matter how long I sing Your glory, I am not satisfied. However much I praise You, I am not satisfied."

Kshana mātra manasāra
Devī pāda smarasida varigen
Ashta siddhi nava nidhi
Gala koduva sura kāmati nallavem

"You bestow the *navanidhis,* the nine kinds of wealth, and the *ashta siddhis*, the eight supernatural powers, on those who remember You even for one second." In one minute there are sixty seconds. If you pray sincerely for even one second, She will grant you the eight powers and the nine treasures the very moment you come to Her doorstep and offer Her your salutations.

For a *Devi bhakta*, a disciple of Divine Mother, even the attainment of *Brahmatvam*, *Vishnutvam* and *Rudratvam* is insignificant. What the true devotee really desires is nearness to Devi. So, it becomes clear how much inner purity is required to meditate on the Divine Mother who grants the extraordinary divine state of *moksha.* An extremely pure heart is required to meditate on the Lord. If any faults are detected, we should rectify them in order to progress in our spiritual life.

Embodiments of Sacred Souls! In the *Lalita Sahasranama* the *Sarvanandamaya bindu sthana* is in the middle of the *Sri Chakra,* within the *trikona,* the innermost triangle. It is man's goal to realize that *bindu,* the *Mula karana shakti,* the Energy which is the *mula* or source of everything in the infinite cosmos. The *sadhaka* has to become inward and realize that this Energy is within himself, in everybody, and in the entire universe.

Yaśyeṣtu jaṭhare sante
Brahmāṇḍa ananta koṭayaḥ

"That Brahmanda Janani, who contains in Her womb countless *brahmandas,* countless universes and innumerable galaxies, was born as the daughter of King Daksha." She told him that She would leave him as soon as he became egoistic. How was She able to tell him this as soon as She was born? Because She could see the future. You may not be able to see what is going to happen in your future, but Mother can actually see, and tell what is going to happen. That is why She told Daksha that She would be born to him as his daughter, but would leave his house the moment he insulted Her. She is born as Daksha vamsha kalika, the beautiful flower bud of the family of Daksha, but She also becomes the Daksha vamsha Kali—She causes the destruction of Daksha's lineage.

Here Amma picks a beautiful name of Divine Mother—She is Dharma samvardhini. The point is, being Dharma samvardhini. She will always establish *dharma,* righteousness, and in order to do so, She will punish Her own father if necessary. Divine Mother does not like anyone to be full of ego. She is Dharma samvardhini. She loves righteousness, and will protect anyone who is *dharmic.* She did not favor Daksha just because he was Her father. This is a point we must understand clearly in our lives. Like Dakshayani, daughter of Daksha, we must be very strict when it comes to *dharma.* Only then can we enter the kingdom of *dharma.* That is why it is important to correct our faults and foster in ourselves the good qualities that we lack.

You must plough the field and plant the seed called *Om*. We cannot repeat twenty or thirty *mantras,* as they are too many. So select one *mantra* that you like, such as the *Narayana mantra,* or any other *mantra*—for God is one, and all names are His—and meditate on God. First you need to remove the weeds of the *arishadvargas* so that the plant of spirituality can grow well. You may already be doing spiritual practices, but it is Amma's desire that you should do them even more intensely, and thus reach the exalted state of bliss. You should not move about in this lower state. When you roam about in these streets, you see ordinary humans, but when you move about in that exalted state you will see *jnanis* like Vyasa and Valmiki and other *paramahamsas*. You must roam in those streets. There are no *arishadvargas* there. You do not encounter egos. Down here it is all *samsara panka*, worldly mire. There is freedom up there. Mother has given you the knowledge to know which is better. You know what will give you stability.

By considering the story of Durvasa and Daksha, we can understand that no matter how high we may have reached, even one small, mean quality can bring us down to a lower state. If we see any such qualities in ourselves, we should reduce them and elevate ourselves spiritually. It is Mother's sincere wish that you should all become inward. You may mingle among many people in many disturbing circumstances, but you must create a separate world within yourselves. Take a singer for instance. He will be in the world of music. A painter will be in the world of painting. A spiritual person will be in the world of inner joy and peace. Everyone is in his or her own world. Do not concern yourself about others, or try to make everyone else a devotee. It is not your concern. Stay in your own world with your Divine Mother and try to become one with Her.

Let me tell you the essence of the extraordinary *Chandi Sapta Shati*. It tells the story of a king who has lost his kingdom, and a *vaishya,* a merchant, who has lost his property and wealth. They both come to a forest, and go to Brahmarshi Sumedhasa. They pray to him, "Although we have lost our kingdom and home, and become separated from our wives and children, we have not overcome our attachment to them. What is the reason for this?"

Sumedhasa Rishi explains, "It is the influence of *maya* upon your mind that makes you attached to people related to you by flesh and blood. Once you are released from this illusory effect of Jagat Janani, you will have the awakening of knowledge." They then ask, "What should we do now?" The *rishi* told them he would give them a *mantra*, but then was not seen for a few days. Suddenly one day he appeared to them and gave them the *mantra*. They meditated on it for three-and-a-half years.

During the first year of their meditation they sustained themselves only on leaves. In the second year they took only water. And in the third year they survived only on air. After three and a half years they continued to meditate even more severely, holding their breath. Eventually, it was *Navaratri* time, the time most pleasing to Mother, and *Durga Ashtami* was on a Friday that year. Durga Devi in Her most glamorous and beautiful form, holding various weapons in Her eighteen hands, and wearing a beautiful red *sari,* seated on a lion, appeared before them. They, however, did not see Her as they were in deep *samadhi*. She called out to them, but they did not hear Her as they were in an elevated state, beyond body, mind and intellect.

She brought them back to physical consciousness and when they opened their eyes, they saw Her. They were very happy to have Her darshan for She had responded to their meditation on Her *mantra*. She asked them, "Ask for whatever you want." The King begged her, "Amma, I lost my entire kingdom. Please grant me back my kingdom. I have been meditating on You for three and a half years. Please make it happen that I get my kingdom, not only in this birth, but in the next one too—in the whole coming *manvantara.*"

Devi granted his wish saying, "In the coming *Vaivasvata manvantara,* you will be born as *Vaivasvata Manu.* As Manu, you will rule over all the people in this entire world. Since you have meditated on me, I will grant you all that you wish."

She then turned to the *vaishya* and asked him what he wished for. He was looking spellbound at *Devi*, amazed at Mother's extraordinary splendor and beauty, Her *tri netra,* three eyes, eighteen arms and Her *trishula* and other weapons. He was overwhelmed, and tears were rolling down his cheeks. He forgot all about his home, his wife and children, and everything else. This shows that his mind had become pure and clear. The king's desires did not decrease even after having the vision of *Devi.* Once again Mother asked the merchant to express his wish.

The *vaishya* replied, "Amma, let me not have any ego, nor the feeling of 'I,' 'me' and 'mine' for even a second for the rest of my life. Always let me be absorbed in Your Consciousness to my last breath. Bless me thus." He did not ask for anything else. Amma kept asking him to wish for more, so that once She left, he would have no regrets about not having asked for enough. Nevertheless, he refused and did not wish for anything more. Amma blessed him according to his wish and disappeared.

We see the same feeling in the biography of Vivekananda. Sri Ramakrishna asked Vivekananda three times to go to *Devi* and ask for what he wished. Each time

Vivekananda, who was Narendra at that time, said: "I just want *jnana*, please give me *jnana*." Ramakrishna reminded him to ask for what he really wanted, which was to relieve his family from dire poverty and debts. Vivekananda refused to ask for these things, he asked only for *jnana*. It is fascinating!

Divine Mother gives courage and appears as the epitome of peace to pure devotees, yet, in the very same form, She appears as the most frightful enemy to the wicked. The same sun appears to be setting on one side of the Earth while it appears to be rising on the other. The same form of *Devi* appears to be a motherly form full of peace and compassion to the aspirant who is himself peaceful but appears as the fierce and destructive Kalika to wicked minded people.

Amma picks another name of Divine Mother, Nritya vinodini:

Mahiśa mastaka ṇṛtya vinodinī

"One who enjoys the sport of dancing on the head of Mahisha." *Nritya, natya,* is dance. Amma says Mother Divine loves to dance on the head of Mahishasura, who symbolizes *ahamkara,* ego. Amma says it is the same as *Kaliya mardana*. The story of Lord Krishna and His *Kaliya mardana* is wellknown. Kaliya is a poisonous multi-headed snake, and Krishna subdues him and dances on his heads.

Likewise, Devi is

Mahiśa mastaka nritya vinodinī

She places Her feet on the ego and dances on it. The moment She places Her feet on the head of Mahisha, his ego is destroyed. In the same way, our arrogance should decline, and we must gain purity. We are very spiritual, but there is no elevation. Therefore develop purity. Pray whenever you get time. If you pray sincerely for even one second you can get *samadhi* like the *vaishya* did.

What is required is not wishing for an empire like Vaivasvata Manu. He may have acquired the empire and ruled over millions of people, but he did not attain that which is truly worthwhile. Both the king and the *vaishya* meditated and had the vision of Devi at the same time, but why were their desires so different?

True knowledge is above and beyond *Brahmatvam, Vishnutvam and Rudratvam.* It is complete, self-luminous, and beyond name and form. Let us take the example of one *shloka* before we conclude:

Amma:

Girāmāhur Devīm Druhiṇa gṛhiṇīm Āgamavido
Hareḥ patnīm padmām Hara sahacarīm Adri tanayām
Turīyā kāpitvam duradhigama niḥ sīma mahimā
Mahā māyā viśwam bhramayasi Para Brahma mahiṣī

Translator: This beautiful *shloka* is the concluding essence of the *Vedas.* Some of the *brahmin pundits* who have studied the *Agama shastras* and *Vedas* are stranded on the street without elevating themselves. For, by praising you as Saraswati they have limited You who are limitless. Is Amma just Saraswati? No, She is not.

Hareḥ patnīm padmām Hara sahacarīm

"Amma is Hari's wife and companion, Padma. She is also the companion of Siva." That is, She is Maha Lakshmi. They see Her as Lakshmi Devi. For some others, She is *Adri tanayam,* that is, She is Parvati, the daughter of Giriraja and the companion of Parameshwara or Siva.

Duradhigama niḥ sīma mahimā

"Nobody really understands You, Mother! Their knowledge of You is as little as a tiny mustard seed."

Mahā Māyā viśwam bhramayasi

"You immerse this entire infinite universe in illusion; You hold the entire cosmos in Your hands and are amused at Your own play, for You are Lila vinodini." We ignorant beings on Earth argue and debate meaninglessly on the *Vedas*. The whole knowledge in the *Vedas* is equal to a pen flashlight. You are the illuminator of a million suns.

Kamala dala vana tapa ruchi

"She roams in this extraordinarily beautiful garden of the universe by placing one foot on the Earth and the other on the moon!" However, when the devotee calls Her sincerely even once, She immediately goes and resides in his heart.

All your talk is related to worldly matters. The matter discussed in the *Lalita Sahasranama* is not at all related to worldly matters but to the cosmos. If you really want to understand this subject you can study the *Purusha Suktam* and the *Sri Suktam*. You can also get this knowledge from the *Vishnu Sahasranama,* hidden in the form of nuclear seed letters. We just do not know the *mantras* which contain those seed letters. We simply read the *sahasranamas,* whether of Vishnu or Lalita, but we do not know the *mantras* containing those nuclear seed letters. There is a nuclear *mantra* in the *Bhagavad Gita*, and the *Chandi Sapta Shati* also has a key *mantra*. Without knowing these *mantra*s it is a waste to read the *Bhagavad Gita,* the *Lalita Sahasranama* the *Vishnu Sahasranama*, or the *Chandi Sapta Shati.*

Amma: The essence of the *Vishnu Sahasranama* can be summarized in this one nuclear *mantra:*

Sri Rāma Rāma Rāmeti Rame Rāme manorame
Sahasranāma tat tulyam Rāma nāma varānane

Translator: The meaning of this *shloka* is that chanting the name of Sri Rama even once is equivalent to saying the *Vishnu Sahasranama* a thousand times. When you say

Sri Rāma Rāma Rāmeti Rame Rāme Manorame

you have said the *Vishnu Sahasranama*, not one thousand, but ten thousand times. Therefore, the advice is to chant at least this one line, if one cannot find time to chant the whole of the *Vishnu Sahasranama*.

Similarly, if you cannot read the *Chandi Sapta Shati* because it is too long, and the Sanskrit in it is too difficult to pronounce, then you can simply chant the following *mantra:*

Amma [sings]:

Śaraṇāgata dīnārta paritrāṇa parāyaṇe
Sarvasyārti hare Devī Nārāyaṇī namōstute

Translator: "Devi, You are entirely devoted to the protection of the helpless and those who surrender to You. Yours is a Mother's heart, and therefore You are always absorbed in protecting the helpless."

Actually, the way Amma speaks, it is always very beautiful, because She remembers the first point with which She started. I don't know how many of you remember, but Amma starts Her talk telling us to go within for enlightenment, and here She is telling us that one can get salvation by chanting just one *mantra,* Sri Rama. You get all the benefits of repeating the *Vishnu Sahasranama* by simply chanting Sri Rama. Similarly Amma says, pray to *Devi.* By praying to *Devi* you will get everything. You will attain the *ashta siddhis* and the *nava nidhis*, for Mother gives everything.

Candraśekhara bhaktārti bhanjanā

When devotees are praying to Parameshwara, He is in meditation. However, Mother wonders why He continues to be in meditation when His devotees are praying to Him. She comes out of His body and rushes to protect the devotees even before they call "Siva." Such is the Mother's heart! If you ask, "Why are You protecting the devotees of Chandrasekhara, Mother?" The answer is "When you call the Father, Mother rushes to your rescue. Such is the Mother's heart!"

Hence the saying,

Duradhi gama nissīma mahimā

The great *pundits* of the *Agama shastras* and *Vedas* do not really understand You, Mother! They are limiting You by calling You Saraswati and Maha Lakshmi. Even the great Vyasa and others are in ignorance about You, Mother. They cannot know You. Even Brahma does not know You, so how can anyone else?

Only You know about Yourself. You are beyond reach because of the power of illusion. You are beyond *srishti, sthiti* and *laya.* You are of the form of *nigraha* and *anugraha.* You pervade the whole cosmos as *Brahmi Shakti* and rule the infinite universes therein. Only the sages who possess the wonderful wealth of *atma jnana* realize this fact, not those who are slaves of the *arishadvargas!*

So, with a pure heart, with your whole heart, remember for at least one second, the divine lotus feet of Mother:

Kshanamātra manasāra
Devī pāda smarasida varigen

Then that Devi who bestows all the *siddhis* and the *nava nidhis* will pour the nectar of *kaivalya* into the container of your heart. That is why I have been telling you that your prayers should come, not superficially from your lips, but from deep within your heart.

Amritattva svarupas, blissful divine souls of the essence of nectar! You have accrued a lot of merits from innumerable previous births and attained devotion, knowledge, selfless service, and this noble life. It is as your birth mother from millions and millions of births that I wish you to evolve to greater heights, shine even more brilliantly, and attain the state of *Brahman*. Do you know the age of Mother? She is Kalpantara sthayini. She is not thirty, forty or fifty years old. Her age is millions of *Brahma kalpas*, meaning She is ageless. So old is Mother.

The child is a cute baby. He does not know anything. Vyasa and Valmiki themselves did not know Mother. What then of you? You commit many mistakes in every second. Mother still continues to shower Her love, forgiveness and affection, and only wishes that you elevate yourselves and attain greater heights. Why do you keep on lying and living without morals? She asks you why you are continuing to roam in these dark streets. When you send children to school, some children sit on the wayside instead. When you pass that way and find the child there, what would you feel? It is the same in your case.

You are all sidetracked and sitting on the wayside instead of going to school, studying and getting certified in *Brahma jnana siddhi*. You need that *nanna!* Mother prods Her child and carries him to school. Similarly, Mother prods you all to go to your school, whichever it may be, for all schools are mine. It does not matter to me which school you go to. All I want is for you to study. My work is to check your progress every evening when you come home from school. All I desire is for each child to go to a good college and get good grades. However, when I look at the progress report, I don't see you getting good marks. They are all very low scores. I see you going to school, but you are getting zero marks. Your anger has not reduced and there is no progress. Study well *nanna!*

Wherever you may go during the day, to whichever office or town you may go for business, you have to return in the evening to your home and sleep. No matter where you may have roamed in your previous lives, you have to come back to Mother one day. Similarly, *janma mrityu jara tapta vishranti sthana* is Mother's lap. The resting-place away from the burning pain of birth, death, old age and disease is in Mother's lap only. You have to come to Mother's lap one day. When you will come depends on the road you take. That is why you should do good *sadhana* and shine brightly with a pure heart.

Amma:

Nirmala hṛdaya virājita caraṇam
Sakala carācara vyāpaka caraṇam
Bhava sāgara uddhāraṇa caraṇam
Devī caraṇam praṇāmāmyaham

Translator: "That which helps you cross the ocean of *samsara*, that which pervades the entire cosmos and that which shines only in the pure heart is the presence of the lotus feet of Janani! Meditate on such a Janani." Plead with Her in all purity, "Mother, give me sanctity for I am standing at the same place without progress. I am stuck where I am, and cannot move ahead. Give me liberation!"

Amma:

Yeshṭeshṭu nodidaru sāladammā
Ishṭārdha gala kuḍuva drishṭānta rahitayā
Yeshṭeshṭu nodidaru yeshṭeshṭu pādidaru
Yeshṭeshṭu pogādidaru sāladammā

Nishṭayol bhajisuvā sishṭa janarigalla
Parama nishṭayol bhajisuvā sishṭa janārigalla
Drishṭi gochara satata srishṭiyola kānadā
Ashṭaishvarya galā drishṭike hari suvā
Vijaya nagarī Meenākshī sutā Swāminiyā
Yeshṭeshṭu....

Translator: Amma concludes by explaining the meaning of *kshama,* forgiveness. It is much more than patience. Earth is said to have the greatest patience. Whenever we talk of *kshama*, we think of the Earth, for the Earth has great *kshama.* And Amma has great forgiveness, our Divine Mother loves us all. She tells us that by chanting the *Lalita Sahasranama Stotra* we will be liberated from birth and death. She says we are all Her children.

Dallas *8 April 1997*

ॐ

SPREAD THE FRAGRANCE OF PEACE

Om taccham yorāvṛṇī mahe
Ghātum yajnāya ghātum yajna pataye
Daivī svastir astu naḥ Svastir mānuśebhyah
Ūrdhvam jigātu bheṣajam
Śam no astu dvipade śam catuṣpade
Om namo Bhagavate Rudrāya

Om Trayambakaṃ yajāmahe
Sugandhim puṣti vardhanam
Urvā rukamiva bandhanāt
Mṛtyor mukṣīya māmṛtāt

Om śānti śānti śāntiḥ

Om lokāḥ samastāḥ sukhino bhavantu (3x)

[The following discourse was given in Telugu to an audience primarily of Indians. This is a translation.]

Blessed Divine Souls!

Amma conveys Her sincere motherly love to you all. It has been the culture of India since ancient times, for many *yugas*, to convey to the whole world, especially on the days of festivals, the teaching that this whole world is like a small family and that we should extend that feeling of love and unity to everyone. Just as we are all sitting here talking affectionately, with a feeling of unity as in a small family gathering, the whole world is really a small family. It is the uniqueness of Indian culture that it has been teaching this concept of extending that feeling of unity and love to all mankind since time immemorial. You are all fortunate and blessed to be born in such a sacred and divine culture. You must all fill your hearts with the light of this divine feeling. As an Indian, it is your responsibility to distribute this love, peace and light to the whole world.

Blissful souls! Till now you have spent your life practicing the most noble spiritual practices and values. When we are reading a book we expect the last page in the book to be good. Therefore the ending of our life should be full of knowledge, maturity and peace. Without maturity there is no balance. In order to have a good ending, one has to climb many more blissful summits and gain knowledge. Wishing that you should all feel a sense of responsibility for the distribution of that knowledge to the whole world, we shall start today's program.

On this occasion of *Ugadi,* the Telugu New Year's day, I convey to you all my good wishes. In India on this occasion, all the Telugu people organize public programs and also have recitations of extemporaneous poetry. Some of the poems are songs celebrating *Ugadi,* but on this occasion of *Ugadi*, we will invite Divine Mother in the form of the luminous Ashta Lakshmi, and ask Her to fill our hearts with peace and the knowledge that dispels darkness and provides light to the whole world. Let us pray that as we commence our life of purity, which is like nectar, She takes us to the banks of peace.

Sacred souls! For the past two days we have been discussing the *Lalita Sahasranama* in terms of spirituality. Ordinarily in India nobody discusses the *Lalita Sahasranama*. Some people talk about the *Sundara kanda*, and some talk of the *Bhagavata*, *Ramayana*, etc., because they are ever new. Similarly they talk more on the *Bhagavad Gita,* because it is the essence of the *Vedas*. However, the *Lalita Sahasranama* is a tough subject.

Nobody really understands it. A few people secretly chant the *Lalita Sahasranama* among themselves, but nothing is done publicly. Therefore, one can say that in the past ten years a sort of movement has taken place regarding this most esoteric *Lalita Sahasranama*. We have been fortunate in the *ashram* to have chanted the *Lalita Sahasranama* sixty crores, or six hundred million times. Imagine how many men and women have participated in this chanting!

A beautiful awareness has come to Indians after reading the *Lalita Sahasranama.* Thousands and thousands of people are also writing the name *Om Sri Lalitambikayai namah.* Many devotees, turning inward in *yoga,* are worshipping Devi, who is seated in their heart as *Advaitamrita varshini*, showering them with the nectar of the bliss of nonduality. Having prayed to Her saying, "Mother, we cannot come to Manidwipa. Will You please consider our hearts to be Manidwipa and come into the temple of our hearts?" they have sanctified their lives with the fragrance of peace, and are spreading that peace to their families and the world at large.

All of you are also chanting the *Lalita Sahasranama* and are therefore uniquely instrumental in spreading that universal peace. It has been said that the *Lalita Sahasranama* is a great instrument for spreading universal peace in the *Kali yuga*.

There was once a great discussion among the *rishis* in Manidwipa. Vyasa, Valmiki and others were all gathered around Jagat Janani, who was sitting in the seat of honor. That is why She is called Guru mandala rupini. She is like the *meru* in the *japamala*. Everybody was asked, "Will you go to the Earth in the *Kali yuga?*" but nobody wanted to go. They said, "In the *Kali yuga* many people will be lying and making a lot of mistakes." Many of the *rishis* and *jnanis* were willing to come to Earth in the *Treta* and *Krita yugas,* but they did not wish to come in the *Kali yuga*. Therefore, the Lord Himself said, "That is okay, I myself will go in the *Kali yuga*." Then they all reflected upon the problem of giving hope to humanity and it was decided that the chanting of the *Lalita Sahasranama* would fill the whole world with peace. World peace can be earned if even one percent of the population meditate on Gayatri.

Today, having discovered the nuclear weapon, we think that if it is used, the whole world will be destroyed. This feeling is low and full of negativity. To be able to serve fellow humans, to be able to love another and shower affection and share in another's sorrow is to be humane. From being humane one becomes divine. When there is no humanity, how can there be divinity? In order to overcome the six enemies in one's heart, one has to chant the divine name of the Lord. And the powerful seed letters are abundantly present in the *Lalita Sahasranama*. Today I wanted to write my notes on seed letters and then tell you about them. However, there is not enough time. At least tomorrow, when I speak again in Telugu, you must definitely listen, because when expressed in Telugu, deeper meanings are conveyed. So, somehow, I will write at least twenty pages quickly and explain them to you. Then you will be afraid to speak—or even think—a single negative thought in your hearts. You will wonder at the power of words, and realize the futility of speaking useless words which bring ruin. It will become clear that it is elevating to use words in a more worthwhile manner.

Divine Mother is also called Mahiyasi. It is only in *bhu loka*, this Earth, that all the poets are praising Divine Mother. Mother loves poetry. She is also called Kavyalapa vinodini. While She is seated in Her swing in Manidwipa, She is enjoying these poetic compositions. She is also said to be Vani Rama sevita. Lakshmi and Saraswati are serving her. While Lakshmi and Saraswati, each on one side of the swing are fanning Her and swinging Her, She is enjoying the beautiful poems composed by various poets. Truly speaking, in order to understand beautiful poetry, you need a broad and mature mind. Otherwise you would be considered to be very dry. Therefore, in order to savor this literary beauty, Mother is said to be Mahiyasi—that is, She protects this Earth. She has an extraordinary relationship with the Earth; She makes Her children scholars of distinction, true children of Sharada Devi, who symbolizes knowledge. They become the authors of astonishing poetry and rare, wonderful compositions of literature.

You must have read the life story of Kalidasa. His nickname was Kaliya. Calling somebody by a nickname is very sweet; it brings about a lot of intimacy. There is a great difference between calling someone Subbanna rather than Subramaniamgaru. As soon as you call "Subbanna," it generates a warm, loving feeling. Similarly we have Kaliya. He was foolish and ignorant and took care of his animals.

There was a great princess who was famous and well known for her remarkable wealth of knowledge of the Self, but her proud behavior exasperated her *Guru* and he wanted to teach her a lesson. So, out of anger he got her married to this innocent and ignorant Kaliya. One can tell whether a person is educated, and how well he is educated, by the way he speaks. There is an additional feature that gives beauty to education—humility, which enhances the fragrance of education.

So, when Kaliya's wife saw him devoid of all these features, she cried to Divine Mother, "Amma, why did you give me such a husband? What did I do to deserve this? Anyway, I am not refusing to accept my husband. Let it be according to Your wish. I only pray to You to give him knowledge."

While she was praying thus in the temple, Kaliya came to the temple and made sounds pronouncing the word, *"Ayi, ayi, ayi,"* in front of Devi. He was making all these sounds, "*Ayi ammora! Ayi ammora!*" in the language of a villager. The word *"ayi"* is the seed letter of Devi. We have just heard the Devi *mantra. Ayim* is the seed letter in combination with the *bindu,* and *ayi* is the seed letter of Saraswati Devi.

When Kaliya, who had a pure inner heart, spoke these words, Divine Mother felt extremely happy with him. Being pleased, She immediately gave him *darshan.* As soon as he had that wonderful *darshan*, Kalidasa started reciting poetry extemporaneously:

Sudhā samudrāntara hṛdayan
Maṇidwīpa samrūḍh bilvāṭavī madhya
Kalpadruma kalpa kādamba
Kāntāra vāsa priye Kṛtti vāsa priye
Sādarārabdha sangīta sambhāvanā lola
Nīpasragā baddha cūli sanā
Dhatrike sānumat putrike

This is only one *shloka.* A man who did not know even a single word sang a hundred and eight *shlokas* extemporaneously!

Viśvadig manḍala vyāpi māṇikya
Teja sphurat kankaṇālankrite
Devī Vāmadibhih Śaktibhiḥ sevite

"On Her left side, *Shakti* is serving the Divine Mother, while millions of *devatas* are surrounding Her." Having witnessed Her cosmic form, Kaliya became Kalidasa: He was Kaliya, then he became Kali, and finally he became Kalidasa, the servant of Kali.

So, *nanna*, you should all become Kalidasa! Right now we are servants of this exceptionally remarkable world and a few trivial dollars. We are servants of our desire for fame. We expect people to praise us and so we are performing meaningless actions, unknowingly and innocently. There is not much difference between Kaliya and us. But when Mother showered Her *kripa*, grace, on him, he experienced that wonderful knowledge of the soul and saw the whole cosmos in Her. How did Kaliya get the ability to compose such beautiful poetry? If he got it by chanting that sacred seed letter only once, then if you chant the *Saraswati mantra* with full knowledge, your words will be full of charm, knowledge, sanctity and truth. What is the power of the word? It is Truth. What gives sanctity to the word? It is Truth. What gives fragrance to the word? It is Truth. Truth is full of knowledge.

Where does that knowledge come from? Mother is said to be *Satya loka nivasini*; therefore, it comes from Mother Herself. What happens to us when we understand Truth? We become exceptionally illumined. Lakshmi has eight forms, known as Ashta Lakshmi. Some of the Lakshmis stay with us temporarily and after a while leave us. An example of this is Santana Lakshmi. There was recently a flood in the Godavari River and one lady lost all her children in the floods. Similarly, another person lost all his possessions in the flood. However, the Lakshmi of *yoga* and knowledge will never leave us. She gives us matchless inner beauty. The other Lakshmis come to us briefly, stay with us for a short while and then depart.

The bliss of the Self or God Consciousness, Yoga Lakshmi, Atma Lakshmi is never destroyed and never leaves us. And when She is with us, all the other Lakshmis also stay with us. Therefore, we should always keep Her with us.

Amma has not asked you to think about God all twenty-four hours of the day. It is not Her intent to force any one principle on you. The main point here is that in the ancient *dharma* of India there are many extraordinary precious gems. You already have them. Amma wants you to once again brighten them and examine them carefully. If we understand the word *atma* in the light of *dharma,* truth, a heart filled with compassion, a life full of knowledge, then we will be blessed.

Indian culture never preached that man should follow some blind beliefs. So what should one do? One should follow one's heart and act accordingly. Believe in yourself. Don't put your mind to sleep. The essence of the *Lalita Sahasranama* is that one should welcome the beauty of life by living in honesty, with high morals and ethics and a shining, pure heart.

It is said that there is a *Sarvananda maya bindu* in the *Sri Chakra.* When you look at the picture of the *Sri Chakra* you will find that there are various kinds of triangles in it. There are four triangles of Siva:

Caturbhiḥ Śrī kaṇṭḥaiḥ
Śiva yuvatībhiḥ pancabhir api

Devi has five forms. The triangles in the *Sri Chakra* are intertwined and it is difficult to distinguish them. However, there is a beautiful and distinct central triangle, and in it is a *bindu* or dot that is unattached to the central triangle. That is the *bindu* of bliss representing the bliss and peace in our lives. We all have that. Unfortunately, we have lost it, just as we lose milk when we put it in a vessel with holes. We do not have the required discipline, inner beauty and spirituality. We have God's grace in abundance, but since we do not have the necessary discipline in our life, all that grace is lost just like milk poured into a sieve. Only when we close all these holes—representing anger, infatuation, greed, and dishonesty—by keeping them under control, will we have success in our spiritual *sadhana,* whatever *yoga* it may be.

I do not mean to say that meditation is the only *yoga.* Some people who like it will take up the *yoga* of meditation. Some people only like to keep their eyes closed. They don't like to keep them open. When you want complete rest, you can only get it by forgetting your body. When you try to sleep, do you keep your eyes open or do you close them? It is only when you close your eyes that you get rest. It is only when you forget your physical body that you get rest.

It is the same in *yoga* also. *Yoga* is a combination of many things. Let us take an example. Consider the Yamuna River, Ganga River and Saraswati River. The meeting point of all these three rivers is called *Triveni Sangam.* It is called *yoga.* In the same way, *yoga* germinates in our life when we obtain this human body, find a *Sadguru,* are given a chosen *mantra* like the *Rama mantra,* meditate on that *mantra* with faith, devotion and discipline, and lead a beautiful inner life without cheating anybody.

However, the seed of *yoga* does not sprout because we are meditating at odd times without any discipline, and are always talking without any control over our speech or behavior. We are servants of our minds, whereas the great souls have the mind in their service. These are the secrets that we have not understood, and therefore we are making mistakes. We can control the mind to act according to our wishes by training it. To cite an example: the elephants and horses in the forest are not willing to carry heavy loads for us in the beginning. Do you think they like picking up all that weight for us? No. They do so because of our training, and because they have no choice. See how huge the elephant is. It can destroy man in a second, but it listens to us because of the training we give it. It is the same with the horse. Initially when a person wants to ride a horse, it will throw him off. A horse becomes submissive when certain parts of its body are touched. It listens to you and lets you ride it. This is written in the *Vedas*.

Ashvarudha tishtha Devi—Devi ascends your horse and rides very fast: This horse is not good, for it rides hither and thither and speaks whatever comes to its mind without any control. Ashvarudha Devi means Ujjayini Maha Kali. She is Kshatriya pujita. Meenakshi Devi is Rajya Shyamala, the minister for Lalita Devi.

Mantrinyamba virachita vishanga vadatoshita: She is the foremost chief minister for Lalita Devi. Rajya Shyamala incarnated as the *Rama avatara*. In this way Devi has many forms in the *Sri Chakra*.

Then you have Kshira Bhavani as in Maheshswara mahakalpa maha tandava sakshini. At the time of the dissolution of the world, when all living beings are being destroyed like ants in a flood, it will not be possible for anyone to watch that destruction. Divine Mother will be agitated seeing the destruction of Her creation.

Such destruction in the *Kali yuga* will come in the future. We are at the end of *Kali yuga*. We must do something for ourselves. We must board the bus to our destination. If you say I will wait, then you will remain where you are. You will be lost in the crowd. It will be wise to procure a good seat in the bus and proceed. You must only perform good actions and keep your hearts very pure. You need to practice sweet devotion, which is full of nectar, for your *yoga* to bear fruit.

Similarly with *karma yoga,* which is sweeter than even *bhakti yoga*: You must practice desireless actions and decrease the ego, the little self in you. *Jnana yoga* is the direct path to God-Realization. The kingly path, *raja yoga,* consists of self-enquiry. It is a very difficult path, but when the mind attains maturity, one will question: "Who am I? Where did I come from? What am I doing? Where am I going?" One will meditate upon these issues.

Finally there is *dhyana yoga*. It is a mistake to think that meditation consists simply of closing one's eyes and sitting idle. In the beginning we meditate to control the mind that is like a horse or elephant. We need to practice persistently and use the *mantra* as a goad. We must keep chanting *mantras* like the *Narayana mantra* or *Vishnu mantra* constantly to control this horse or elephant. Later, when it is restrained, it will listen to us. Right now the mind is not listening to us. Instead, we are listening to its commands. The mind is like the horse—it is not letting us ride it. The more we try, the more it throws us off and does not let us sit on it. Therefore, in India, there is a beautiful comment in the *Vedas*, which you might have read. It says that in the ancient times the ladies in India had mounted the horse that is beyond control. Even the *rishis* did not understand what horse they were talking about. The horse that is referred to is symbolic of the mind. They had completely controlled their minds. They did not listen to their minds but their minds listened to them.

So meditate on God with the power of *buddhi*, the intellect. *Dhiyo yonah*—it is the intellect that shows the path to the knowledge of *Parabrahma*. That is why we pray to Mother to illumine our intellect and give us knowledge of the Self when we chant the *Gayatri mantra.* This is the meaning of the *Gayatri mantra*. It is necessary to brighten our intellect with a one-pointed mind.

Just as we travel in a ship with the help of a compass, we need spiritual discipline in our lives. Without discipline we can never expect spirituality. Discipline helps one walk a beautiful path. Therefore a life of discipline radiates a lot of fragrance. Discipline is required in getting up from sleep, in speech and behavior, and in many other things. We have to watch our every word, our every deed, our every thought and our self. All this can be achieved only through discipline. Therefore, without discipline our life will be like a garden full of the weeds of anger, greed, jealousy and pride.

Consciousness is like an infinite *Veda vriksha*, the tree of the *Vedas,* the Tree of Knowledge. It touches the ultimate heights of the cosmos. Due to these weeds, it is suppressed and buried somewhere in the ground like something that cannot be seen, buried under the snow. It is like a plant that is frozen under the ice. So let us all try now—let us remove the snow and reveal that Tree of Knowledge. Let us clear up all the weeds in the garden so Amma can stroll in that garden. When you invite someone to your house, you decorate it and you wish to cook something tasty. Similarly, how can you invite Jagat Janani into your heart without cleaning it and decorating it?

So pray to Divine Mother, "Amma, I have a great deal of anger even though I am fifty years old. I don't need it anymore, so please reduce this feeling of anger in me, Mother." Amma will tune it. Sometimes when you listen to the radio you hear a lot of static, and it needs to be tuned in order to hear the program. Similarly, Amma will tune your heart. So right now we are hearing a lot of unnecessary blurred sounds full of negativity—like anger, jealousy and greed.

Mother is said to be Krodha nashini, Lobha nashini, and Moha nashini. She is said to be Nirlobha, free of greed. She destroys your greed. She is Kama- Krodha- Lobha- and Moha-Nashini. It is clearly mentioned in the *Lalita*

Sahasranama that She will destroy all these qualities. We are reading the *Lalita Sahasranama* but are unable to destroy these qualities. We need to read it with intense desire, and pray to Mother to remove these negative qualities. She will definitely come into our heart and remove all these weeds. This is the truth.

Who else can remove these weeds? Will a mother ever be intolerant and hate her child? No matter how disgusting the child, a mother will never dislike her child. After all, she is the one, not the father, who takes care of the child from infancy, and bathes him with great love, and raises him despite all unpleasant circumstances. A father may also do this, I am not saying he does not. But the major responsibility falls upon the mother up to the age of one or two.

Who else can take care of the child? It is only the mother. She serves her child twenty-four hours of the day. Similarly the Mother of everyone for millions of births does not concentrate Her mind on all the impurities within Her child who is so small—of seventy or eighty years. She has existed for millions and millions of *kalpas* and has taken countless forms through the *yugas*. Divine Mother's age cannot be calculated. Her age is not in terms of years but in millions of *yugas*. Therefore, even if Her child has committed murders and the most abominable crimes like *go hatya*, killing a cow or *stri hatya,* killing a woman, She does not focus on those factors. As soon as She sees any *dharmic* traits arise in Her child, She wishes to encourage them, and grants him the knowledge of the Self.

That is why the first nabme we hear in the *Lalita Sahasranama* is *matri*—Sri Mata. This name indicates Her three responsibilities: Firstly, She loves and nourishes like a mother. No matter how great She may be, once She comes to Her child, She is Vatsalya amrita varshini; that is, She showers the nectar of Her divine love and affection on Her child. The responsibility of a mother toward her child is indescribable and beyond words. Secondly, like a father, She explains correct and appropriate action in this world. And thirdly, like a *Guru,* She teaches discrimination between good and evil, true and false. The word Sri Mata contains all these three aspects.

The second word is Sri Maharajni. Mother is the great queen. Srimat simhasaneshwari: She is seated on the throne of *dharma*. So, how is this great queen?

Mukund Brahmendra sphuṭa makuṭa
nīrājita padam

A constant *arati* is being performed to the Mother as Brahma, Vishnu, Maheshwara. All the three million *devatas* bow down to Her lotus feet, and the jewels in their crowns are radiating their brilliance as *arati* to Her. So how does that radiance appear?

Viśwadig manḍala vyāpi maṇikya
Teja sphurat kankaṇālankrite

Her feet are adorned with jingling anklets, which contain billions of galaxies in them. And the radiance emanating from Her feet illumines million of suns. Extraordinary is the power of Mother!

Nakha didhiti sanchanna namajjana tamoguna: The radiance emanating from Her toenails destroys any *tamo guna* in us as soon as we bow down to Her lotus feet. She is *tama harini, bhaya harini, sanjivani, divya sanjivani*. She destroys *tamo guna*, removes all fears and confers extraordinary divine power even on one who is dying. If you take a wilted flower and sprinkle water on it, after an hour it will start to revive. Our life is similarly wilted. So what can we do to refresh it? It will be refreshed only when Mother showers Her bliss.

That is why, in considering the second *mantra,* when it is asked, "Who is this Mother sitting on the throne of *dharma*," it is said: Brahmopendra Mahendradi deva samstuta vaibhava.

Brahmādi pipīlakānta Jananī

The lotus feet of this great Goddess are constantly praised by Brahma, Indra, and millions of *devatas,* all the *munis, siddhas, gandharvas, yakshas, kinnaras, kim-purushas* and all the other classes of beings, as well as by the *Vedas, Upanishads, Agamas* and *Nigama shastras.* So great are the lotus feet of *Devi!*

Those feet have the power to make even Brahma serve them, so great are they. You will read in the *Vedas* that those divine lotus feet are pervading the entire animate and inanimate worlds, and the millions of *brahmandas* or galaxies are below the lotus feet of Divine Mother. It is clearly stated that the millions of *brahmandas* are revolving under the feet of Divine Mother, and a brilliant glow constantly radiates from them. Simply remembering those lotus feet destroys one's *tamas.* Divine Mother is *mantra svarupini,* Sarva mantratmike—the soul of all *mantras.* She is Sarva yantratmike—the soul of all *yantras.* She is Sarva yajnatmike—the soul of all *yajnas.* She is Sarva pithatmike—She resides in all the *pithas*—the *ashthadasha,* eighteen, *pithas* and *dvadasha,* twelve, *pithas.*

When you ask Mother, "Mother which *pitha* do you like most to reside in? Do you like to reside in Manidwipa?"

Velli virisenu ni prabhāvamu
Vishnu lokamunanduna

"A small spark of Your brilliance is residing in Vishnu loka in the form of Vishnu, as Maha Lakshmi and as Vaishnavi Devi."

Pallavinchenu nidu bhāvamu
Brahma lokamunanduna

"Another spark from You is residing in Brahma loka as Saraswati Devi."

Tellamuga Kailāsamanduna
Mūdu lōkamulanduna

"Another spark has come into Kailasa as Maha Parvati Devi."

Chellunamma triloka pāvani

"You reside in all the three worlds at the same time. It is possible for You alone to do so."

You ask again, "Amma, considering the above mentioned three *pithas* and the *pithas* in India and all the *pithas* in the world, which *pitha* do You like most to reside in? You are known as Aditya mandala pada gamini, so do You like to reside in the sun? Or do You like to reside in the moon on the full moon day as Nitya kala svarupini, as Nitya shodashika rupa Sri Kanthardha sharirini?" (In the *Lalita Sahasranama,* it is required that one read all the *mantras* without breaking them. However, this name should be separated and pronounced as Sri Kantha ardha sharirini, meaning that She is present in Sri Kantha, Siva, as *ardha sharirini,* half His body.) "Do you like to be in that *pitha*?" To this She replies:

Nāham tīrthe na Kailāśa Vaikunṭhe
Vasāmi kintum jnāni hṛdayāmbhoja madhyame

This is a beautiful Sanskrit *shloka,* and Mother has made Her answer clear in it: *Naham tirthe*—"I am present in all the *tirthas* as *Tirtha svarupini,*"—in the Ganga, Yamuna, Godavari, Krishna, Brahmaputra and Kaveri. The Godavari River is truly beautiful! It can feed the whole world with its waters alone. It is so full of nectar. And the southern Ganga, the Krishna River, has made this whole Earth fertile.

We have polluted all those rivers. You all must come to India and clean all the roads and plant good grass. India is not clean and that worries me a lot. When I am walking in America, I comment to Swami, "Aren't these roads beautiful, Swami?" And he says, "Yes, Amma." We should awaken this awareness of cleanliness in India. Temples are also polluted with writing and advertisements. We visited a temple recently in Sri Sailam. It would cost over two hundred million dollars today to rebuild it. It is an ancient temple. All the shopkeepers have messed up the temple by writing their advertisements on its walls. Now they are trying to renovate it by cementing it again. It required over two million to do so. One poor man has taken up this project. It is a wonderful project. We have polluted all this sacred wealth by our thoughts and ignorance. This Earth should be kept clean. So also our minds and lives.

Mother has told us clearly when She will come and reside in our heart. She has said: "*Na ham tirthe*—I am present in *tirtha*, holy water. I am in the form of all the sacred rivers. I am present in Gangotri and all the other holy rivers. I like to be in Kailasa and I am also present in Vaikuntha. I am in all the *pithas* and *brahmandas,* but there is one special place I like to reside in."

"Where Mother?"

Vasāmi kintum jnāni hṛdayāmbhoja madhyame

"I love to reside in the heart of one who is refined with real devotion and knowledge and who constantly remembers me."

See how beautiful it is! She prefers to be in your heart rather than in Gangotri. Can there be anger and jealousy and other negative qualities in such a heart? Can there be ego in such a heart? No! But we keep all these things, and try to have devotion. However, now we understand, and so let us do some gardening and remove these weeds which are really small and useless.

Your mind is not something great. To control it is just like controlling an elephant with an *ankusha.* Mother is Krodhakar ankush ojjvala. There are innumerable thoughts running through our minds every second. Do not bother about the mind—don't listen to it. To control the anger, just take Mother's *ankusha* and poke the elephant. As you keep doing that, the elephant will be controlled. However heavy an object, the mind will carry it. If you ask it to stand, it will stand, and if you ask it to sit, it will sit. It will listen to whatever we say. Therefore, we should control our mind, which is like a wild horse, and refine it. And we should make this sentence a reality:

Vasāmi kintum jnāni hṛdayāmbhoja madhyame

You should make it a reality. You should have the feeling that Mother resides within you, and that when you take a bath, She Herself is being bathed; when you are taking your meals, food is being offered in all the *pithas* as *naivedya* and the bells are ringing in all the temples. All the poor, starving people who visit the temple are fed from that one meal and are able to tolerate their hunger better. Therefore, you should do every action with a *yogic* feeling—as an offering of *naivedya*, offering your entire life to Mother in the form of *yajna.* This is the *Bharatiya* culture.

We cannot read about all the *tantras* and *pithas,* or do all the *yogas, yagas* and *mantras* now. So, whatever we can do, even if it is five minutes of meditation, it is Amma's wish that we should do it with a sincere feeling. Your prayer should be hundred percent perfect. There should be no deception in it. Neither should there be any desire behind it, because it is said that devotion with desire is *adham bhakti*, the lowest form of *bhakti. Nishkama bhakti*, devotion without any desire at all for the fruit of actions, is considered the best

All the dirt from many births comes up in our minds in the form of desires. A question arises—who is the enemy of our peace? Our desire is the enemy of our peace. As soon as a desire arises in our mind, we become restless. When we have no desires, we are peaceful. Therefore, let us minimize our desires. We should not have too many desires. Let us cut down our desires so we can live a little peacefully. Devotion that is *nishkama,* desireless, with no desire at all for the fruit of action, will lead man to a life of peace and glory.

In the *Lalita Sahasranama* we have this *mantra:* Shuddha vidyankurakara dvija pankti dvayojjvala. *Shuddha vidya* means, "of the form of *Brahma vidya."* This indicates that in order to know this *Brahma vidya* it is necessary for a human to have a one-pointed mind. The meditation on Divine Mother is remarkable: Muladharaika nilaya Brahma granthi vibhedini: "When you practice the *yoga* of meditation with intensity, it opens up the knot called *Brahma granthi."* Manipuranta rudita Vishnu granthi vibhedini: That is the second knot. Ajna chakrabja nilaya Rudra granthi vibhedini: the third knot.

There are three main knots in our body—*Brahma granthi, Vishnu granthi* and *Rudra granthi*. When we open these three knots, we will find Amba shining brightly in the *sahasrara*. The *atma jnani* opens these marvelous *yogic* flowers and allows us to attain the vision of the *atma.* At that time in the tenth gate, the *sahasrara*, the universal lotus, we find Viswa Janani, Universal Mother, residing within and experience *Brahman* in all beings in the world. This is the highest state, not attainable in one day. A lot of *sadhana*, regular practice, and most importantly divine grace is required to achieve this state. Therefore, on this auspicious *Ugadi* day, let us make a resolution to put in at least some effort, uphold this great ideal, and embark on the journey to achieve that ideal.

It is essential to have an aim in our lives. When we ask a student, "What are you studying," and he in turn asks you, "What should I study?" you cannot really tell him what to study. Whether he wants to be an engineer, doctor or computer scientist, the student must decide for himself, and have a definite aim in life. Similarly, you are a student in God's school of life, the world. This is a cosmic college. If you have zero marks, you will not be admitted into this cosmic college. Just as some schools look at your merit certificate to see if you are qualified, the good schools would reject your application if you submit a certificate with low marks, because their standards are high.

Similarly, you read daily *Brahma vidya, Shuddha vidya, Maha vidya, Atma vidya,* in your *Lalita Sahasranama*. In order to obtain this *Shuddha vidya, Brahma vidya, Maha vidya,* and *Atma vidya* that is *Vedatita*, beyond the *Vedas*, you require extreme purity. Therefore, we have always said that purity is the gate to wisdom. Purity is the *simha dvara,* the lion's gate, the grand entrance gate to freedom. When we do not have purity we cannot gain entry through that lion's gate, and we are sent back like Durvasa. Therefore, we must purify our minds.

Get up early in the morning and pray for forty days with utmost discipline. In America getting up early means 6 o'clock according to the standards here. Getting up early in India means 3:30 am. There are *lakhs* of people in India, I know many women, who get up at 3:30 and do meditation. I have a cabinet full of files with applications for attending my retreats from people who say that they meditate from 3:30 to 6:30 every morning. They then get down to the daily household chores, which are many. They do not have any other desires. People from other cities wish to come to me during the *Navaratri* festivals and reject invitations to other events such as marriages, etc.

During *Rama avatara*, the *rishis* requested to come down to Earth again with Him, and Rama promised them that they could do so when He incarnated again. So they came as *gopikas* when He came as the *Krishna avatara.* The *gopikas* had a lot of work from morning till evening. They had to do many chores, like collecting cow dung, milking the cows and cleaning the cowsheds. So who were these people who were collecting the cow dung and cleaning the cowsheds? They were *rishis*, not ordinary people. They felt like crying when asked to do these chores. Nobody likes to do that kind of work. They were very pained at this situation and cried. Even Radha was confined to her home when all doors were closed and guards were posted outside to make sure she wouldn't go out. When someone asked, "How come Radha hasn't come today?" they said, "She cannot come. The people in her house have made it impossible for her to come." Then Balarama, with the help of a few others, went to her house, cut through the ceiling, got her out, and took her to sport with Krishna. That is the power of love. It cannot be controlled. It is a torrential flow.

Everybody cries to Krishna:

Sārahinamaina ee samsāra yātra lo
Ni sanga sukhamokkate gopānganā

"In this meaningless journey of life, Your company is the only happiness." From morning to evening, they wait for Krishna to come so they can sit with Him. Every second feels like a million *yugas*. Everybody old and young, and even children, wants to sit near God. An eighty-year-old person as well as a five-year-old child wants to sit near

God. There is no age difference. There is no distinction of any kind, no gender difference, for God Consciousness is beyond all these. No matter how much of it one sees, it is not satisfying; no matter how much one listens, it is not gratifying enough. Such is the nature of God Consciousness. No matter how much you absorb of it, it is never enough. So the *gopikas* were crying to Krishna that they had come down in this *yuga* to experience God Consciousness and not to do work. They wanted Him. So Krishna said, "Then you must forget your body."

So when Uddhava and others came and tried to preach the knowledge of *jnana* and *dhyana* to the *gopikas,* they were unmindful of it and could not understand any of it, for they had become completely absorbed in Krishna Consciousness. One has to achieve this kind of consciousness. That is the essence of all *yogas*. How can an ordinary human attain such consciousness? One cannot get this kind of *gopi bhakti*—it is boundless and immeasurable. It is difficult for even *rishis* to get *gopi bhakti.* In order to get this kind of devotion one must have done *tapas* in millions of births. It is not so easy to obtain it.

Nanna, we cannot do all those things now. So when you get up early in the morning, whether it is five, six or seven o'clock, take a bath and sit in your prayer room and cry in front of God. "Must I bear so many difficulties when I have come here to get happiness?" We wanted to get some kind of happiness, but having come here we are laboring and working like machines. This is the supreme truth, equal to the Truth in the *Vedas*. So what you call happiness is very little. For a meal you take one sandwich and a glass of orange juice. For this you are toiling so much. You do not even have a hot meal. You are under a lot of pressures and apprehensions and taking medicines for your anxiety. If you repeat the *Gayatri mantra,* you will not require any medicines for anxiety. I have received thousands of letters in America telling me about all these medicines that people are taking to control their anxieties and worries. They say that they have a lot of stress and the medicines are not helping to reduce their anxiety. This was new to me. I did not know that there is such a thing as a medicine for anxiety.

I said, "Why don't you do meditation or chant some *Vishnu Sahasranama Stotra,* etc.?" So they replied, "We have no time, Amma." True, in this country you do not have time. So that means you came to this country for some happiness and have to work so hard for it. Stay here for some time, and then come back to India. Don't stay here too long. The end of your life should be good and sweet like going to Mother's lap—sweet. You are all working very hard and mechanically. You have no certainty of when you will lose your house or job, or anything else for that matter. You are not sure when your children will leave you, or your husband, or your wife, or your life. There is so much insecurity that it can cause a heart attack. Our genes cannot bear this. We desire peace.

When we go to India we feel so much affection. Once when I was travelling in the night at 8:30, the car broke down and we had to stop on the wayside near a temple. While we were sitting and waiting outside the temple, an old man came out from a hut and saw us. He immediately went into his house and came back with a rope and climbed a nearby coconut tree. He got some coconuts from the tree and gave us all the water from the coconuts. However, he was not satisfied with doing just that, so he went back to his house and got us some parched rice to eat. Then he brought us some buffalo milk and we drank it. We didn't even talk to him, but he did all this for us and was still not satisfied. We had no relationship with him and didn't even talk much to him.

Why then was he so hospitable? He was an elderly man and climbed the coconut tree late in the night so he could give us coconuts, and then he gave parched rice, and then he milked the buffalo so he could give us milk. He did all this for us without expecting anything in return. We were strangers, travelers, yet he was so concerned about our welfare. He didn't even expect a *rupee* from us. Such is *Bharatiya samskriti*, Indian culture. Let us salute it a million times and put the dust of the feet of that old man on our heads because where there is love and *dharma*, we find God. A man with such endearing love and crazy affection should be saluted and one should bow down at his feet.

There is a celestial power behind love. Love without any commercial motive has divine power. The moment love is linked to money, it brings about the downfall of humanity. When we have love without expectation we have divinity, *dharma* and *shanti*. We do not have any need to recite the *Lalita Sahasranama* or *Vishnu Sahasranama* nor be devoted to anyone. It awakens sincere compassion, soul culture and humanity within our hearts. Humanity sanctifies a human being.

No matter how much one searches, there isn't a *Veda bhumi*, *karma bhumi*, and *nishkama bhumi* like your land of India. It is full of the wealth of the knowledge of the Self, capable of instilling one with the spirit of sacrifice which makes one give to others without any thought of oneself. Such is your land, consisting of truly wealthy people! Your land consists of people with such meritorious actions. They may be scattered under trees, in huts and other places, but they have the ornament of morality in their hearts. They have *jnana, dharma* and effulgent devotion. They may not be educated, but in every region, whether it is Assam, Karnataka or Kerala, they are given this philosophy in the form of small *shlokas*. They cannot read high philosophies such as the *Vedas*, *Upanishads* and the *Gita*, therefore, they are handed out small, simple, easy to understand *shlokas* to study. In this way they are given the essence of the *Vedas* in the form of small verses and songs. Our grandmothers do not stray from the path of *dharma* because they are constantly singing these potent messages through songs such as lullabies, and verses from the *Gita Govindam* that they sing while cooking. Immeasurable is their devotion and faith. When they invite ten people for a meal, they actually cook for a hundred people! Nobody will ever say, "Why didn't you tell me you were coming?"

You must have heard the story of the man named Megasthenes who came to India and traveled through the region of the Yamuna River. He once stopped at a house and asked the lady of the house for water. She went in and got him milk. He again asked her for water, and she then brought him buttermilk. He repeated, "I want water," and she replied angrily, "Please get water from the Yamuna River. It is not courteous to serve water to our guests. We prefer to give something special. How can I simply give you plain water and let you go?" He was so surprised at her hospitality in giving milk to a total stranger that he started calculating the cost of the milk. She, however, placed no value on the milk. It was not a matter of money. However, love has great value. If you find anybody counting his money, people will say, "He is not an Indian." An Indian will not measure anything in terms of money.

Thus we never put a cost on the love of the birth mother, the love of the birth father, the teachings of the *Guru* and the treatment of a guest. We will give them anything they ask for, including our heart and our life. Such an attitude of sacrifice is nectar; it shows exceptional human values! The root cause of such illustrious, revitalizing values is Truth, because their seed is Truth. If the seeds were false you would not have had these *dharmic* values for so long. It is due to their unifying form and the shelter of Truth that nothing could mar it. Being from such an invigorating culture, you should not be struggling like this for happiness. Even if you are struggling now, have a definite aim, and stay here for five, six or ten years or whatever, do your *japa* and Gayatri meditation and Saraswati meditation regularly, and illumine your inner Self. Then with an attitude of *nishkama seva*, return to India and serve the poor and downtrodden. The world is said to be *vasudhaika kutumbam*. Wherever you may be, you have to serve. That is what we need.

The Abala gopa vidita *mantram* in *Lalita Sahasranama* asks you to unite everyone. Devi as Mahishasura mardini is standing with a million hands. In the battle with Mahishasura, the ocean comes and gives Mother a *pasham*. Varuna Devata gives Her a lotus. Yama Devata gives an *ankusham*. In this way each *devata* comes and gives Devi a weapon. Vishnu Bhagavan gives a discus, while Shankara Bhagavan gives a *trishul*a. Devi stands with all these weapons in Her hands. What does this story indicate? We have offered a lot of fruits to Amma. They have accumulated with Her, but when Amma distributes them, one fruit goes to each person.

When I stand here with two hands and someone else comes and stands behind me, then I have four hands. When another person stands behind both of us, then I have six hands. In this manner, with each person coming and standing behind me, my hands have become a million! In this way, when all hands are joined in unity and start a battle, we can gain victory over ignorance. This indicates that a person by himself as an individual cannot accomplish much. The inner meaning of Mahishasura mardini is that there is great power in unity.

In the *Ramayana,* family values are exemplified, because family values are very important in human life.

One cannot think of oneself only in any country in the world. If the husband doesn't feel well, it is hard for a wife to eat without him. When both are at peace and they eat together, then they are happy even if there is only a little food. Therefore, in the *Krita yuga* itself the great importance of family values was emphasized.

The quality of a society is reflected in the behavior of the people of that society. In the great battle of the *Mahabharata*, we see that Duryodhana had no love for society. If he did, he would have cared about so many people dying in the battle. He would have said, "I don't want any kingdom, I will renounce everything and go away to the forest." Since he had no love for society or relatives, and no fear of God, his heart was empty and he was prepared for the destruction of his society. The second epic, the *Mahabharata*, indicates that it should not be so.

In the first epic, the *Ramayana,* we see that when Kabandha touched Sita Devi, his arms were cut off. And when Ravana touched Sita, his whole dynasty was destroyed. Whoever touched Sita was burnt to ashes. These incidents signify that woman is sacred and as powerful as fire. Therefore, one should approach any woman other than one's wife with the same attitude of reverence as is owed to Divine Mother Jagan Mata. By doing so, our culture teaches men not to get entangled with women, but to be good and respectful to them. One should not view them with any bad or improper intentions. Such ethics and morals have been well thought out.

When you consider the story of Harishchandra, you will find that even the *rishis* could not make the king tell a lie, even at the expense of the loss of his wife, children and kingdom. He gave that much importance to the value of truth. Then you have the other story, where the king, in order to protect the pigeon that came to him for refuge, gave up his own body part by part to keep his promise of protecting that pigeon. When you consider the sentiments and values in these stories, you can keep them as jewels in your heart. To maintain these jewels one needs to have a great deal of dedication and sacrifice.

Society has given us a lot. A huge hospital has been built. Many famous doctors and nurses, after having studied long, work hard in that hospital for many years. We spend about ten or twenty thousand *rupees* in a marriage. Later, when we get sick and are admitted into a hospital to get relief from our ailments, the doctors, nurses and other staff members show us a lot of affection, love and responsibility, using all the sophisticated equipment. For all the service they have extended, do you think a few *rupees* can be enough? The hospital is useful for so many people. Some of the nurses give such good treatment and some doctors take so much responsibility on behalf of patients. Many doctors get up at midnight and go to see the patients without getting irritated, and comfort them with a lot of love.

Consider the *avadhutas*. If you go to them, they will throw stones at you. They will not comfort you. They will ask you not to come close to them because you are in body consciousness. However, if you go to spiritual people who are *avataras*, they will comfort you. In some ways you can call them psychiatrists. They comfort and elevate those who come to them by asking them not to worry or have fear regarding their problems. Doctors do the same. In this way, when we consider the contributions of society, we have to ask ourselves how we are repaying it. We must repay society in some way—at least a little bit. It is our duty to do so, for the sake of humanity, without the feeling of doership. So, cultivate purity, and then there is no doubt you will contribute to the light in society.

Divine Blessed Souls! On this occasion of the *Ugadi* festival, Amma conveys Her good wishes to you all. You should ascend the highest peaks of the noblest and best humanity and Divine Knowledge. Become great *paramahamsas* and attain the state of the *Sarvanandamaya bindu sthana*, the center of peace in your heart. It is my wish that you should not lose patience, tolerance, forgiveness and inner purity. You should have a definite aim and think, "I will live at least one day of glorious splendor and brilliance." It is my sincere and heartfelt desire as your very own birth mother that with this in mind you should progress in your life without any setbacks. *Hari Om Tat Sat*.

May universal peace thrive. May all the people in this world who are helpless, distressed and troubled, and those who think they have nobody—including the wealthy who have many troubles—get peace, happiness and contentment. May there never be any battles on this Earth. May there be abundant crops and may the planets continue to give shining light to this Earth. May feelings of anger and ego never arise in the human heart and may there definitely be everlasting peace. These feelings were expressed in the chants of the *Veda mantras* many *yugas* ago. Let us all become a small light the size of a fingernail in the mountain of the Light of God and be absorbed in His light. This is Amma's desire in thought, word and deed.

Hari Om Tat Sat

Dallas *9 April 1997*

ॐ

DRINK THE ELIXIR OF RAMA'S NAME

[This discourse has been translated from Telugu]

Blessed Divine Souls,

One must elevate oneself to a higher level in order to understand the significance of rituals. On this *Ugadi* festival day, a condiment containing the *nava rasas,* the nine tastes, called the *Ugadi pacchadi* is prepared with ingredients of bitter taste, such as the *neem* flowers. The *neem* flower should be consumed today for good health, but this is not possible here.

When the *Mrityunjaya homa* is done, a creeper called *amrita valli* is used. If the fresh leaves of this *amrita valli* creeper are given for forty days to children with mental retardation, the illness will be cured. The leaves must be fresh. Even if we bring that plant here, it will not thrive due to the climate. Another problem is that we cannot bring plants into America. If we could bring these herbs here, they would be very useful to people here. *Amrita valli* has one hundred and eighty medicinal uses. One variety has the odor of *ghee*, and is used for the *Mrityunjaya homa.*

Another herb grows on the Vindhyavat Mountain in the Himalayas, also called Gayatri or *somalata* or *amrita valli. Soma* and *amrita* have the same meaning. Those people who have chanted the *Gayatri mantra* one hundred thousand times with great discipline go to this mountain, and collect the leaves of the *amrita valli* on the day of *Kartika Pournami,* the full moon day in the month of *Kartika.* This creeper puts forth a leaf every day and is in full bloom by the day of the full moon. By the time it is *amavasya,* the new moon day, the creeper sheds all its leaves and becomes bare. When it sprouts new leaves, it looks like Devi Parvati, and when it sheds all its leaves, it is bare like Lord Siva. That is amazing!

In ancient times, when people did *Gayatri japa*, they obtained the leaves of this creeper, crushed them and made *soma* juice. They used this *soma* juice in the *homa* and drank what was left over as *prasada. Soma rasa* cured blindness, developed intelligence, purified and increased healthy blood cells—these herbs have so many properties. Whatever is in the cosmos is also in our bodies. So the sages who had deep knowledge about all these herbs had great reverence for Mother Nature.

It has been shown by scientific research that radium rays spread to a radius of two hundred feet around the *tulasi* plant. These rays destroy bacteria. So when a *tulasi* leaf is put into water, within fractions of a second it destroys all the bacteria in it, and we take this fresh water as *tirtha,* holy water. It can prevent cancer; it is very good for health. The *bilva* leaf has similar properties.

There is a special variety of the *amrita valli* creeper that grows in our forests. It is not visible to everyone. When Amma tells people that She saw the *amrita valli* in a certain place in the forest, they reply that they searched for two hours and could not find it there. But when Amma went looking for it, She found it. It is said that these creepers hide. When Hanumana went to the Himalayan Mountains to look for the *sanjivani* plant, it concealed itself. Then Hanumana assured it that he had not come to get it for selfish reasons, he needed the *sanjivani* herb for Lord Rama's brother, who was wounded in battle.

There is a herb called *sandhana karini* which heals broken bones—this herb exists. Similarly there is a herb called *vishalya karini*, which removes foreign objects like iron particles in the body. Amazing medicines exist! Great sages have the knowledge of these medicines. They chant the *Gayatri mantra* and soak the *amrita valli* herb in milk overnight in the correct proportion. Then they perform the *Mrityunjaya homa* with this herbal milk, which is excellent for good health. In India it is called the *Ayusha homa*; here we call it the *Mrityunjaya homa*. In India, when a patient is bedridden and seriously ill, this *Ayusha homa* is performed in temples and the patient gets immediate relief from his illness. The vibrations from this *homa* reach the patient and give him life-energy. God grants extension of the patient's lifespan. You should all have *purna ayusha,* a full lifespan.

When people ask Amma, "Why this long life?" Amma says, "Children, there is a definite aim to this life on Earth." You have forgotten it and have been wasting your time. If life ends without fulfilling that aim, we have to return with all the toxic seeds of our *samskaras* and suffer all over again. Just as weeds that have not been removed will sprout again after the rainy season, our *samskaras* will sprout in our next birth. That is why we have to remove them now.

First of all we have to remove anger. Anger is born of desire.

Kāmād sanjāyate krodhaḥ

"Anger arises because of unfulfilled desire." Secondly,

Krodhāt bhavati sammohaḥ

"Delusion arises because of that anger." When man is overcome by delusion, he loses awareness of right and wrong action, and remains in the darkness of ignorance.

Sammohāt smṛti vibhramaḥ

"Delusion causes loss of memory." A person's mind is confused, and he develops a very low attitude.

Smṛti bhramśād buddhi nāśo

"When the mind becomes confused, the intellect is weakened and man gets deeply immersed in darkness." That is why we need a full lifespan. Amma wants you to live well for a hundred years. Children, you need to live a complete life, because the goal of your life has not yet been achieved. You must study well for the goal to be attained. Even if you do not perform spiritual practices, it is okay, but you must reduce anger, attachment, and gradually reduce all your negative *samskaras* or tendencies. It is in your culture that you must gain maturity by the age of forty. All world cultures focus on the same truth—honesty and love for all. Hatred is not great—the power of love is the greatest. So develop the power of love in your life. This can be done by praying to the God of your choice. All Gods are one, but you can choose to pray to God in any form you like. Like Mirabai, offer everything to God with a pure heart.

So, on this auspicious *Ugadi* day, we will take the nine *rasas* of the *pacchadi*, but we will not take the *krodha rasa,* the juice of anger, and the *moha rasa,* the juice of attachment. *Shringara rasa*, a passionate state, and *vira rasa*, a violent, warrior-like state—these emotions are not good for a long duration.

Pibare Rama rasam—imbibe the elixir, the *rasa* of Rama's name. It is really delicious. This is a song by Sadasiva Brahmendra. Where can this nectar be found, who have partaken of this elixir?

Piba re Rāma rasam rasane
Piba re Rāma rasam
Dūrīkṛta pātaka samsargam
Pūrita nānā vidha phala vargam
Piba re...

Janana maraṇa bhaya śoka vidūram
Sakala śāstra nigamāgama sāram
Piba re...
Paripālita sarasija garbhāndam
Parama pavitrīkṛta pāśāṇam
Piba re...
Śuddha Paramahamsa āśram gītam
Śuka Saunaka Kauśika mukha pītam
Piba re..

When you drink the elixir of Rama's name, it immediately destroys the bad *karmas* of innumerable births. You do not have to repeat it many times; even if you utter Lord Rama's name once with heartfelt devotion, it removes the bad *karma* of innumerable lives and bestows wondrous blessings—the blessings of wisdom, peace and spiritual wealth. Instead of drinking this nectar, why are you imbibing the *rasas* of anger, attachment and ignorance? These worldly *rasas* are drenched with ignorance; do not take them. Drink only the nectar of godliness and be blessed.

Śuka Saunaka Kauśika mukha pītam

Maharshi Shuka drank this nectar. His status is higher than that of great *jnanis* such as Vishvamitra, Vasishtha, Vyasa and Parashara. It is well known that Maharshi Shuka went away to perform penance soon after he was born. He was such a great soul that his holiness is beyond description. He was *digambara*—he wore no clothes; the directions were his garments. He was of incomparable beauty, and devoid of passion.

Maharshi Shuka had no knowledge of low qualities such as anger and greed, and no bondage. He was completely devoid of the *arishadvargas*—the six weeds or negative qualities. With great discipline and a hundred percent purity, he went to the Himalayas at a very young age and performed great *tapas,* and with the blessing of Mother Kundalini blossomed the thousand-petal lotus in the *sahasrara* and attained the Supreme State. Maharshi Shuka is incomparable. So, this nectar of the divine name of Lord Rama was enjoyed by Shuka and Saunaka, who were very great sages, and who became *jivan muktas,* liberated while still in their human bodies. They attained freedom from anger, greed, jealousy, etc.

In this *yuga*, people are not liberated; they are bound by many negative qualities. These qualities are very low compared to the divine qualities of the *atma*. We are bound by the lower qualities because we do not understand the value of the divine spiritual qualities.

So, where can we obtain this elixir?

Śuddha paramahamsa āśram gītam

In the divine cosmic *Lalita Sahasranama,* Divine Mother Adi Para Shakti is called Maha virendra varada. This is the *mantra* of the Divine Mother Adi Para Shakti in the form of Sita. She manifested as a special divine Light. Sita is *Para Shakti*; She descended on this Earth and came to live in the *ashram* of Sage Valmiki for fourteen years. Sage Valmiki meditated on God all his life and composed the great epic *Ramayana.* In fact, we cannot think of the *Ramayana* without Valmiki's name:

Kūjantam Rāma Rāmeti
Madhuram madhurākṣaram

The cuckoo is perched on the tree of *Rama rasa,* singing "Rama Rama." That bird is Valmiki. Divine Mother came to that *koyala*. She stayed in his *ashram* for fourteen years. Mother resides in the *ashrams* of these great souls. Mother also resides in the hearts of all those who have attained the greatest purity. As Valmiki is not physically present today, Divine Mother has to reside in the *ashrams* of those souls who have attained perfect purity of heart.

When we go beyond the four *ashrams*, the four stages of life—*brahmacharya*, *grihastha*, *vanaprastha* and *sannyasa*—and attain the state of *paramahamsas*, Mother comes to stay in our heart and sings the eternal song of *Om*. Now we are saying *Om*, but when Mother enters our heart and sings that eternal *Om*, that inner song experienced within is

Śuddha paramahamsa āśram gītam

Where did they obtain this elixir of *Rama rasa*? Where did it originate?

Paripālita sarasija garbhāṇḍam

It is a mistake to think that it came from King Dasharatha or Queen Kaushalya. This is a very limited notion, because this nectar originated from way beyond. The immense tree of *dharma* was being uprooted, and to re-establish *dharma* on Earth, this nectar incarnated from the cosmos as Sri Rama.

Hari Om Tat Sat

Dallas *9 April 1997*

ॐ

COME TO MOTHER WITH EMPTY HANDS

Beloved Divine Souls,

The *Lalita Sahasranama* has the power to cause changes in the cosmos. During the *Treta* and *Krita yugas*, the great sages had a discussion and they declared that in the *Kali yuga*, it would be possible to obtain world peace simply by chanting the *Lalita Sahasranama*. The vibrations of the *bijaksharas,* seed letters, of this *stotra* have the amazing power to move planets. These facts have been spiritually and scientifically proven. So when you chant the *Lalita Sahasranama*, the *shakti* or energy of even one of these names, excluding the remaining nine hundred and ninety-nine *mantras*, has the capability of affecting not just you, but the entire cosmos.

There is so much *shakti* in the *Lalita Sahasranama*; it elevates man to the highest level. All of you should chant the *Lalita Sahasranama* every Friday. It is very auspicious to chant it daily. Mother is very gracious on *pournami*, the full moon day, so chant the *Lalita Sahasranama* on full moon days also.

Chant *Om Sri Lalitamba* mentally. Bring your notebooks and I will start writing this *mantra* in them for you, and you can continue in any language—Hindi, English, or any other language. Do this for world peace. We can give monetary assistance, that is good, but writing the divine name with our own hands is very powerful. You are not required to write a certain number of pages. You can write the *nama* five, ten, a hundred, or a thousand times, depending on your own interest. There is no compulsion in this; even one name is enough.

It has been declared in the *Lalita Sahasranama* that even one name of the Divine Mother has the power to destroy the sins of all humanity from the beginning of creation. The multitude of sins of all people committed in their millions of births—terrible sins, like the killing of cows, women, teachers, *brahmins*, the knowers of *Brahman*—all these are completely destroyed by the utterance of just one of Divine Mother's names.

Viśṇu nāma sahasrācca
Śiva nāmaikam uttamam
Śiva nāma sahasrācca
Devī nāmaikam uttamam

This has been declared in the scriptures. So *Devi's* name has the power to turn you inward. The *Lalita Sahasranama* balances the mind, turns it inward and bestows inner beauty, because She is a Mother. A mother does not put soiled garments on her child; she dresses the child in beautiful clothes before she takes him out. Similarly, in every birth Mother gives you a beautiful new dress, and you go out and soil it with ink within five minutes.

How many times am I to change your clothes? I am dressing you in clean clothes many, many times, but you soil them with anger, attachment and egotism. This is like you coming back crying after pouring ink over your clean clothes. Each time Mother takes you back, changes you into another clean dress and gives you a new birth. (This coming back is not death or destruction, it is *tirodhana*, being taken back by Mother). So now you have to keep this dress clean and return to Amma with the same *chinmaya sharira,* an unblemished body of pure consciousness.

Amma [laughs and asks a devotee]**:** Baby, have you spoilt your dress? No, no, no, my children are sweet, they never spoil their life.

Swamiji: Each new birth is another opportunity given to us by Divine Mother. We get this human form after being born in eighty four *lakhs*—that is, eighty four hundred thousand —plant, insect, and animal life forms. In the *Viveka Chudamani*, Adi Shankaracharya has also said that birth in this human form is *durlabham*, difficult to obtain. Having obtained it, the intense desire to attain God is rare, and getting the blessings and guidance of a *Sad Guru* is even more rare. Only the *Sad Guru* can remove all the obstacles on the spiritual path and protect you, no matter where you may be. He never leaves you.

Amma: In the *Sama Veda* it is said that a small boy comes to Divine Mother's abode. The *rishis* deny him entrance. Because he has not chanted any *mantras*, studied the *Vedas*, or conducted any sacrifices, they say he is not qualified.

Swamiji: If some highly educated people like doctors are in a conference and a lay person without any qualifications walks in, they do not allow him to participate in the conference. Similarly, the *rishis* did not allow this ordinary boy to be among them. Great and illustrious sages like Valmiki, who had performed severe penance, were present, and they questioned this ordinary boy about his worthiness. He had not chanted the divine name of Lord Rama in twenty-four thousand songs like Thyagaraja, or worshipped God with beautiful musical compositions like Ramadasa, the greatest king of music, or written great poetry like Mahakavi Kalidasa, or magnificent epics like Vyasa Mahamuni. Neither had he done any meditation or *japa* or given donations to charity. The *rishis* advised the boy to do something worthy in his life to gain entrance to such a sacred place. For example, if we go to a bank where we do not have an account, the bank authorities will ask us why we are there. So the *rishis* had the right to question the boy's presence. He had not done any *sadhana* to deserve this eternal *Brahmic* bliss. The sages advised him to perform spiritual *sadhana* and come back.

As the boy realizes that he is not worthy of the esteemed company of the *rishis* and turns back, he hears the Divine Mother's soft, delicate, tender voice from the eternal cosmic silence. She comes running swiftly, leaping from planet to planet, appears before him, grasps his hand and takes him away to Her wondrous abode of transcendental consciousness. Mother looks for inner purity only, nothing else matters to Her. We have to remember this.

The boy did not grasp Mother's hand. Mother grasped his hand. She left Her glorious throne and came running to hold Her child's hand even though he did not meditate on Her for even one day. Why did Mother come and hold the child's hand? In this *yuga*, we cannot do great deeds like Vyasa who wrote the great epic *Mahabharata*, or Valmiki who did severe penance, or Shankaracharya who attained extraordinary *vedic* knowledge by his eighth year, or Shuka who did *tapas* right after he was born. These illustrious people are beyond comparison. We cannot compose divine songs like Saint Thyagaraja or Purandara dasa, but still we wish for God's grace. There is nothing wrong in desiring grace. Mother knows our desire.

Amma:

Sanākadi munidrulu ni charaṇāmbuja dāsalu
Dinulagu anadhalu ni divya kripā patrulu
Amma ani piluvagane kshanamu niluva jalavu
Karuṇā rasa drishtito vodini cercu konduvu
Neevu kani demi kaladu bhuvini dayāsāgari
Neevu chandāmāmā vagunu velugu bratuku reyi

Life is like *amavasya,* the new moon night, in pitch darkness—the path cannot be seen. We need at least one day of brightness like the *pournami,* the night of the full moon. The unhappy boy knows he is unworthy. In his despair, with total self-surrender and with utmost intense devotion, he just calls out "Amma!" As soon as he calls "Amma," Divine Mother comes swiftly from far, far away and holds his hand. She tells the *rishis*, "This boy is also my child. When I am feeding so many, how can I send away this one child?"

Divine Mother's love is inexhaustible, sweeter than nectar. She is Vatsalya amrita varshini; She showers the ambrosia of tender motherly love. She is Guna mani, the bright jewel of divine qualities. She is Amrita varshini; She showers the nectar of bliss on all. She will not reject a child because he did not perform *tapas*. We are all Her children. So even if we are immersed in ignorance, if we just call out "Amma," She does not hesitate for even a second. When the boy called out to Her with intense love, She came running. She looks upon all, from great sages to helpless orphans, with equal vision. She is the One who grants liberation. If Divine Mother wills, She can take you to the highest of all states in a moment. She comes and holds the hand of the devotee who longs intensely for Her love. It is not just that we have to surrender to the Divine Mother, but we have to find a place in Her heart. The Divine Mother may be in everyone's heart, but we must try to have a place in Mother's heart.

On this auspicious New Year's day, all of you should make a resolution to start a spiritual practice. For example, you can resolve to chant the *Sahasranama* for forty days, or write the *Om Sri Lalitamba mantra* or *Om Sri Rama mantra* daily—any one practice is fine. You should not spend all your time in worldly pursuits such as eating and sleeping only. You should have a regular spiritual activity. Do not advertise it; perform your spiritual practice in silence—it is between you and Mother. Mother is aware of everything. Nothing escapes Her eyes; even the movements of an ant are noticed by Mother. Her vision encompasses this entire cosmos.

You do not understand this because you see things from a human level. If you elevate yourself to a higher state, you will understand. That is why the *rishis* say that those who are always caught up in the turbulence of worldly life pollute the sacred environment, so they do not allow such people to enter. Do swans allow a crow to join their group? The sages know that worldly people bring all their mundane troubles into a sacred place, so they tell them to first get rid of all their baskets of problems before they enter.

One of my daughters once dreamt that she was coming to Mother with baskets full of sweets and beautiful clothes. But Mother says you cannot bring anything to Her, you have to go to Mother empty-handed. You cannot give anything to Mother; you can only receive from Her. So you cannot take your basket of negativities like ego and anger into the land of *Brahmic* bliss. You have to throw away all your baskets of anger, attachment and greed and go to Divine Mother with empty hands.

Hari Om Tat Sat

Dallas *9 April 1997*

ॐ

ONENESS IS THE ESSENCE OF SPIRITUALITY

Swamiji: I will mention a few points from Amma's talk yesterday before we start.

Amma said that when we add two hands to two, it makes four hands. If we add two more hands, we get six. The point is, as Amma brought out beautifully, we must stand united. If we stand united we can accomplish anything.

Amma told us yesterday that the epic *Ramayana* teaches us correct family values. It is the story of Lord Rama, His brothers and His wife, and shows us how *dharmic* His behavior was toward his father, and even toward his stepmother—it is a classic. We don't know of any other classic that brings out the same aspects. Similarly, the *Mahabharata*, as Amma said, is about societal values. It is the epitome of the daily conflicts we go through every day. The *Mahabharata* is so good at bringing out societal values that one of the jokes we have in our part of the world is, if you have conflicts with the neighbors or people in the same village, or anyone else, we say, "There is a *Mahabharata* going on." The reason is that you can always refer to the *Mahabharata* and find a similar incident, and probably find a solution as well. So you must read both of them. You need to have societal values as well as family values.

Here we don't have much time. One of the most wonderful and generous givers in our folklore was the Emperor Sibi. He gave away his own flesh to save the life of a dove that was being chased by an eagle. We don't have time to go into all the details, but Sibi took a knife and said,

"I will give you a quantity of my own flesh equal to the weight of this dove to satisfy your hunger." Actually it was Indra who had come in the form of the eagle to test the emperor.

The point is that the spirit of giving must be ingrained in you to the extent that you even offer your own body or limbs—your very life if need be—to help others. At the end of the discourse, Amma said that when we stay in a hospital, sometimes we don't appreciate the incredible service provided by the physicians, the surgeons and the nurses. They hardly ever complain, because they do selfless service, and they give us comfort. We should do the same. We should see them as role models, and ask ourselves how we can repay society even in the smallest way.

In conclusion, Amma said, "Today is *Ugadi*. Make a fresh beginning." Amma gives us all Her blessings. Amma encourages us all to sit on the highest throne at the top of the spiritual ladder. She wants every one of us to climb up step by step. Even one day of complete truthfulness and purity is great. Start that day today. And Amma wants *vishwa shanti*, world peace. Amma says we should all pray for world peace, for the material and spiritual prosperity of the rich and poor; pray for the whole *brahmanda,* even the ants; pray that there should be no wars, that there should be plenty for everyone to eat. But most importantly, pray for the illumination of everyone's mind, and for everyone to be on the righteous path. *Hari Om Tat Sat. Jai Karunamayi!*

****

Swamiji: We worship the lotus feet of a divine person because spiritual energy is always concentrated in and flows from the lotus feet of the holy ones. That is why whenever we prostrate or offer our respects to divine persons, we touch their feet. And when we do so, that energy flows into our bodies. In this *pada puja* first we will wash the *Guru's* feet with water, and then with milk, yogurt, honey, sugar and fruit juice. When all these have been offered to the lotus feet, the vibrations and the energy which emanate from the divine sacred feet are absorbed into all these items. It has also been scientifically proved that when we partake of these items which are saturated with the spiritual energy of the divine person's holy feet, as *prasadam* we get a lot of energy.

Divine persons can transmit energy to us in many different ways, even by a look. If they look at us once, spiritual energy will be passed to us through their eyes. When they touch us or bless us and when they apply *kumkum* or *vibhuti* to our forehead, they give us their energy. Through their divine message, too, they pass us energy. And in this *pada puja,* not only will the persons who actually perform the *pada puja* be blessed, but all who are witnessing this *pada puja* today will also get this greatest energy. So you are all very fortunate to be here today and to witness this *Maha pada puja* to our Divine Mother, Bhagavati Sri Sri Sri Vijayeswari Devi.

Just now Srimati L. sang two beautiful songs, one in Tamil, the other in Telugu. The essence of the first song is: "You are the only person who can take complete care of me. I have come and taken refuge at Your feet, I have completely surrendered to Your feet, so You have to take care of me now." This is the essence of the song. In the second song, the devotee says: "I have come at last to Your lotus feet. I have been in this world-play for so long, but have never called You. Now ultimately I have come to You, so You have to talk to me, O Mother! I have come to You as Your child, so You have to take complete responsibility for me." That is not only her prayer, but the prayer of all of us here. So now let us start the *pada puja,* first with a prayer:

[Swamiji chants several shlokas and the *pada puja* is performed.]

Amma's Discourse:

Embodiments of Divine Souls, Amma's Most Beloved Children,

I am so happy to see all my children here, on this pleasant evening in Houston. Children, when there is spiritual elevation in our heart due to meditation, we expand our life, our heart and our love. We start our day with cosmic love, throughout the day we give the same love, and at the end of the day before going to bed, the fragrance of that cosmic love beautifies our entire life. However, this cosmic love cannot grow in our heart because of the six weeds growing there—weeds such as anger, greed, jealousy and hatred, which are truly little weeds. Really they are very small weeds.

Maya is very subtle. When *maya* disappears there is no hatred at all. Where there is hatred, there is no truth. Where there is truth, there only will be wisdom, because truth is the gateway to wisdom. Truth alone beautifies all mankind with so many divine attributes. Children, develop truth, develop cosmic love and be always in divine wisdom, be always in wisdom.

We use our wisdom in so many ways—in the office, in society, in family life and also in our heart. Nevertheless, when we try to practice truth, we find that it is really very difficult to do so in this *Kali yuga.* You know this *yuga* is polluted, but if we really practice at least the truth, we will enjoy divinity in our hearts, have elevation in our lives and achieve Self-Realization in this very birth. The main aim of human life is the realization of Truth. Children, develop your divine attributes even more, and elevate yourself, expand your self and beautify your entire life with the fragrance of divinity, Truth and wisdom.

So, embodiments of Divine Souls, you are not this body, you are not this mind and this limited intellect. Your self is truth, your self is tranquility and your self is attributeless, indivisible, indestructible power. You are wisdom. Your self is everywhere. But we have limited ourselves to this mortal frame. When we meditate and understand the Truth, all mankind will be elevated to the highest peak of desirelessness, which is the pinnacle of purity.

So reduce your desires, limit them, and have the beautiful desire to see God everywhere—not only in the church and temple. It is not amazing to see divinity in the good. However, if you see divinity in the bad and the good, everywhere, all the time, you will become a highly elevated spiritual soul.

So have a definite aim. You must have a definite aim. Ask, "What is the aim of my life?" Go within and enquire, and develop inner beauty. External beauty is not important, inner beauty is important. So develop compassion, kindness, equal vision, wisdom, tranquility and all these divine attributes. Our entire life is beautified by the fragrance of these divine qualities.

Children, reduce anger, temptation, lust, greed and hatred, for all these are forms of *maya.* When *maya* disappears, you are so peaceful, and you have inner vision. Those who have inner vision will be able to understand this universe. Develop that inner vision. Try to understand reality. What is reality? Truth is the only reality. This entire life is only a dream. When we elevate to the highest peak of truth, we have a beautiful vision. That vision is knowledge—divine knowledge. So, have true devotion and faith in God—one hundred percent faith, not ninety-nine point nine percent. You must have one hundred percent faith. Faith does not mean blind faith, not just following anything blindly. Have discriminating faith, one hundred per cent discriminating faith. Then only will you have dispassion in your heart, and all the beautiful inner qualities will bloom.

Meditate. God is only one. There are innumerable paths in this world in the form of innumerable religions. The great *Sanatana Dharma* teaches beautiful righteousness. It has existed for millions of years from *yuga* to *yuga. Dharma* stands alone without any support. So have that righteousness in your heart and understand reality. Develop your divine qualities more and more. Go inside, inside, inside. Have inner vision and try to listen to the inner voice in meditation. Meditation develops our spirituality and elevates all mankind. Meditation is nothing but purification of our body, our mind, our soul, everything.

The universe can be divided into three parts: One is *jiva,* the individual, the second *jagat,* the universe, and the third Ishwara or Absolute Bliss. We make these divisions of *jiva, jagat* and Ishwara because of our ignorance. When we attain God-Realization, these divisions of *jiva, jagat* and the Absolute disappear, and we see that everything is the Absolute. This happens stage by stage. It does not happen in one day or in one meditation or even in one birth. Innumerable births spent in spirituality lead to this knowledge. So make this realization your goal, utilize this birth and try to achieve your true destiny at least in this birth. Innumerable births have been wasted in so many small and useless activities—just eating, talking, and walking—with the same anger, the same lust, the same greediness.

The world is always changing. So many things are always changing. However, truth does not change. Truth is Absolute. Meditate on Truth only. Whatever path you may follow, do not get stuck at any one point. Do not think, "This religion is good, that religion is bad." Do not limit yourself to anything in this world. That is also one sort of bond. We lose our wisdom in such bonds. Go beyond all these things. Be always in wisdom. Do not be limited by Amma's words either; do not be bound to Her love either. Elevate yourself to the Absolute. Listen to the decision of your heart and proceed on your path.

There are so many exits on the road of life. When you miss your exit, you go off into a very different direction. So do not miss your exit. Have a correct map and reach your destination—God-Realization. Do not be bound to anything in this world. See only divinity everywhere. That is real spiritual elevation. Seeing divinity only in the church and temple, only in fathers, in holy mothers and good people, is really not amazing, because they *are* good. They live a noble life. They have love and affection for all; they are pure people. If you really want the highest elevation, go beyond opposites and merge in the Eternal, merge in the Eternal.

The sun is one, the moon is one, Mother Earth is one, air is one, fire is one, and mankind is one. All true *Gurus* are also only one. Go to every *Guru,* pay your respects, listen to the words of the teacher, and practice the teachings.

Practice is really important, not just listening, or just reading some books. Do not get stuck in details. That is not true spirituality. Spirituality is wisdom. Be always in wisdom. Look at the galaxies in the cosmos. All the planets are in the sky, but they are not attached to each other. They have individual personalities. The sky is like a little pond, in which the sun is a diamond flower, the moon is a silver flower, Saturn is a blue sapphire flower, so beautiful, and Venus is another flower. All the planets are beautiful flowers. They are all blooming in the cosmos with their individual personalities.

So let your consciousness bloom with beautiful devotion, true devotion, one hundred per cent devotion, not just a show of devotion. Let discrimination bloom, and develop all the beautiful inner qualities. They will beautify your whole life and fill your heart with more and more fragrance. Develop not only divine love but cosmic love. Develop cosmic love, children. Remove all these weeds. Anger is not good, it is not sweet, it is very bitter. Hatred is not good. When *maya* disappears, hatred also disappears. When hatred is there, *maya* is still in our hearts. If we hate one person and like another, that is not good. See divinity everywhere—that is true devotion; that is real spirituality. So remove *maya* or illusion permanently from your heart.

"Why is there this illusion, Amma?" you may ask.

We have had only one great problem in our innumerable births, only one. What is that problem, children? Ego—our ego is very big and strong. When you have an ego problem, if anyone comes to you and touches you, can you bear that touch? Never. Patience and tolerance are like big pillars. Where there is tolerance, where there is real patience, you have sweetness in life. Tolerance gives immense strength and immense peace. In the beginning tolerance is not sweet and may even seem useless. However, in the end it turns out to be very, very powerful.

Tolerance is the jewel of *sattvic* people. It brings purity and joy. Decorate your entire inner life with these beautiful gems and jewels, children. Have love, more love. Love elevates you. Love not only elevates the giver; it also elevates the seeker and connects him to the Absolute. Our aim in spiritual life is to understand and experience Truth, the Absolute.

The *Bhagavad Gita* is from *Dvapara yuga* and is five thousand years old. The *Ramayana* is more ancient, from *Krita yuga*, and the *Vedas* are even more ancient than the

Ramayana. So from *vedic* times, through innumerable *yugas,* Truth has remained changeless and permanent. Truth is Eternal and Absolute. It is benediction, it is indestructible power.

Have a definite aim in your life, and remember that whatever form of God you pray to, God is only one. The sun is one but the rays are innumerable. You cannot say that the ray is the sun. The Absolute is everywhere. In Sanskrit it is called *dharma,* righteousness, very beautiful. Righteousness is not really an appropriate word for *dharma,* but it is close to its meaning. *Dharma* is like a banyan tree. Do you know the banyan tree?

A child asks, pointing to a branch, "Amma, what is that? Is this branch the tree?"

"No, no, son, this is a branch, not the tree."

"And what is this?"

"This is a leaf, a tender leaf, and these are fruits, and these are flowers. This is the bark. This is the mother root and these are side roots, and this is a stem—all these together make the tree."

In the same way, righteousness, truth, courage, patience, tolerance, equal vision, wisdom—all these are called *dharma,* very beautiful. Everyone has the right to be established in *dharma. Dharma* is one, the Absolute. It is eternal peace.

So pray to God early in the morning. Actually, morning time is very pleasant. Having worked continuously the previous day, after five or six hours of rest at night, your brain is very fresh. You have no restlessness at that time and it is easy to concentrate. So pray to God from the bottom of your heart. Pray to God with tears. Prayer must not come from the lips but must always come from the bottom of the heart. Such a prayer reaches divinity. So children, try to pray, meditate and concentrate. Give your love to everyone. That is important. If you are not praying, it's okay. I do not bother much about prayers. However, you must not lose your wisdom, righteousness, and humanity —that would be really bad. Keep giving your love. Give selfless service, the kind where the self is less.

Meditation purifies us of our sense of "I," "me," "mine," and gradually removes all the black curtains. These black curtains are pollution. This pollution is gradually burnt by the purity of the divine fire of meditation, the fire within us. We have so many fires—hunger is one sort of fire; anger is another fire. Meditation is a good fire. It purifies each and every cell of our body and elevates the soul to the Absolute. So children, remove the weeds, the six weeds.

You have a beautiful cosmic tree inside your heart. It touches the cosmos, but it is in the garden of the soul. It stays under the ground because of these weeds. These weeds are very small. Try to understand the *maya* which is in you. Analyze your nature. If you have anger and lust, your nature is *rajasic* and *tamasic*. So control the *rajasic* and *tamasic* natures, and improve your spiritual quality, that is, your inner beauty, and elevate yourself to the *sattvic* state. From the *sattvic* to the *vishuddha sattvic* state you must have one hundred per cent purity. This is also mentioned in the *Rig Veda* very beautifully.

In this *yuga,* we have polluted this entire Earth with so many impurities—polluted the rivers with contaminants from factories, lead pollution, so many kinds of pollution. The most important pollution is our negativity. Our negative thoughts pollute the entire universe. So, it is said very beautifully in the *Rig Veda*, in the first canto, "Let noble thoughts come to us from every side." Only noble thoughts—not good thoughts, beautiful thoughts, but noble thoughts must come to us. Nobility leads to purity and purity to divine wisdom. When you have both purity and wisdom, you attain God-Realization and your life becomes so beautiful with absolute wisdom.

So children, this is the essence of the entire *Sanatana Dharma.* It is so beautiful. It teaches wisdom, truthfulness, honesty and so many beautiful things which are useful for all mankind. Amma wants to share that love, cosmic love, with the entire universe, with Her children, whom She calls Her babies. O my babies! Come! Come to Mother!

"How can I elevate myself, Mother?"

"Oh, you must cultivate all the good qualities in your heart. Pull out all the little weeds."

Anger is a very small weed—compared to the Absolute, is it a big weed? It is not. We give so much importance to our anger, lust, greed, hatred and jealousy, which are all very mean qualities. Send them out permanently from your heart and elevate your soul to the highest peak of Truth, children!

Meditate regularly in the morning. Prayer or meditation must be one hundred per cent truthful. Be honest in meditation and have faith in meditation. But remember that meditation is only a path, not the destination. You must understand this point clearly. Give your selfless service, where the self is less, one hundred per cent less, and give it with love. Whatever service you perform, it must be without any expectation from anyone. That is *nishkama karma yoga,* or true selfless service. It is the greatest *yoga* for all mankind to merge with the Eternal.

So elevate yourselves and go beyond this mortal frame. Meditation, spirituality, devotion—all these lead you to immortality. Without discipline, no one can attain spirituality. Spirituality is dependent on daily discipline.

Have discipline, and learn the language of the divine—absolute silence. Freeing the mind from the source of all thoughts is meditation. Thoughts may be positive, negative, good, ordinary, low, or noble. Meditation means going beyond even noble thoughts. Go beyond all thought and merge with the Eternal, children!

Mother is eternal, attributeless, divisionless. Oneness is the essence of spirituality, not duality. So merge with your Mother. She is everywhere. Open your heart and open your third eye. Opening the third eye means the attainment of true knowledge—seeing God everywhere, all the time—first in yourself and then in the entire universe, in the whole cosmos.

Your spiritual college is not in this world. It is a cosmic college. You are a cosmic student. So remove all the weeds within. If you really want to have a cosmic education, elevate. Elevate, expand, and meditate, meditate, meditate. Learn silence, learn silence, learn silence. Listen to the inner voice, open the third eye of knowledge and see divinity everywhere in this universe. That is the highest aim of human life.

So, embodiments of divinity, children, do not walk on the mud path of worldliness! Always walk on the path of rose petals. Have real devotion and faith in whatever path you follow. All religions are the same. Every religion leads to the same goal. So have faith. All mankind belongs to you—the entire bird kingdom, animal kingdom, Mother Earth, the five elements, air, fire, everything, and all the religions and the entire cosmos belong to you. You are everything—what are you not? So children, merge with your Mother!

Hari Om Tat Sat

Houston *11 April 1997*

ॐ

GOD DWELLS IN THE TEMPLE OF THE HEART

Embodiment of Divine Souls,

There are innumerable religions in this world. The essence of all religions is contained in two *shlokas* of the ancient *Sanatana Dharma.* The first *shloka* is from the *Bhagavad Gita,* which contains the essence of the *Upanishads* in seven hundred *shlokas:*

Anayāścintayanto mām
Ye janā paryupāsate
Teṣām nityābhyuktānām
Yoga kṣemam vahāmyaham

This nuclear *shloka means,* "If anyone surrenders to me totally, one hundred per cent, I will never leave him, and I will always take care of my child." There is a nuclear *shloka* in *Vishnu Sahasranama* that is at the end of the prayer.

Sri Rāma Rāma Rāmeti
Rame Rāme Manorame
Sahasra nāma tatulyam
Rāma nāma Varānane

The second *shloka* is from the *Chandi Sapta Shati,* which sings the glory of Divine Mother in seven hundred *shlokas.* It is chanted particularly during the *Navaratri* celebrations. The beautiful nuclear *shloka* from this holy book is:

Om śaraṇāgata dīnārtā
Paritrāṇa parāyaṇe
Sarvasyārti hare Devī
Nārāyaṇī namōstute

"O Mother! I do not pray for myself alone. Go to all Your children who have problems, Amma, and give them Your cosmic love and compassion. Elevate all Your children to the ultimate state of peace and bliss." If you recite this *mantra* either two, five or seven times every day, the power of the *mantra* will bring peace to the universe. Pray to Mother for peace in the whole universe. This universe is yours, it belongs to you. Nature gives you so much. It is your duty to repay nature's bounty by praying for universal peace.

Pray from the bottom of your heart for humility, purity and wisdom. Beg Mother to remove your negative qualities. Prayer from the heart is heard in a fraction of a second, for God dwells in the temple of the heart. Develop sincere devotion and equal vision, cultivate righteousness, compassion and tranquility. These are the beautiful ornaments of a spiritual seeker. Let all these jewels beautify your heart. Then the *atma jyoti*, the flame of the lamp of devotion, will not tremble or flicker. If our devotion is strong we will have bliss, patience, courage, and righteousness. And if we have all these divine attributes in our heart, our love will never be shaken under any circumstances. This is the essence of the *Bhagavad Gita* and *Sanatana Dharma:*

Anayāścintayanto mam
Ye janā paryupāsate
Teṣām nityābhyuktānām
Yoga kṣemam vahāmyaham

When the devotee surrenders completely:

Anyathā śaraṇam nāsti
Tvameka ṣaraṇam mama
Tasmāt kāruṇya bhāvena
Rakṣya rakṣya Janārdanī

The deity responds: "I never leave one who worships me with a hundred per cent faith, under any circumstances whatsoever."

The *Sharanagata dinarta mantra* in the *Chandi Sapta Shati* also shows the attitude of the devotee. It is a beautiful *mantra* with very powerful seed letters, and is also a universal prayer. In ancient times, the wise ones knew that people would be full of negativity in this *Kali yuga.* So all these innumerable prayers were created for universal peace.

You may ask, "Amma we can only pray for peace in our area, how can our prayers bring universal peace?"

Suppose we were to take some chillies and put them in the fire, what would happen in this room? The chillies would immediately give out a strong and pungent odor, and it would become very difficult even to breathe. Just a few chillies would affect the atmosphere of the entire room. In the same way, if we were to put some incense in the fire, the whole room would be filled with fragrance.

When we chant *Om* once, what happens? Positive vibrations are created which spread through the whole cosmos. Suppose we throw a small stone into the pond, what happens? It creates vibrations and waves, which touch the outer edges of the whole pond. Likewise, when we pray to Mother with *mantra*s such as the *Om mantra*, the *Rama mantra* or any *mantra* with faith—what happens? There are seven *lokas* in our body, connected to the *Sapta Sri Mandala,* the seven worlds of Divine Mother. The vibrations of *Om* connect our mortal body to the Immortal. When we meditate, from the tips of our toes to the *Brahma randhra* at the top of the head, the *Om* sound travels through all the seven *chakras,* and we are connected to the entire cosmos. So the negative vibrations in the cosmos are controlled by the power of the positive vibrations of the primal seed letter *Om.* If the positive vibrations are fifty percent and negative vibrations are also fifty percent, the two are balanced. But when there are only one per cent, half percent, or just a quarter per cent of positive vibrations, there is no balance of morality in the universe. So if we pray with any *mantra,* the *Gayatri mantra*, *Om mantra*, or any other *mantra,* the power of the seed letters in that *mantra* will burn all the impurities in the universe. It will also purify the heart of the devotee and elevate him to the highest peak of desirelessness.

In the beginning, we pray to God for the fulfillment of desires. Gradually, after some years there are no desires. Where do all these desires go? They are burnt by the power of purity. We are not even aware when these useless desires are burnt. So children, make your prayer pure. Be like a pure bee and drink the elixir in the divine cosmic lotus, the *vishva kamala,* the universal lotus in the *sahasrara.*

So when we pray with the *Om mantra,* all the *chakras* in our body—there are nine *chakras*—begin to bloom. These *chakras* are also mentioned in the *Vedas:*

Caturbhiḥ Śrī Kaṇṭhaiḥ Śiva
Yuvatibhiḥ pancabhir api
Prabhinnābhiḥ Śambhor navabhir
Api mūla Prakṛtibhiḥ
Catuṣ catvārimśad vasudala
Kalāśca tri valaya
Tri rekhābhiḥ sārdham
Tava śaraṇa koṇāḥ pariṇatāḥ

Mother's *chakra*s are five—the *pancha bhutas.* Four *chakra*s are Siva's. This combination of nine *chakra*s is the human body. So why do we need meditation? So that we can remodel ourselves. The art of remodeling life into divinity is called meditation. We want to remodel our life; we want to purify our life with meditation. In the place of anger have peace; in the place of selfishness, selflessness;

in the place of desire, desirelessness. So we need to remodel everything—our mind and our whole life. All these divine attributes, like gems and pearls in our hearts, shine when we always dwell in peace.

Children, always meditate for divine knowledge. Ask Mother, "O Mother! Please grant me a grand life. My life is filled with poverty—poverty in knowledge, poverty in devotion, poverty in peace of mind and in so many aspects. Please give me real wealth—wealth in devotion, wealth in peace, wealth in health, wealth in satisfaction, in contentment, and in so many things." That is the real wealth.

Do you know a *stotra* called *Daridrya dahana stotra?* Generally in India they sing the *Daridrya dahana stotra* for the attainment of wealth, but that is not the real meaning. At the spiritual level, the meanings change. Spiritually the prayer is for the wealth of peace, contentment, equal vision, purity and elevation to the highest level. However, in practical life, it is very hard to achieve this elevation. So meditate early in the morning. If this is not possible because of the many tensions in your life, try to meditate before going to bed. Summarize the day, understand your mistakes. Meditators should not have even a little ego.

Children, meditate on the Truth; cultivate inner beauty. Start the day with divine cosmic love, fill the day with divine love, and end the day with divine love. One with inner beauty never hurts people. There are so many steps for you to climb. Do not stop your eternal journey. Go forward fast, and attain God-Realization, because the main aim of this human life is Self-Realization. The Self is Truth, Self is wisdom, Self is tranquility, Self is indestructible power, Self is only One—God is only One, all the real *gurus* are also only One. There is no diffference between all the true *gurus*. Mother is One, Mother Earth is

One, air is One, fire is One. All the elements are One. Cosmic love is also only One. So elevate yourself to the highest peak of purity. Pray for purity, purity, complete purification, and meditate, meditate, meditate! Evolve and elevate yourself to the highest peak and expand your *atma* to the entire cosmos.

In *Sanatana Dharma,* there are *shanti mantras,* or prayers for the welfare of all humanity. Who will pray for others? Because you are a pure soul, you pray for your brothers and sisters in this universe. Never see any difference between anyone in this universe. In the *Vedas* it is said in beautiful *shloka*s that the entire universe is *vasudhaika kutumbam,* only one family. So all humans are your brothers and sisters. The feeling of oneness in spiritual people is just like my feeling towards you—you are nothing but my flesh, my blood, my bones and my soul. That is my feeling. I feel that you are separate from me only in body. The feeling that you belong to this country, I belong to that country and so on, is very limited. If your feeling is elevated to the highest level, you will feel that all mankind is mine, all religions belong to me. This is not the little egoistic "me," it is my soul. So every living being is my soul, nothing but my flesh, my blood, my bones and my soul. That is true spirituality. So, children, there are such beautiful steps in spirituality. We need to go beyond confusion and ego, and cultivate all the good qualities.

We never go inside and search for Reality because we are living in a speed wave. That is why we cannot achieve anything. If we just sit in silence, go within, and attain inner vision, then only will we be able to understand the inner Reality in our life. That is possible only in meditation. Meditation makes our mind silent, and we can observe ourselves: "O, my thoughts are very wrong, very sick. I am very proud, this is not good; and I have anger too—this is also not good. I must try to control myself. But how can I control myself?" You can do it by chanting *Rama nama,* by chanting Divine Mother's name—Lalita Devi's name, any divine name, or just *Om.* By the power of the seed letters in these names, the cosmic flowers, the *chakras,* bloom in the body, which is like a beautiful pond of nectar. In this beautiful pond, the divine cosmic flowers are present. Try to bloom them with divine knowledge. When the sun of knowledge shines on those flowers, they bloom. So cultivate knowledge, compassion and righteousness and attain God-Realization. How will this be possible? By the constant practice of meditation and by spiritual discipline. Do not give up meditation for even one day, for without discipline there is no spirituality. Discipline is extremely important for spirituality.

Have contentment—contentment is the greatest treasure. It is called *shashvata aishvarya*—permanent wealth. If there is no contentment at all in our life, we are always materialistic, sad and unhappy. You know more than Amma about this world. For just a little happiness, we are working and working and working like machines, and we get so tired. Working so hard, we have frustrations, anxiety, so much stress and fear—why this fear? Everywhere we see fear, fear and fear. This is because we do not have wisdom in our life.

Spirituality is the only solution to this problem. So if you come and ask Amma for a solution, I will give you a response, but it will be a temporary solution. I think of it as a spoon-feeding process. Some time later you may have another problem. Where will you go then? If you talk about your problem to anyone, it is not good for you also. They may criticize you, laugh at you, or talk about you to others. So you must not tell anyone about your problems. Because I am your Mother, you come to Amma, and it is my responsibility to listen to your problems, so I will talk to you for five or ten minutes. In that little time, you feel so happy. Who will talk with us in this world? Who has the time? If anyone gives you a little compassion, just a very tiny bit of love, you become so happy, so happy, because life is like that in the world.

So children, how can we cultivate contentment in our life? We must have a permanent connection with Mother Divine through meditation. If you meditate, you have a connection with Mother Divine. Whenever you pray, immediately you will get a response in your heart, telling you, "Do this, do that, do not go now, go right now! " In this way you have intuition in your heart, which is a message from Mother.

Only meditation will give you a permanent solution to the small problems of this temporary life. This life of forty or seventy years is only a long play. So you will get a solution, but there is a destiny. We have a definite aim in life. That aim is *moksha,* salvation. We need permanent liberation from all these problems, so we want *moksha,* the *jivana mukta sthiti,* the state of liberation in this very life. Beautiful words! There are so many words in Sanskrit for salvation—*moksha, jivana mukta sthiti, mukta sthiti, moksha sthiti, jnana sthiti, Brahma sthiti, Brahmi sthiti.* So many words which mean salvation. There is only one word in English. How can we attain this state? If we are always at the spoon-feeding stage, there can be no salvation. Meditation leads you to salvation. You have a permanent connection with Divinity, and your entire life is remodeled. Then you can hear the inner voice of intuition wherever you may be. You enjoy Divinity in the form of peace. The divine fragrance of peace is ever with you. Children, be always in that divine fragrance—it is so beautiful!

Your soul is the light of all lights. In this cosmos there are so many suns, and your soul gives light to all the suns in the galaxy! Such is the supreme power hidden in your body. Open the heart, open your heart, and dispel egoism permanently by your prayer. Have real devotion, humility and one hundred per cent discriminating faith—not ninety-nine point nine percent faith, but a hundred percent faith. Not ninety-nine point nine and a quarter percent, but a hundred percent faith. Not blind faith; it must be, we must have, discriminating knowledge in our life.

Why do we chant the *Om mantra* at the beginning of our program? The *Om mantra* purifies the physical body, the mental body and the intellectual body, and gives connections to the cosmos. That is the power of the seed letter in *Omkara*. He who chants the *Om mantra* will attain God-Realization in this birth.

There are thousands and thousands of *shlokas* in the *Vedas* about the *Om mantra*. Just the *Om mantra* is enough to purify each and every cell of our body, our mind and thoughts—there are so many bad thoughts. Remove all these thoughts, burn all the bad thoughts. Always have noble thoughts, pure thoughts, positive thoughts and good thoughts only. That is humanity, not divinity. First begin with humanity and then raise yourself to divinity. If there is no humanity, how can you expect divinity? So elevate yourself from *manavatva*—qualities of a human, to *Madhavatva*—qualities of Madhava, Vishnu.

These are ornaments for a spiritual seeker. Whatever faith he may have in his life, for whatever reason, that is not the question. Go beyond all limitations and do not get stuck in constraints. Sometimes we can get stuck at some points. When we put a cassette into a tape recorder, it can get stuck at one place, so that we cannot listen to the songs after that point. In the same way, if we are stuck in some blind beliefs, some points, then we begin to think, "Only this is true; only that is true." That is also a sort of egoism.

Go beyond all these little limits. Listen only to the decision of your heart; act according to the voice of your heart. The decisions must be made at the right time, not after several years. Life is wasted by prolonging the matter endlessly. So take the decisions in time—at the right time—and have a peaceful, good life.

We are in this body, but we are liberated from all these qualities. We are always in the fragrance of peace; and we have contentment when we have decorated this beautiful temple with all the divine attributes. When you meditate with these divine attributes, you can achieve the state of *samadhi.* Do you know that eleven seconds of silence is *samadhi?* Without any thought—only eleven seconds—but it is not possible. Even in one second we have a thousand thoughts, for the mind is always working. From the mind, innumerable thoughts arise spontaneously. Burn all these *rajasic, tamasic* and *sattvic* thoughts, seek meditation without these thoughts and enjoy *samadhi*—at least for eleven seconds! Is it possible in this birth? Yes, it is possible. It depends on our interest in meditation and on our devotion. It must be possible, no problem. Amma encourages all Her children, and says it is possible, possible, possible. Try to come. This path is so far away, but I will accompany you with my thousand hands. I will hold all my children with all these hands. Come! and be not afraid of anything. Be not afraid of anger or any of these little things. Do not see them.

Forgiveness, *kshama,* is divine. It beautifies our life. Where there is forgiveness, there only is Divine Mother. There only is compassion, and there only is real spiritual wisdom. We have no wisdom in this life. We are under the control of the mind; we are like slaves—always under the control of anger and greed. So send them away, children. Send them away permanently from your lives and be one with Mother. Have a different aim.

Start your eternal journey and have devotion. Don't just sit in meditation and become dry. That is not good. Have devotion. Make your heart tender like butter. That happens in devotion only when your feelings become so delicate that you are unable to even cut a flower. You are not even able to walk on the grass. You can hear the grass cry, "O! Who is walking on my back?" You can feel its pain. You hear the voice of nature everywhere. Have a tender heart so that even flowers can say to you, "I have come to you all the way, offer me to God." Then we can have tender feelings in our heart. Now we have dry feelings. We are always using harsh words.

The *Saraswati mantra* purifies our words, our tongue, our heart, and gives one hundred percent tenderness in our life. Whatever is in our heart comes out in our words. So have a pure heart, always speak softly, smoothly, gently, truthfully and kindly. That is Saraswati. Saraswati is revealed in our behavior. Mother Saraswati changes our behavior. Saraswati is not just sitting on a lotus and playing the *vina*—that is not Saraswati. Saraswati is in your life in the form of knowledge, in the form of humility, in the form of good behavior, good character, moral values and humanity. She beautifies us with all the divine attributes and gradually helps us attain the highest peak of attributelessness. That is Saraswati.

We chant the *Saraswati Mantra* for elevation. "O Mother elevate me in knowledge, I want knowledge. I have knowledge about this world, but my knowledge is not enough for God-Realization. I want to be elevated to that highest peak. So I pray to You with this *Saraswati mantra*, please give me liberation from all these natures. Fill my heart with good virtues, and elevate me to the highest peak of desirelessness. My enemies are my desires. So remove these enemies from my heart, send all the dark forces from my heart and open my heart, make it pure and give me awareness. Let my thoughts, my deeds, my every action be purified by divine knowledge. Please grant me all this, Mother." Divine Mother will grant you all these, children. Pray to Mother and get these beautiful attributes in your life.

Children, all these things are easy to say but very hard to practice. To have Truth is to remove anger and egoism from our heart, which is very difficult. By the grace of Divinity, anything is possible in our life. Our mind and intellect are powerless before divine grace. What is our intellect? Divinity controls the cosmos. So where is our knowledge? It is really powerless before divine grace. Pray always for divine grace. Being alone in your room and facing east is very good for meditation. There is a reason for this. The magnetic waves travel on Earth from east to west and from north to south. If you sit in other directions you will not be able to sit for a long time in meditation. Facing east is very good for salvation, and so is northeast. So try to face east wherever you are in your room. Facing north or northeast is also very good. Never sit in meditation facing west or south—those directions counter the vibrations in our body.

When we meditate with *mantra*s, our whole body is stimulated and the vibrations of the power of *mantra* stimulate all the *chakras*. There is a beautiful reasoning to the power of *mantra*s. So next time we will discuss all these things. The recent fifty years of scientific research has shown how the *Om mantra* and the *Ayim mantra* work in our body. The *Ayim* seed letter works in the mouth and at the *vishuddha chakra*. The *Srim* seed letter works in the eyes, forehead, the ear and also the throat. The *Hrim* seed letter in particular gives a lot of energy. Sometimes, when you feel weak, just chant mentally, *"Hrim, Hrim, Hrim."* Immediately you will get lots of energy from Mother. *Hrim* is the source of energy. And when you say *Om*, from the tip of your foot to the top of your head, the entire nervous system is stimulated in a fraction of a second. When we repeat the *Om mantra* only once, it purifies the blood, and we never get paralysis or stroke and we never get a heart attack. So these seed letters work beautifully for the mental body and our nervous system.

If you meditate on the *Saraswati mantra* a hundred and eight times, it will probably take five to six minutes, not much more. The *Saraswati mantra* purifies the seeker and bestows him with divine knowledge. Pray alone in your room facing east or north and your prayer must always be from the bottom of your heart. Pray for purification—purification in words, deeds, and in your entire life. I want elevation from mortality to Immortality. That is our aim. The main aim of our life is only Self-Realization. You already understand that. So be a practical meditator—practice meditation every day. That is very important. When we chant the *Mrityunjaya Mantra* now, keep your concentration between your eyebrows. That is the knowledge-place, the third eye place. Withdraw your mind from all external forces and focus your mind between the two eyebrows at the *ajna chakra*. There is a great junction point between our two eyebrows. We attain God Realization and we have inner vision in the place between our two eyebrows only, in this very body.

[Chanting of the *Mrityunjaya mantra*]

Swamiji: So this is great! Actually, yesterday at the Yoga Center, Amma was saying that we need mental healing; this is very important. Before we detect ailments in our physical body, our mental body is destroyed because of mental illness. So mentally we have to be cured and mentally we have to be healed. So this greatest healing and the energy Amma gives are not just for the physical ailments, as many of you may be thinking. Amma gives us hope, She elevates us, She consoles us and She gives Her blessings for our spiritual upliftment also.

[Amma speaks in Telugu]

Swamiji [translating]: *Jai Karunamayi!* Amma was saying that some devotees are interested in doing *likhita japa.* Remembering God and repeating God's name is *japa.* Writing the divine name is also one kind of *japa,* and is called *likhita japa.* Some of the devotees have been telling Amma that they want to write the name of God, the name of the Divine Mother Lalitambika. So if you all bring notebooks tomorrow at the evening session, Amma will bless them by writing the first *nama* in your notebooks. Amma is saying that even if it is a single *nama*, it has a lot of energy and power and if you do this kind of *likhita japa,* it is very powerful and it will elevate you. So one by one you can all line up now and take Amma's blessings. *Jai Karunamayi!*

Houston *13 April 1997*

ॐ

MEDITATION RESHAPES MAN FROM MORTALITY TO DIVINITY

Embodiments of Divine Souls, Children,

Look at the wild flowers. Even in the desert, where there is no water or manure and the climate is very hot and dry, the cactus flowers bloom so beautifully with fragrance. There are so many flowers in our body: the root *chakra* or *muladhara* flower, the *svadhishthana* flower, the *manipura* flower, the *anahata maha* flower, the great heart flower, the *vishuddhi* flower, the *ajna chakra* flower and the thousand-petal *sahasrara kamala,* the universal lotus in the tenth gate of our body. So let all those flowers bloom, children. Bloom them immediately. Offer them to Mother Divine. That is the real *puja:*

Bhavet pūjā pūjā tava caraṇayor yā viracitām....

Brahma, Vishnu, Siva, the great *Trimurtis*, and all the *devatas* bow to Mother's lotus feet. They offer so many sweet, fragrant flowers to Mother, but She likes one flower:

Caitanya kusumārādhyā caitanya kusuma priyā

Kusuma is a Sanskrit word which means a beautiful, delicate flower. *Chaitanya kusuma* is the cosmic flower. Mother loves the cosmic lotus, the thousand-petal *sahasrara* lotus. So all the great *devatas*, *rishis*, sages, the *Trimurtis*, all come to Mother with their hands full of flowers, and offer them to Her. But Mother says,

Bhavet pūjā pūjā....

"There is only one true *puja,*" the greatest *puja* in the universe—offering the inner flowers to Mother. Bloom all these inner flowers for Mother. Do not hurt the flowers, they cry when you cut them. So bloom the real inner flowers, bloom the universal lotus, the *sahasrara* lotus of a thousand petals in the tenth gate of the body, and offer that cosmic flower to Mother Divine.

The *muladhara chakra* is the first *chakra* at the base of the spine. *Mula* means the main; *adhara* means the base or foundation. It is also known as the root *chakra*. It is a beautiful, luminous, four-petal lotus of orange hue. The color is indescribable. In that *chakra* of four petals, there is a triangle in which lies the serpent power *kundalini* with closed eyes. It is always in a sleepy state. When we meditate with a *mantra* such as the *Om mantra* or the *Saraswati mantra*, the *kundalini* wakes up.

The second *chakra* is the *svadhishthana chakra*. When the *kundalini* is in the *svadhishthana chakra*, we have many attachments. I am just giving you some information on the surface level, not in detail.

The third is the *manipura chakra,* When the *kundalini* is in this *chakra*, we criticize people: "Only my path is good, I have respect only for my *Guru*, I don't care for anyone else." We get stuck in these beliefs, repeating ourselves like a cassette in the tape recorder: "I believe only in Devi, I have faith only in Saraswati." O children, this is very pathetic, really a thousand times pathetic, because we are stuck at one particular point. Divinity belongs to the entire universe. Your Self belongs to the entire universe. Do not be in this pathetic position, babies. Elevate, elevate, elevate. No holy person in this universe will allow their children to be stuck at one point. They want them to be elevated, to touch the cosmos and be in bliss—that is their wish for all mankind.

The fourth is the heart *chakra* or *anahata maha chakra*. When *kundalini* is in the heart *chakra* we have humility, pure devotion and wisdom. So many people who are on the spiritual path have no wisdom. They say, "Do not go there, do not read this book, do not look at those things." Even spiritual, holy persons can be limited by such ideas. This shows no wisdom at all. So be always in wisdom, my babies, be always in wisdom. Have liberation from all the six inner enemies and cultivate one hundred percent humility. When the energy stabilizes in the heart *chakra*, you are in perfect silence. When you speak, you speak only spiritual words, you have self control and there are no more doubts in your mind:

Bhidyate hṛdaya granthiḥ chinna samṣayaḥ

"When the *hridaya granthi,* the knot of the heart, is pierced, all doubts disappear." Sometimes there are many clouds in the sky. When the sun shines, there are no clouds. All these clouds appear when we limit ourselves to the body, mind and intellect. When the sun of divine knowledge shines in the heart, there are no clouds at all.

When the heart *chakra* is blooming with devotion, we have one hundred percent humility and all the divine attributes bloom within. Gradually we enjoy peace, truth, wisdom and tranquility in our life. We become silent, with absolutely no negative emotions at all—no anger, lust, or any of these immoral qualities. We are full of purity and discriminative knowledge about Divinity. We understand that God is One, all beliefs are One, Divinity is One, all the real *gurus* are also One, the sun is One, the moon is One, the Earth is One, all humanity is One. Why do we see differences between people? Only because of *maya,* illusion.

When the *anahata maha chakra* blooms, we have no disease at all, we are beyond desires and our thoughts, words and deeds are a hundred percent pure.

At the base of the throat is the *vishuddhi chakra*. When the *vishuddhi chakra* blooms, our entire life is purified, we have a hundred percent devotion and we experience *samadhi.*

The *ajna chakra* is between the two eyebrows. This is the spot which Amma touched yesterday when She gave each and every one of you Her blessing. It is called the third eye place, the place of divine knowledge. *Omkara* ends here. When the energy reaches this *chakra,* we have self-illumination. Now we have knowledge about this world, but no knowledge about Divinity. When the *kundalini* comes to this *chakra,* you have a hundred percent knowledge about Divinity, about pure consciousness. So, when the third eye is opened, you bless this entire universe—you overflow with forgiveness and compassion. You are beyond compassion, beyond attributes, and you yourself are Divine. You merge with Divinity—you go from this mortal frame to immortality—you attain Self-Realization. But sometimes when the energy is in the *ajna chakra,* there is still a transparent curtain.

However, when the energy reaches the *sahasrara,* the universal *kamala,* the thousand-petal lotus on the crown of the head, there are no more curtains. There are no names or forms, only absolute silence, bliss, self-illumination, and *samadhi.* You realize, "This entire cosmos belongs to my soul only."

So, embodiments of Divine Souls, be always in bliss! Come, come back to your Mother's sweet home, the place of divine grace, to the universal lotus, the tenth gate of the body, the *sahasrara*. That is peace, that is eternal peace.

[Amma speaks in Telugu]

Swamiji [translating]: *Jai Karunamayi!* Before our meditations we learned *pranayama*. When we practice *pranayama* and do it before meditation, this *pranayama* helps to awaken the spiritual energy, the *kundalini,* which lies asleep in the *muladhara*. So *pranayama* is very important.

Amma: Children, what is the definition of meditation? What is your feeling about meditation?

Yogaḥ citta vṛtti nirodhaḥ

The *Patanjali Yoga Sutras* were written by that pure soul, Patanjali Maharshi, who is considered to be the manifested form of the serpent power *kundalini*. Did you see that beautiful idol of Nataraja yesterday in the Yoga Center? Well, there is a beautiful temple with a thousand pillars in Chidambara, India, which is considered to be Nataraja's place. Patanjali Maharshi conducted a meditation session there like the one we are having today. About one thousand disciples attended.

He was a very strict *rishi,* so he had admonished his disciples: "Do not speak, do not argue, do not do anything. Close your eyes, meditate, and just listen to me, to my message." Some people opened their eyes and were immediately reduced to ashes because of the intense rays of self-illumination from the *kundalini*. Only one disciple remained. He learned the *Patanjali Yoga Sutras*—that is, the hundred *Yoga Sutras*.

Patanjali never burned those people. Ishwara also never burned Manmatha, the God of Desire. Patanjali was sending the powerful spiritual energy in his body, the lighting, the vibrations, to the seekers. When they opened their eyes with anxiety, without truthfulness in the heart—what happened? They were reduced to ashes. But the spiritual energy passed from Patanjali to the seeker who kept his eyes closed. So truthfulness is also very important for a spiritual aspirant. Patanjali Maharshi, in spite of having one thousand people who wanted to learn meditation, gave the message of the *Yoga Sutras* only to one seeker out of the one thousand. It has been said in those *Yoga Sutras:*

Yogaḥ citta vṛtti nirodhaḥ

Yoga means to control the thoughts, to free the mind of thoughts. Meditation is the art of remodeling man into Divinity. Now we are in human form, the mortal form. So meditation is the art of remodeling man to Divinity, immortality. Meditation purifies our mind, life, thoughts and deeds. Meditation is the fastest path to God-Realization. We chant divine names for countless years. How many people chant these divine names from the bottom of their heart? We are often just looking here and there, and singing some *bhajans*. There is no inwardness at all. If we really have inwardness, our heart becomes purified by the fire of just one repetition of any divine name such as *Om namah Sivaya* or Rama. But we chant only with our lips, not from the bottom of our heart. If we chant with intense feeling, we are very fortunate.

So, children, meditation gives you inwardness. We close our eyes, but our mind is working, it is full of thoughts. Gradually, as we repeat these *mantras*—the *Om mantra* or the *Saraswati mantra*—these thoughts are destroyed from the root, as if by a laser, and we are free from the load of *karma*. The *karma* load is very heavy. It is like a mountain—not one mountain but millions of mountains. The *karma* load of innumerable births is the cause of all the pain and misery in this life. This load is quickly destroyed as the seeker chants the *mantra* during meditation. Each and every repetition of the *mantra* burns the thoughts at the root.

Every thought becomes an action. If it is a good thought it is okay. But if it is a bad thought, a poisonous thought—such as the thoughts of people who want wars, like Duryodhana—even if it is only one thought, it causes impurity in the entire universe. So destroy the thought. Watch your thoughts, and burn any negative thought at the root itself. That is important. This will happen in meditation.

Meditation will give you self-confidence, self-control, and improve your will power. You will have good health, equal vision, balance of mind, peace in your life, and balance in thinking—all these good things—and a positive way of thinking leading to positive actions. Anger is gradually reduced by meditation. We develop a one hundred percent balanced mind through meditation only, no doubt. Meditation is the art of remodeling man into divinity. It is so beautiful.

Remodeling the man: If our house is in very bad condition we remodel it and beautify it with new construction. Likewise, through innumerable births in this world, human nature is again and again being remodeled by meditation. Anxiety, hatred, jealousy—all these little, little qualities are destroyed and replaced by peace of mind, equal vision, compassion and divinity in our life. So, meditation is undoubtedly the great art which remodels man into divinity.

So when we plan a meditation retreat for ten days or one week, keep all your vacations for Amma. Do not waste time going here and there but spend your time in the spiritual path, children. Meditate on your Self only. Siva meditates on His Self. Self is pure, Self is Bliss, Self is Absolute, Self is wisdom—meditation on the Self is the greatest *yoga.* And we must have devotion. Without devotion how will you sit in meditation? It is a waste of effort. So we must have devotion, faith and a spiritual bent of mind. We also need knowledge—*jnana*—the understanding that we have to search for the secret in our own Self. Thus we need a combination of *jnana*, meditation and *karma*. You must stop all external *karmas* and do only one *karma*—meditation.

All the *yogas* are integrated here. First of all you must have devotion and faith. Next, you must learn the value of meditation and silence. And third, perform meditation in order to experience Reality—*karma*. Meditation on the Self should be done only for true wisdom, not for any powers or *siddhis*.

No doubt meditation is the way to remodel yourself from mortality to divinity. At present we are mortal. Gradually the black curtains of illusion are removed from our eyes and the third eye is opened in meditation. These curtains also cover our heart. These black curtains in the form of thoughts are permanently removed by meditation. We are then able to open our heart with pure devotion to the wisdom within.

So evolve and expand yourself—inquire and discover divinity. These are little words—evolve, try to elevate yourself, and expand. The nature, or *atma lakshana* of *atma* is expansion—like air. Air is always expanding. So *atma* is *vyapaka*—it is all pervading, not limited to a small pot. It is in *atma's* nature to expand to the entire cosmos. So your Self is *atma*. Why do you limit yourself to a particular religion or a particular country, or particularly to this body, this mind, and limited intellect? Before divine grace, our limited intellect and mind are really powerless. Before divine grace our limited intellect is powerless. They have no power at all. Divinity is higher than anything in this world. So, children, do not be limited to the mind, body and the limited intellect. The spirit is self-illumination, power and contentment. When we experience *samadhi,* we feel that contentment.

Meditation includes all the *yogas.* It is *bhakti yoga* and selflessness. Selfless means our self is less, our ego is reduced in meditation. We never think about ourselves. And it is knowledge—that is *jnana yoga.* We are searching for the inner reality, the inner secret. We want to listen to the inner voice, and we want to see the divinity inside our heart—in our heart *chakra.* And finally we want *samadhi.* That is how it is. All the spiritual books and all the sages, the great souls, say that *samadhi* is the greatest peak of spirituality.

Only those who have experienced *samadhi* understand what it is. Eleven seconds of being in the thoughtless state is *samadhi*—only eleven seconds. How many seconds are there in a minute? Sixty seconds. Not even one minute is needed to achieve *samadhi*—only eleven seconds! Even when we are in the sleeping state the mind is still working in the form of dreams. We move around, walk, talk—so many things happen to us in our dreams. The mind is not still. But *samadhi* is absolute silence. There are no thoughts at all. There is no *karma* load.

The entire *karma* is burned by the power of the seed letters in your *mantra*—in the *Saraswati mantra*, in the *Om mantra,* in the *Rama mantra.* The *karma* is burned from the root. If the roots of a plant remain in the ground, and if we just remove the weeds from the surface, they grow again. So send the laser rays of *mantra* power into the roots of all the weeds and burn all your *karmas* permanently.

This is possible through meditation. We have many *chakras* in our body, but they are not visible to the human eye. When our third eye is opened, the innumerable junction points of our body, and the greatest *chakras*—especially the *shat chakras,* the six most important *chakras* in our body—all bloom in meditation when the *kundalini* awakens and rises from the root *chakra.*

So in *pranayama* when we breathe deeply, the *sushumna* opens, and our breath touches the root *chakra.* The pressure caused by the deep breath we take awakens the *kundalini,* the serpent power lying asleep in the root *chakra.* Oxygen is the main source of energy. Without oxygen there is no life at all. This oxygen, this vital energy, touches the subtle form of the *kundalini,* which wakes up by the pressure of *pranayama.* This does not happen in one day, ten days, forty days or even after one year of meditation. Very slowly and very gradually, with constant practice of meditation, we achieve the power to awaken *kundalini* in the root *chakra* and make the *muladhara* lotus bloom.

What happens when the root *chakra* blooms? If you sit on thorns or nails it never hurts you, for your body becomes as light as a cotton ball—weightless. So when the root *chakra* opens, it connects to the *sushumna* and the *kundalini* starts its eternal journey. It rises from the *muladhara chakra* to the *svadhishthana chakra.* When the *svadhishthana chakra* opens, you have a divine vision of the moon, and you are able to walk on water.

Many sages in India are able to sleep and walk on water. Even in modern times there are many such sages. One of them lives near Chitoor in South India. He is a great *avadhuta.* Some sages can control the second element, water, and others can control all five. By the way, the element of the root *chakra* is earth. When the *kundalini* reaches the *manipura chakra,* you control the power of the sun—*agni*, fire. Even if you sit on fire it never burns the body.

There are innumerable scientific reasons for these *chakras* blooming. Now you are taking down notes, but all these points are beyond your understanding. You may even find them amazing. At present you can only meditate for one or two hours daily. This is baby meditation. But when you meditate for longer periods—ten hours, twelve hours every day—your mind is silenced and you begin to understand and capture the truths in the *chakras* when they bloom.

The element of the heart *chakra* is *akasha,* the sky, symbol of the mind. We control the mind only in this *chakra.* The sky is pervaded by air, oxygen. Oxygen is always only in our heart *chakra.* It purifies the blood. This *chakra* controls *prana,* vital energy. When we go beyond the five elements, then only can we touch *prana*—that is the soul, the Absolute. The *bijakshara* of *vayu* is *yam.* It is a very powerful *bijakshara.*

Do you know Anjaneya Swami in the *Ramayana?* His mother is Anjani Devi. She prayed, concentrating particularly on the heart *chakra,* to Vayu, the Wind God—the power of air, that is, oxygen. She wanted a very powerful son. Anjaneya is the son of Vayu, *Vayu putra.* He is very, very powerful. His body has the power of thousands and thousands of elephants. He has tremendous will power. So when we concentrate and particularly meditate on this heart *chakra*, we have great will power and energy.

The *vishuddhi chakra* is the throat *chakra.* It is mentioned in the *Lalita Sahasranama.* By the way children, if possible try to learn the *Lalita Sahasranama.* So many New York children do *parayana,* daily chanting of the *Lalita Sahasranama.* The seed letters in the *Lalita Sahasranama* touch the cosmos. Such is the power of the seed letters. First listen to Amma's cassette and gradually practice line by line. Thus you will be able to learn the whole *Sahasranama.* It may take one year. Don't hurry. It purifies the *karma* of innumerable births. That is the power of the *Lalita Sahasranama.*

These *chakras* are mentioned in the *Lalita Sahasranama*:

> *Mulādhāraika nilayā*
> *Brahma granthi vibhedinī*

Brahma granthi means the root *chakra*. "Mother! You are always in the *muladhara chakra,* in the abode of *kundalini*. You are sleeping there. When we meditate, You wake up and bloom all the *chakras* in our body." The second *granthi* is:

> *Manipūrāntaruḍitā*
> *Visṇu granthi vibhedinī*

The *manipura chakra,* the *chakra* of the sun, contains the full power of fire. When we open this *chakra,* we control the five elements and go beyond. This is described in the *Lalita Sahasranama:*

> *Panca pretāsanāsīnā*
> *Panca Brahma svarūpinī*

These *pancha brahmas*—sky, air, fire, water and earth, all the five elements—are Your forms only. You Yourself are the source of their energy. When You withdraw Your energy from them, all the elements become powerless. So You are the main source of these five elements.

Mother is in the *vishuddhi chakra* as the levels of speech—*para, vak*, *pashyanti*, *madhyama* and *vaikhari.* There are five nervous systems in our body. When *para* is working, we always speak sweet words, good words, divine words, and we think spiritually. We are very pure in our conversation. When we are in worldly consciousness, we hurt people, and our thoughts and words have a low quality. Our way of thinking is also not good. This is an indication that this nervous system is not working in the *vishuddhi chakra*. When Mother comes to the *vishuddhi chakra*, all the five systems bloom and we are always in purity. Whatever is in our heart manifests in our words. So this is the purity of the *vishuddhi chakra*. We become a hundred percent purified in thoughts, words and deeds.

This is the *ajna chakra* here. [Amma points on the diagram]. It is the place of Saraswati—see the sun and moon? There are two nervous systems—we have two beautiful videotapes about them. [Amma points to the nose] Indians women wear nose studs in their nostrils. The nerve on the right is called *pingala,* the sun *nadi;* the one on the left is *ida*, the moon *nadi.* These two nervous systems are connected to the *sushumna,* the elixir *nadi.* When these two nerves combine here [pointing to a point between the eyebrows]—new moon and full moon—that is the *samadhi* experience. This is according to the *Yoga Shastras,* which go into greater detail. I am just touching on some points.

See the moon and sun here? Women wear a pearl stud here [pointing to the left nostril], and a diamond stud here [pointing to the right nostril]. The diamond represents the sun, while the pearl represents the moon.

The *nava ratnas,* nine gems, are worn in rings for the nine planets, as are the nine colors—did you know that? In olden times some people wore the *nava ratnas* daily. One of my sons yesterday asked me whether metal has the power to control rheumatism and other ailments. We do wear bangles of *pancha dhatu,* the five metals. There is a beautiful meaning to the worship of idols. Idols of silver, silver plating, and other metals are charged with the lighting, rays, from the entire cosmos, which is then transferred to our body. So people wore, and some even now wear, diamonds on Sunday. On Monday, they wear white clothes and pearl jewelry; Tuesday they wear *pushya raga,* citrine, of a very light, golden color. It gives and preserves wealth—it is very beneficial. Wednesday they wear emeralds and green-colored clothes. On Thursday—the day of *Guru graha* or Jupiter—red clothes and *padma ragas,* rubies are worn, and on Friday—Mother's day—they wear all the *nava ratnas,* the nine gems. Saturday is for sapphires and blue diamonds and dark blue clothes.

[Amma continues in Telugu]

Swamiji [translating]**:** From ancient times in India, it was customary to wear different kinds of jewelry set with precious gems. Every precious stone has an effect on the body, for it stimulates the junction points of the nervous system. So jewelry was worn at all such important points in the body: Round pendants were worn on the forehead, necklaces around the neck, ear studs in the ear lobes, bangles and bracelets round the wrists, rings on the fingers and toes. They also wore ornaments around the waist and ankles, and a special one on top of the head at the *sahasrara.* Each piece of jewelry has its own significance—it stimulates the nervous system and energizes the *chakras* in the body.

Color therapy and stone therapy have been discovered only recently in modern times, but from ancient times in India they knew the significance of wearing precious stones, and the effect that different colors had on the body.

In olden days in India people did not use iron plates for food, because iron attracts the rays of Saturn. They used only silver plates. Otherwise they used to eat food on leaves, especially the banana leaf. Why is food eaten from banana leaves? Amma is asking a question.

This is done because it is healthy to eat from leaves. It is a direct way of taking the chlorophyll from them. As you know, the green part of the leaf contains chlorophyll. The leaf is washed, and hot food is served on it. The chlorophyll in the leaf is absorbed by the hot food, and thus we take chlorophyll directly into our body. This is the scientific reason for taking food from the banana leaf. *Palasha* and banyan leaves are also used for serving food.

The breaths inhaled and exhaled during *pranayama* through the *ida* and *pingala,* that is, through the left and the right nostrils, converge at one point between the eye brows—at the *ajna chakra,* the third eye place—and stimulate the *sushumna.* Every *chakra* has a *bijakshara,* seed syllable. The *bijakshara* of the *ajna chakra* is *Om,* the *Pranava mantra.* Every *chakra* also has a presiding deity. Here it is Lord Siva Himself. When one reaches this stage, when the serpent power, the *kundalini* energy, reaches this *chakra,* Siva and Shakti unite and become one. There are no two at all. And when one reaches this place, when the energy transcends and reaches this point, the *sahasrara,* then only can we experience this oneness.

The *Guru's* main responsibility is to initiate a *sadhaka.* But after initiation, the *Guru* has to explain everything, make the disciple sit near him, and make him practice the *sadhana.* In each and every *chakra* there are blockages and a lot of pollution from previous births. This has to be washed away and the blockages removed. So the *Guru's* work is to clear all our doubts, and lead us on the right path. We must first understand what *sadhana* we are doing and we must have no doubts at all. The duty of the *Guru* is to clear all doubts. Just initiating is not enough. He has to teach you and lead you to the *sahasrara.*

There is a forty-five minute videotape showing all these *chakras*, and Amma has explained it very beautifully. She describes each and every *chakra* with its presiding deities, and what the nature of a seeker will be when he reaches a particular *chakra* in the body. So a person's spiritual progress can be determined by examining his nature. We will bring that video and show it to you next time.

Amma: To continue...

The *Sri Chakra* is a representation of Divine Mother Herself. It is Divine Mother's crown, it is Divine Mother's throne, and it is a diagrammatical representation of the abode of Divine Energy. In the picture of the *Sri Chakra* shown here in the *Lalita Sahasranama* book, there are nine triangles—five pointing upward and four pointing downward. In the central triangle pointing downward you can see the *bindu.*

When people say: "Amma, how can we draw that mathematical design?" it hurts me. People get stuck on the wrong point. They see the *Sri Chakra* as a mere geometrical drawing. But those who know about the *Sri Chakra* in India are able to draw it in beautiful colors on the ground during the *Navaratri* festivals. All of our children can draw the *Sri Chakra* on the ground. Yet it is impossible for a scientist with a lot of equipment to draw it easily—it might take him eight to nine hours.

Swamiji [pointing]**:** This figure is very small, but you can see the nine triangles are intersecting at many different points. At these points again some more triangles are formed. Thus there are sixty four triangles in all. In the center you can see an inverted triangle with a center point, the *bindu*. You can all take a look. Just pass it on.

Amma [pointing]**:** This is the tenth gate. When we meditate, the tenth gate opens and the *sahasrara kamala,* the universal lotus, blooms. There are so many reasons for meditating, children. It is not just a blind belief. Some people say, "What is there in meditation?" They are stuck in some point of view and they are not able to understand the significance of meditation.

obThis is the picture of the main *Sri Chakra* which is worshipped in Amma's *ashram* in Bangalore. [Showing the picture] It is a gold *Sri Chakra* and is one of the biggest *Sri Chakras* in the world. It is four feet square, while most *Sri Chakras* are only small ones. This is because bigger ones cannot be easily worshipped. This one is sixteen square feet. Here we can see the nine triangles very clearly drawn on the sheet of gold. And here in the center is the *bindu* in the innermost inverted triangle.

See, this is the *ajna chakra*. There are the two forms of Siva and Shakti. Gradually, at the *sahasrara,* these two forms merge and shower nectar, elixir, like the full moon. When we attain *samadhi*, all of our *vasanas,* our negative thoughts and tendencies such as anger and jealousy, are erased. "O Mother! My handwriting is very bad. [Amma laughs] "I have written negative things in my heart. So erase, Amma, all those things. Erase, erase, erase. Remove all the negativity and bloom this thousand-petal lotus one petal at a time, so that I can attain *samadhi,* God-Realization."

So this is beautiful, *nanna*. It is not possible for you to understand more details about how these *chakras* open in meditation just by listening to talks on this subject. If we meditate daily for at least four to five hours, we can develop a little understanding about the *kundalini.* Just seeing these pictures or reading books is not enough. We have to experience it.

In India, there are no teachings, no lectures, nothing. In the morning, at 3:30 a.m., Amma just comes to the prayer hall, blesses all the people and then leaves. They sit in meditation until evening. In between we have some breaks for lunch and I come and give some *prasada* to them. Especially because the *prasada* touches Amma's hand, it becomes elixir. *Prasada* is divine; it is not just rice or curd *bhat*. We prepare it with love and devotion, praying with the *Gayatri mantra*. We give that *prasada* to each and every one—whether there are a hundred people or a thousand. It gives fulfillment and lots of contentment inside. They don't feel the need to eat even one piece of bread after taking the *prasada*.

The people at the retreat have contentment. This is because of the rest they get in meditation. One hour of meditation gives the equivalent of eight hours of rest to the body. So it is not necessary to take rest. The only problem is joint pain caused by age. They relax for five or ten minutes then go back to meditation. They are in silence and meditate very well.

In the evening at the end of the program, we show a video about one *chakra*—not all the *chakras*—with all the details about that *chakra*. In one week we cover the spiritual aspects. The second week we may talk about the scientific logic regarding the *chakras*, as there are many scientists and students also among the *sadhakas*. So we talk about the colors, what happens when the *sadhaka* concentrates, how the *chakra* blooms, and other details about the *chakras*. It will take about six to seven months to cover all the aspects of *chakra* meditation—just listening to the different topics—not practicing *chakra* meditation.

Nanna, I have condensed the milk—I condensed that milk and made it into cream because we have so little time here. So next time when I come we will have a beautiful meditation program, and whoever is really interested in meditation can attend it. We will meditate from morning to evening, and at the end of the program in the evening you will have a little information about meditation—just like a road map. Talking is only a road map. Experience is different.

Egoism is the main problem. Where there is egoism there is darkness. Where there is egoism there is darkness. The ego has been our main problem through innumerable births. Children, kill this ego with meditation. Your first enemy is only egoism. A meditator opens his eyes and understands who his enemy is: "O, my ego is my real enemy." We have no enemies in this world, we only think they are our enemies. That is also one sort of ignorance, an illusion. Our enemy is within us, the "I," "me," "my" ego problem. So your first enemy is only egoism.

Humility is the enemy of egoism. Humility is the enemy of egoism. Therefore children, make friendship with humility, and send egoism permanently from your heart. Make friendship with humility and courage. Have contentment in your heart and banish the ego forever. Because of this problem, through innumerable births we are in the darkness of a shell. It is not beautiful. So give up egoism permanently and make your life self-illuminated. Then you can have a connection with Divinity. When there is egoism there can be no connection with Divinity.

Where there is no egoism, there only we have the divine connection with humility. Where there is humility, there is inner beauty and we have compassion, real devotion, faith, forgiveness and all these divine attributes in our life. We have a divine connection with the spirit. So if your heart is pure, you will be free from lust, anger, hatred, jealousy, egoism and vengeance.

Children, worldly objects are very beautiful, but even more beautiful is your Self. And more and more and more beautiful still is the soul! The soul is more beautiful than anything else in this universe. So taste that beauty. The *atman* is infinite beauty, beauty of beauties. Matter, that is, the *annamaya kosha*—the physical body as explained in the scriptures, is only a cover for the *atma.* We are not this dress, this body.

This body is only a dress. You wear a black dress one day; a blue dress or a purple dress another day. You have so many dresses. There are so many dresses for our soul also. Innumerable dresses—so many different bodies. So remember, the soul is the main source. The body is a dress for the soul. The soul is the beauty of beauties.

Prana means vital breath, our life; and *manas* is the mind. Mind is nothing but a bundle of thoughts—*rajasic* thoughts, *tamasic* thoughts, and *sattvic* thoughts—good thoughts, bad thoughts, pure thoughts, devotional thoughts—and in meditation we are thoughtless. We must minimize the thoughts, *rajasic, tamasic* and *sattvic* too. Then we will reach the stage when we never even have second thoughts. If any good opportunity comes to us, we say immediately: "Oh, I will do that." We never have a second thought, for we are in pure consciousness.

When we are in pure consciousness, there is no second thought at all, because we are so pure. We are in the *vishuddhi chakra.* There are no second thoughts, not even *sattvic* thoughts. We are in pure consciousness. And these thoughts are filtered from *tamas* to *rajas, rajas* to *sattva,* and *sattva* to *vishuddha sattva. Vishuddha sattva* means one hundred percent purity. From *vishuddha sattva* we are in pure consciousness, that is, the thoughtless stage—*samadhi.* Freeing the mind from thoughts is real meditation.

So in the *Saraswati mantra* cassette, the *Saraswati mantra* is repeated five times followed by a period of silence. The silence part is the real meditation. Why this *mantra*? Because the mind is wandering here and there. We focus our mind in between our eyebrows; that is the best place for meditation. If you are not able to meditate on this particular point—if you feel strain—try to focus your mind on the heart *chakra*. Why? There is a reason for this. For example, when you take a white paper and a lens, and focus the rays of the sun onto the paper, after a few minutes the concentrated rays of the sun burn the paper. The third eye is like the lens, and the *chakras* like the paper. The *chakras* are black with the *karmas,* bad deeds, not from this birth alone but from innumerable previous births also. A blocked root *chakra* means a person is filled with low desires. A blocked heart *chakra* leads to great anxiety, frustration, pain, fear, etc. A clouded throat *chakra* results in the use of bad words, and in mean thinking. So all the *chakras* are black with these qualities or the *arishadvargas,* our six inner enemies.

Chief among these enemies is egoism. If we send egoism permanently from our heart, we have humility, divine humility. Humility is very beautiful. Where there is knowledge, there only is humility. Once you understand that the reality of your life is divinity, you will never keep egoism in your heart. Egoism leads to nothing other than anger, lust and all those low natures—very low thinking with bad words, bad thinking, and desires. And all the *chakras* are blackened with this dust.

When we particularly concentrate on the *chakras*, it is called *chakra dhyana*. Then after some years, we gradually learn the *laya dhyana*. *Laya* means to merge. We merge our individuality in the universal Personality. It doesn't happen in one year or two years, *nanna*. According to the *Yoga Shastra*, if you have a very good *Guru*, at each and every stage he will take the responsibility of your spiritual life, giving good guidance and notes, and making sure that you have so many sittings of meditation. Only then will you have a little spiritual elevation in your life. For three years you will have many obstacles in *yoga.* In the fourth year you will conquer your mind by the power of the seed letters in your *mantra.*

So how to focus the mind? Where? When? What is the best time for meditation? Which direction to face? Direction is also very important. Magnetic waves always travel on the Earth from east to west and north to south. You know that. So when you sit in meditation against these waves, you will feel restless and you will not be able to meditate for a long time. So sit in meditation according to the vibrations of these magnetic waves. Facing east is very good for meditation and also north. Facing east or the northeast is for salvation.

In the olden days, the great sages were able to sit in meditation for a long time—not one or two hours but a hundred years. Anthills surrounded their bodies. They were able to leave the body there, while they were in pure consciousness. That is the power of meditation. Those who do not have this understanding of meditation may say "Oh, what is meditation? Just closing the eyes. I never find any joy in meditation. My mind is so restless." Yes, it is natural. When we sit in meditation, the impurities come from our mind spontaneously. Millions of thoughts spontaneously come to the mind throughout our life.

This is our problem because the mind is nothing but thoughts only. These thoughts are from previous births filled with good and bad deeds. If our deeds were good, we have pure thoughts, spiritual thoughts and selfless thoughts. If our deeds were bad, our thoughts also will be so impure and restless, filled with frustration, etc. So if anything is happening in your life do not think about it. Forget all those things. Start a new life—start a new diary, and start the page with *Om.* Fill your entire life with pure thoughts, good deeds, and with selfless service.

So meditate, children. Meditate with devotion, meditate with selfless service—self means the egoistic self. Make it less, less, less—one hundred percent less. And with discriminating knowledge, *jnana,* and meditation, *dhyana,* remodel your life to divinity. This is very beautiful. Meditation is beautifying and remodeling your entire life to divinity. Now we have anger and jealousy and there is no beauty at all in our life. So when we meditate, we beautify our life, remodel our entire life and we are in divinity. That is the art of meditation. All *yogas* are hidden in the *Lalita Sahasranama.* If you learn the *Lalita Sahasranama,* by listening to the cassette and chanting it, you will very easily develop the capacity to understand the question: "What is *yoga*?" The essence of all *yogas* is contained in the *Lalita Sahasranama.*

Viśuddhi cakra nilayā
Ārakta varṇā Trilocanā

The *chakras* are also mentioned in the *Lalita Sahasranama.* We have a high elevation in the *Lalita Sahasranama, nanna.* I experienced this all over the world. Whoever is chanting the *Lalita Sahasranama* has a balanced mind. Everyone has problems and troubles in their life, but they are very balanced, they never care for the problems and pains in their life. They take things very easily and they are always in the Supreme Consciousness of Mother Divine. They are in prayers and they have a lot of humility. They never care for anything in this world. That means not egoistic things. They never expect anything from this world. They always want to be like a baby who loves its mother, putting themselves in Mother's unseen hands. This is because unseen Mother's hands are embracing the cosmos. So open your third eye, children. Go beyond all the things in this world, and experience the oneness that is the essence of meditation.

[A question from the audience: "Will you please explain more about *yajna?"*]

Amma: *Yajna, nanna,* is very beautiful. Do you know Telugu? Listen to Amma's tape on *Divya Bharatiya Dharma Samskriti,* or Divine Indian Moral Culture.

[Amma speaks in Telugu]

Translator: *Yajna bhavana* is the feeling with which a *yajna* is performed. The intention of *yajna* or *homa* is sharing with others—whether it is wealth or knowledge. For example, if I have a great deal of money such as two million dollars, and I use it for a good deed, I am sharing that money with others. In ancient times, whatever people had they shared with everybody.

If a place is dirty or dusty, we use some cleaning fluid to clean it up. It usually takes twenty to thirty minutes to kill the bacteria. But when we do a *homa,* the smoke which comes from the *yajna* fire spreads in two or three seconds to kill the invisible bacteria from the walls, floor, ceiling, and the atmosphere. There is so much pollution everywhere...

Amma: There are so many illnesses due to lack of oxygen.

Translator: Amma also mentioned that the stagnation of oxygen is responsible for some of the ailments. Dirt, dust, carpet dust, cats, dogs—all these pollute the atmosphere and cause allergy problems. The smoke of the *yajna* purifies every atom of the atmosphere.

And we all live in enclosed spaces—that is the lifestyle here. We keep the doors and windows of the house always closed and the air conditioning running. Thus we re-breathe the same air—whether we are sitting here or in our offices or cars. There is no circulation of *prana,* the vital energy of natural air—there is no oxygen. Cells in our body form, grow and decay on their own. If you give them oxygen, the decayed cells will be reborn again. Since we don't get enough oxygen, all of us are getting sick both physically and psychologically. At least in this country you are maintaining your health by eating healthy food.

For us it feels like a prison to stay indoors. We find it so hard. But I guess you have to live like this because of the weather. If you have good tropical weather, you can go outside for walks or other healthy activities. Here you cannot do any outdoor activities, because there are so many problems in the atmosphere. You are afraid to go out. People are afraid of each other.

Because of the presence of a layer of impurity in the atmosphere, rains don't come. Whatever we offer into the *yajna* fire burns, and that smoke goes into the atmosphere, where it breaks that barrier and rain is once again able to fall. Rain helps to grow our crops. The *yajna* fire purifies all the five elements in nature, and the whole environment is also cleansed.

When we do *yajna* we all assemble in one place. This helps develop unity amongst us. When we do *yajna* in India we donate cattle, clothes, etc. to everybody. We give out about five hundred *saris* and we feed everybody. This is a way of preventing the concentration of money in one place.

In the same way we invite all great saints and scholars to our homes, so that they share their knowledge with all of us. We all know that in the olden days, saints like Shirdi Baba came for alms to everybody's homes. When they come to these houses, they do not come to beg. These saints belong to the whole community and they do not do their own cooking. All homes are their homes.

Amma [laughing]**:** That is the feeling.

Translator: In return they give *vedic* knowledge—they transform it into clear and simple language for ordinary people.

Even now a lot of *swamis* and saints come for alms. We still have that tradition. When a saint comes to our house, we give him the best seat in the house and offer him some food. In return what can he give us? He has nothing. So he will sing a song:

"O Mother, You are everywhere in this universe! Wherever I look, You are there. You pervade the whole universe. If I don't believe in You how can I gain knowledge or anything else?"

Such songs leave a strong and lasting impression even on the mind of a person who is not on the spiritual path. In India, people sing simple songs about God in their local languages. The knowledge of the great *Vedas* was condensed into aphorisms in the *Brahma Sutras*, then explained in the *Upanishads*, and again in the *Bhagavad Gita* in the form of *shlokas*. These eventually became small songs like *bhajans*, slogans, lullabies, etc., sung in local languages. In this way everybody sings the concepts of the *Vedas* in an easy way at their own intellectual level.

That is why the feeling of *homa* is so fulfilling. We accomplish everything because of *homa*. We share both knowledge and wealth. Everyone benefits from it—not just the person who performs the *homa*.

There was a lot of research done on the *homa* and *homa* therapy. Because of the smoke from the *yajna,* we get cured of diseases like asthma, bronchitis, etc. Our lungs and blood get purified. It makes us all healthy. It increases our lifespan. In India we throw this *homa* ash on trees if they have any diseases. We do not use any antibiotics there. This *homa* ash helps to cure them. We use *vibhuti,* ash from the *homa,* or sandalwood powder to purify the blood and to stimulate the nerves. They improve our overall health.

Even in olden times people wanted a peaceful society. Everybody knows that without mental contentment there is no physical contentment. That is why we need these *homas*, *mantras*, prayers, meditations, etc. They give overall satisfaction to people. If you look at the poor people in India, even though their lifestyle is stressful and disturbed, they are always happy and content. They lead a moral and ethical life. Since ancient times, society was designed and based on these concepts. This was not done in one day or by one person.

God appeared in different times in the form of different sages, *yogis*, saints, etc. He taught us how to lead a moral and ethical life. He warned us how much we would be hurt if we did not do so. He also told us how happy, content and satisfied we would be if we were virtuous. The *Vedas* are very great. I did so many programs on the *Vedas*. In India, the Tirumala Tirupati Devasthanam conducts many universal *vedic* conferences. Here also people conduct so many *vedic* conferences, but they do not know as much about the *Vedas*. In India the sages have tremendous knowledge of the *Vedas*. There are many learned *pundits* in Antarvedipalem, Rajamundry in the Godavari District, Andhra Pradesh and also at the Benares Hindu University.

A lot of *vedic pundits* from different cultures come to Amma's *ashram*. They like Amma's *ashram* because there is no artificial creation there, everything is natural. They like to sit on the stones under the trees in the moonlight and hold *vedic* conferences. We invite so many people —perhaps one hundred or two hundred—including poor and illiterate people. Usually these conferences are held in Sanskrit, but we translate them into Telugu so that everybody can understand about the *Vedas*.

Also Amma has made so many cassettes on the essence of the *Vedas,* such as the Essence of the *Sama Veda,* the *Rig Veda,* etc. Since these are not in English, I did not bring them here. Next time I will try to bring them. I have also made cassettes on the *Gayatri mantra, Viveka Chudamani, Bhajagovindam,* etc. All this material is to communicate to everybody the need for purity, and that the feeling in life is more important than language and grammar.

Another thing to remember is that there is a difference between literature and spirituality. In literature the feeling is at a low level, while in spirituality it is highly elevated. In literature we get stuck with grammar and other things, but it is not so in spirituality. We travel like a rocket and reach the cosmos in no time. Even though the language may not be well expressed, the feeling is very high.

When we do *Ganapati homa,* eight different kinds of ingredients are normally used. Some of them are not available here—a sweet made with rice flour, parched rice, brown sugar, sugar cane, etc.

And we use special grass and one hundred and eight pieces of firewood. The person performing the *homa* offers exactly one hundred and eight pieces of firewood to the *homa* fire. That is not possible here, so we are circumventing that and doing it in a shortened, abbreviated way. Amma wants to bring these particular fragrant types of firewood to the States, but the Customs won't allow it.

Amma also mentioned that when we do *yajna,* cosmic radiation is attracted here into the fire.

Any food that was consumed before should not be offered to the *homa.* One forbidden thing is salt. Salt should never be put in the *homa.* This will result in leprosy.

Hari Om Tat Sat

Houston *13 April 1997*

ॐ

DHARMA IS THE JEWEL

Om namaste astu Bhagavan
Viśveśvarāya Mahādevāya
Trayambakāya Tripurāntakāya
Trikāgni Kālāya Kālāgni Rudrāya
Nilakaṇṭhāya Mṛtyunjayāya
Sarveśvarāya Sadāśivāya
Śriman Mahā devāya namaḥ

Om ātmā tvam Girijā matiḥ sahacarāḥ
Prāṇāḥ śarīram gṛham
Pūjā te viṣayopa bhoga racanā
Nidrā samādhi sthitiḥ
Sañcāraḥ padayoḥ pradakṣiṇā vidhiḥ
Stotrāṇi sarvā giro
Yadyat karma karōmi tat tad akhilam
Śambho tavārādhanam

Om śānti śānti śāntiḥ

Embodiments of Divine Souls, Amma's Most Beloved Children,

Yesterday we covered a few points about meditation. Really meditation is nothing but remodeling our lives, developing the divine attributes more and more and achieving the state of bliss—the state with no attributes —and then attaining God-Realization. There are so many stages in the spiritual path. It has been concluded that all paths are the same. We have the paths of *karma yoga, bhakti yoga, dhyana yoga, jnana yoga,* and others. If we do not have an intense desire to achieve the greatest state of spiritual enlightenment, then it is just blind belief, and we are on our path walking very slowly like an ant. When we have that intense desire in our lives we have the great virtue of *dharma.*

Dharma is the jewel. Where there is *dharma* there only is wisdom. Wisdom is the gateway of *dharma.* It is the greatest virtue. *Dharma* is the greatest wisdom. So, for the spiritual aspirant to receive the *Brahmic* Consciousness in this birth itself one must wear some beautiful ornaments in one's life such as contentment, wisdom, truth, forgiveness, *samata*—equal vision—and selfless service. Selfless service toward all beings of this world is the greatest *yoga* to merge with the Eternal, and eternal bliss is the ultimate aim of spirituality. There are so many steps.

In *karma yoga* we never expect anything from anyone. If we expect thanks or anything of the sort, our *karma yoga* has failed because there is still the self, the ego. There are three types of ego—*sattvic, tamasic* and *rajasic.* With a *tamasic* ego we force others to praise us. We say: "I did this and I did that." In *rajasic* ego, there is a lot of expectation from others even if we do a little service for them. With a *sattvic* ego also we have expectations and say: "He never even said thanks to me even though I did so much."

In *vishuddha sattva* we are always behind the curtain. We never expect even a little bit of thanks for anything. We do only service to mankind because it is a *yoga. Yoga* is a beautiful word in Sanskrit. There are three rivers in India—the Ganga, the Yamuna and the Saraswati—which meet in Haridwar. The combining of these three rivers is called *yoga.* And in medicine, a combination of different herbs is called *yoga* in *Ayurveda,* the Indian science of healing. *Veda* means *yoga,* because *yoga* comes from *Veda.*

In meditation we need the human body. This is a temple for divinity, for this beautiful divine soul. Every human body, every living being is a temple for God. We do not have that awareness because of some stages that we are in. If we have that *Brahmic* awareness in our hearts we understand the immoral qualities in us such as anger, which is not sweet. Other qualities such as lust, hatred, jealousy, and criticism of others are also not beautiful. Even if anyone does so much for us, we are always finding fault. All these are very mean qualities.

If a real spiritual person is always in pure love and pure consciousness he never touches the *tamas* or *rajas* nature and is always in the *sattva* nature. This is also not enough. He must go beyond this state, to the state of the spirit, and that is *vishuddha sattva*. When we are in *vishuddha sattva*, we never criticize others under any circumstances. If anyone comes and injures us we only give love in return, because according to our science—for every action there is an equal and opposite reaction. You give your love to others because you are a meditator. You are a spiritual person. You have all the gems and jewels in your heart such as patience and discriminative knowledge. Without discriminative knowledge life is very childish. There is no mental growth at all. Our mind is stuck in these little points—anger, greed and lust.

So we are always in a small mortal frame in all these immoral qualities. If we achieve the divine bliss with truth and wisdom, we have a lot of peace in our heart. We ourselves enjoy the fragrance of peace and contentment within. Contentment is the greatest wealth and treasure. It is hidden in our hearts. When we open our hearts with *Brahmic* awareness, we are always in the Supreme Consciousness of bliss. So that is the essence.

There is a question in the *Vedas*, "What is the essence of human life?" The essence of human life is selfless service. Make our self one hundred percent *less*, *less*, *less*.

Be always behind the curtain and give your service. In India the women know this. They don't even go into the halls where the public programs are going on and crowds of people come. Instead they remain in the kitchen and prepare so many items. And from behind the curtain they send all the sweets and other preparations for them, and never expect anything in return. If anyone comes and says the dishes are very good and praises them, they simply reply that they are so blessed that they were given this opportunity to serve and therefore, thank them in return for coming to their house and taking all those sweets. That is so beautiful.

Where there is a hundred percent less self, there only is selfless service. So the essence of human life is make our self less, less, less. Do not expect anything even if you give your eyes, donate your kidney, donate your life, give your blood or give your entire wealth. Even in your heart never expect anything in return. In any nook and corner of your heart, even in the most secret place in your heart also, never expect even a word of thanks from this world. That is selfless service. This selfless service makes us so beautiful. We enjoy the real service in our heart.

Nature gives us so much. We never repay anything to this nature. So children first we must learn selfless service. How is this possible? When we keep on meditating and go inside our life, inside our heart, we have awareness about this beautiful consciousness. The world is beautiful, all creation is beautiful. But just as beautiful is your mind if it is full of good thoughts and good deeds. Your intellect is beautiful but the Spirit is more beautiful than all these things. The Spirit is a hundred percent beautiful. So, we meditate on that Spirit only. Where is this spirit? It is in our heart. It beautifies our life with divine attributes and makes us desireless. That is the highest peak of purity.

Try to control and limit all the ordinary low-level desires and gradually have one good desire—*dharma.* Righteousness is also not the appropriate word to explain *dharma.* There are hundreds of gems in *dharma. Dharma* is extremely powerful. In Sanskrit there is a beautiful saying in one of the *Vedas:*

Dharmaḥ rakṣati rakṣatiḥ

If we have *dharma* in our hearts, that *dharma* itself protects us from all the problems in this world. Nothing touches you because of the power of *dharma.* That is the greatest fire, the fire of self-illumination. If any problem comes, it just burns in that fire. Nothing happens to us. That is the power of *dharma.* So, have *dharma. Dharma* alone leads this entire universe. That *dharma* itself is the Spirit and divine soul. Even when all these five elements—fire, water, etc.—after hundreds and millions and billions of years disappear, *dharma* never disappears because *dharma* is attributeless and indivisible. *Dharma* is for this entire universe and *dharma* rules this entire universe. *Dharma* is Truth, *dharma* is wisdom, *dharma* is a hundred percent pure. *Dharma* is only one—there is no second.

So children, meditate. Meditate on your *Ishta Deva.* Go in your own path and achieve the destiny, the bliss in your Self. Give your selfless service to this universe. Be always truthful, faithful and vigilant. Be always in pure consciousness. Enjoy peace always inside. Give cosmic love to this world. Never hurt anyone's religious feeling. Give respect to every religion—that is our *dharma.* People have their own feelings. Never injure anyone's feelings under any circumstances and give respect. Attain God-Realization. Try to meditate on your Self. You are not sure.why? [Amma points to a picture of Lord Siva]. Look at Lord Siva. He is always in meditation. You may feel: "O Siva! You are the Lord. You are divine. What is your meditation for? What is your destiny in meditation?" He meditates on His purity only. Likewise, you meditate on your pure soul only. Everyone meditates on Truth.

So children, try to understand the value of this human life and do not waste your time in meaningless work, and do not use unnecessary words. Speak little. Our words should always be like the holy basil. Every word must be holy and sweeter than honey. Speak sweetly and gently. Never speak any vulgar word. That is the pollution of the mouth. Do not pollute your mouth. Always speak the truth only. If we are in the habit of always telling lies, gradually we forget what we said yesterday or even today. If you always speak the truth, then you don't have to say many times: "This is the truth." So, in the beginning, truth is very bitter and hard to hear, but in the end it is elixir. Truth is elixir. Where there is truth there only is divine *dharma*. Where there is divine *dharma*, there only is attributeless Divinity. You yourself will become the Attributeless.

Attain pure consciousness. A real aspirant will never outwardly show his devotion to this world. It is not necessary. Be a real seeker. Keep your devotion in the secret place, in your inner temple. This temple has four pillars. The first one is compassion, the second is righteousness, the third is cosmic love and the fourth is wisdom. In this temple, bliss is always just like a self-lit lamp. Its light and fragrance fill the entire universe. So children go to that highest peak. Go beyond this body. This body is a cage, and in this cage there is another cage—the mind. And in that mind there is one more cage—our limited intellect, called *buddhi* in Sanskrit. In the *Gayatri mantra* you pray to Mother Gayatri:

Bhargo devasya dhīmahi
Dhiyo yonaḥ pracodayāt

"O Amma, grant me divine grace. Through this limited intellect, I want to understand the Truth. Give me real Knowledge." We pray in the *Gayatri mantra* for true knowledge. We have so much knowledge about different things in this world. But this knowledge is not enough to understand the inner reality. We understand the outward reality. The outward reality is good, but the inner reality is much more beautiful. Everything we see in the outward reality is a dream, but the inner reality is the Truth.

This birth is the result of innumerable lives of prayer. This spiritual meditation and this spirituality in your life do not come to you by accident. They have a very big and strong foundation. So sit on that foundation and achieve the highest peak of *samadhi. "Dhi"* means "where you find this bliss." You must see divinity in each and every being in this world. Now we see divinity only in holy people, in temples, in churches and in good things.

When we achieve divine bliss, we are in the consciousness of seeing God in every living being in this world—in earth, in air, in fire, in mankind, in the bird kingdom, in the animal kingdom, in the cosmos—everywhere. So at that time your soul comes out of this little cage and touches the cosmos. Your body becomes so subtle and you realize: "O, I myself am wisdom!" You have that *Brahmic* awareness: "I am the Truth. I am time. I am divine wisdom. What is there that I am not in this world?" You realize that everything in this world belongs to you only. Then you understand nature. Once you reach that state, can you expect anything from anyone in this world? You are beyond *Veda*. You are beyond time—past, present and future. We never expect any thanks or anything from anyone in this world. You alone are the giver. You are the realized person, you have realized your Self! You are perfectly pure, you are attributeless. You are the individual as well as the Indivisible. You are consciousness. You yourself are tranquility, you yourself are benediction, you are *Omkara!*

Children, that is so sweet. The mind is always thinking: "I, me, my." Our anger, our hate is not sweet. These are little weeds. So vacuum these weeds. Send them permanently away from your hearts, from your life. Meditation burns all of these little immoral qualities from our hearts and leads this mortal life to immortality.

In this mortal life meditation is a ladder. In this mortal frame, we climb so many steps in the ladder. We have humility, we have purity, and we have a lot of inner beauty. If our heart is like crystal, it reflects divinity. So divinize your thoughts. Divinize your thoughts by reading good books, but do not get stuck at any one point—do not always be reading good books, or doing *japa* and being in body consciousness. Go beyond all these things, beyond the *Vedas* also. Go beyond this world. Then only will you be able to understand the Truth in your Self. Truth is so sweet. It is elixir. So children, let us taste the sweetness. If we sit in meditation, there is one *shloka:*

Bhadram karṇebhi sṛuṇuyāma Devāḥ
Bhadram pasyemām akṣyabhirya jatrāḥ
Sthirair angaiḥ tuṣtu vāgam sastanubhiḥ
Vyaśema Deva hitam yadāyuḥ

It is a peace *mantra.* In India in the olden days in the *Gurukula pathashalas*—the spiritual centers—this prayer preceded the *Veda parayana,* the chanting of the *Vedas.* The meaning of this *shloka* is very beautifully expressed with tender feelings, tender devotion. This *shloka* was recited by the great sages like Vasishtha Maharshi or Vishwamitra, before starting the class. What is the prayer in this *shloka?* They pray to the Divine Mother: "O Mother

Gayatri, give me good eyes to see you everywhere and never to see negativity in bad things also. Whatever I hear must be positive. Even if it is negative, I must consider only the positive in the negative. Give me that positive attitude in my heart." If my heart is not pure, no matter what you say, even if it is good, I will think it is bad for me. Because my viewfinder is so small. With that limited egoistic viewfinder if you say something good also, I think it is bad.

So pray to Mother: "O Mother Divine, O Gayatri, O Mahadevi, You have five heads:

Muktā vidruma hema nīla dhavalā....

"The entire cosmos is in your Self, Mother. Grant me a great virtue and that is positivity. Burn the negativity immediately from my heart." So whatever we see, whatever we take into our heart, whatever we hear, whatever we do, must always be positive. We must not do bad deeds. To be always good, sweet and humble is most important.

This Earth is a pilgrim center, it is not our home. You are from the cosmos, so that is your place. You are a traveler in this limited world. You are here for only forty, fifty, or ninety years in this play on the Earth—this is a very limited dream. From point of view of holy people, this life is only a dream. Last night you had a dream. In that dream you saw a panther or tiger and you were so frightened. But when you woke up there was no tiger, no panther and you found yourself in your bedroom! During the dream you were so afraid of that panther but when you woke up from your dream there was no panther at all.

Duality—the feeling of "you" and "me"—creates all these problems and so much fear in our life. It has been our problem from innumerable births and is caused by our ego. When we understand the reality in our meditations, there is no ego at all. Gradually all the curtains are removed and burnt permanently. There are no weeds at all. Then we realize, "I myself am consciousness. Gayatri is in this temple. Mother is in this temple."

Only Mother sustains this entire universe. She pervades this whole universe. She is the main source of energy for this entire universe. She is Govinda rupini, Rudra rupini and Brahma rupini. She is Pancha kritya parayana. There are five actions of Mother. The first three being—creation, maintenance, and dissolution. Dissolution is not death, our soul never dies. We go back to our true home. In Sanskrit we call it *tirodhana* which is a beautiful word. *Tirodhana* means "coming back to your Mother's sweet home." Where is Mother's home, children? *Omkara* is Mother's abode. This world is only a hostel. In this limited life many times we have negative thoughts and sometimes bad thoughts also. So from now onward never speak negatively or speak ill of anyone. Never criticize anybody. That is the pollution of the mouth.

So we chant the *Saraswati mantra.* Saraswati is Self-illumination, Mother of Knowledge, divine Knowledge. Mother will give so much inspiration in your heart. Then you will write so many good things like Valmiki, Yogi Vemana and Kalidasa. They were below normal and very ignorant at first, but by the grace of Saraswati Devi, they became the greatest poets in the universe. Brahma, who created these people, also wondered about this, for they became immortal because of their writings. It is Saraswati's nature to share with the entire universe the arts such as music, dance, writing, poetry and sculpture. And She teaches us to do the same with each other.

So, knowledge is elixir. Without discriminating knowledge, our life is really meaningless and we are very childish. Children, learn to do good actions and meditate on

Truth. Pray to God for purity. "Amma, I want only purity, pure devotion, a hundred percent devotion, a hundred percent discriminating faith. I want to understand Reality a hundred percent and achieve *samadhi.*" The thoughtless state is *samadhi.* So bloom all these *chakras* by meditation and offer these flowers with beautiful fragrance, these self-luminous flowers to Mother Divine:

Mahā padma vanāntasthe kāraṇa ānanda vigrahe
Sarva bhūta hite Mātaḥ yehi yehi Parameśwarī

This is a beautiful prayer calling Mother: "O Mother, you are in the cosmos. Come to me, Amma. Please come to me in my meditation and in my prayer and bloom all these inner flowers and the universal lotus, the *sahasrara kamala.* Please be seated on that *kamala* and give me peace. Make this birth my last."

No more births. We have had innumerable births but we are in the same class or grade experiencing anger, lust, etc., which are so meaningless. So children, send away the little immoral qualities and develop these beautiful divine attributes—dispassion, and discriminating knowledge. Pray for purity and inner beauty. Have inner beauty more and more. If we give love to others again and again we have more and more of the same. If you hate, then that is what results. So do not hate anyone. See divinity everywhere —this is the achievement of *dharma.*

If we are in the shade of the beautiful, greatest *dharma,* we have great peace and immense strength. We think power is strength, money is strength. No. For any nation or any man, or any religion, his faith toward God is the main power. That is the main power, not the power of money or physical strength. Willpower is very important. When you meditate, you have a lot of willpower. You have wisdom. You are able to understand Truth in your life and this world gets changed in your viewfinder. And then you understand the *rishis'* prayer: "O Mother Divine, O Gayatri, O Devi, please give me always a positive outlook because my life in this world is very limited. In this short life, in the beginning I was a student and did not know anything about spiritual activities. Afterwards came *samsara,* the family life with so many ups and downs. Even now I understand very little." It is enough. It is said in the *Upanishads* that it is enough. If you have just a little *dharma*, righteousness, in your heart, it burns all the impurities in your life and elevates you to the highest peak of the spirit, that is Soul, Maha Purusha, Gayatri, Devi, *Om*—call it by any name. All the names are only one. They are the same.

So children, have real devotion, pray to God for truth early in the morning between five and six o'clock. Give respect to every religion in this world. Never injure anyone under any circumstances. If you do not like any custom or religion, do not say anything, just keep silent. They have their feelings, they have their right. Only in spirituality do we have the wisdom not to criticize anyone. So practice these beautiful virtues.

In the beginning it is difficult. When we train this wild horse—our mind—gradually this wild horse listens to us. Because of lack of training it is wandering here and there. When we give our mind proper training, it listens to our words and becomes our slave. Now we are slaves at the mercy of the mind. A *yogi* controls his mind and makes the mind his slave. That is beautiful. So do not listen to your mind. Today it will say: "He is my best friend," and tomorrow it will say: "Never talk to him." So the mind changes like this but the intellect says: "O, if I want to go and pluck any flower from another's garden I will look here and there." Why? Because the intellect says: "Look here and there because you are stealing a flower." So the intellect is telling you: "This is not good, this is wrong, so see if anyone is there." And the mind says: "Do it. There's no problem." So never listen to your mind. It always goes up and down. The decisions of the mind are not correct. So surrender to God one hundred percent.

Om śaraṇāgata dīnārtā paritrāṇa parāyaṇe
Sarvasyārti hare Devī Nārāyanī namōstute

This *shloka* contains the essence of the *Chandi Sapta Shati.* It is the main nuclear *shloka.* In this *shloka* we are saying: "I surrender to You a hundred percent. Only You can send me messages and tune my life. Send me the message that is best for me and lead me to the right path."

Your body is an instrument for Mother Divine. You work according to Her wish in this world. Nothing is in your hands. Mother is working in this world with Her million hands. What can you do with your two hands? So surrender a hundred percent. Pray: "O Mother, lead me. Lead me to the right path."

I have a box of candy. If I say, "Please come baby, take some chocolates," the baby can take only two or three candies with his small hands. But if I give candies with my own hands I can give ten to twenty because my hand is big. If you keep asking Mother continually, "Give me this, give me that," your thoughts and mind are very limited. You will not ask for the right things. But if you surrender a hundred percent to Mother Divine, She will give with full hands and supply everything good for you. So surrender. This is the essence of the *Bhagavad Gita.*

Krishna has given many messages in about seven hundred *shlokas* in the *Bhagavad Gita.* Arjuna is very confused. He represents this entire mankind. So at the end of the discourse Arjuna says: "Krishna, I am not able to understand all these *shlokas.* This *karma yoga,* selfless *yoga,* this *jnana yoga,* this meditation *yoga* and *sannyasa yoga, moksha.* Of all these *yogas* I am not able to understand even one word. O my Lord, just tell me what to do and I will do it. That is enough for me." So, you must have this kind of total surrender, a hundred percent surrender. Surrender your entire life, surrender it just like you would offer a flower. Bloom this inner flower and offer it to Mother. It is mentioned beautifully in the *Lalita Sahasranama.*

Durvasa was one of the many great sages who prayed to Mother Divine. He was a great *rishi* but he had a lot of anger. Because of his anger he was unable to enter Mother's abode. With innumerable flowers he prayed and worshipped Mother daily. But as it is mentioned in the *Lalita Sahasranama,* Mother is worshipped with one special flower. Mother Divine is Chaitanya kusuma aradhya, One who is worshipped with the flower of consciousness, and Chaitanya kusuma priya, One who loves the flower of consciousness. What is that flower? We are not able to understand that *Chaitanya* means consciousness—beautiful divine consciousness. So in these two *mantras* from the *Lalita Sahasranama,* Mother wants you to bloom and offer your inner flower of consciousness. *Kusuma* means flower, the flower of spiritual consciousness—fragrant with silence, truth, wisdom and peace. So, if we have these fragrances in our heart then our heart flower is blooming. So children, bloom that flower immediately. Do not offer these physical flowers which dry up after one or two hours or one or two days. But the inner flowers never fade and are always blooming so that their beautiful fragrances fill this entire universe. I want that flower from you. Offer your entire life as *prasada* to Mother.

We offer coconut after breaking it. The coconut is a symbol of our ego. Do not allow ego to enter your life. If there is still ego, send it away permanently. Give retirement to the ego immediately.

Maha padma vananthaste

Maha padma means innumerable lotuses are there in the cosmos. Mother puts Her feet on those lotuses and planets and comes to you all the way as your own near and dear Mother. She never expects anything from this universe. Mother is always only a giver. So, my immortal children, go beyond this mortal frame and climb the ladder of meditation, and selfless service, follow the path of devotion, the path of knowledge, or any other path. Go beyond this body, mind and limited intellect and focus your mind always on silence and bliss. In prayer we talk with God. In meditation—there is a difference in meditation—God talks with us. We have a message from the cosmos. You may say prayers such as this one in Sanskrit:

Anyathā śaraṇam nāsti tvameka śaraṇam mama
Tasmāt kāruṇya bhāvena rakṣya rakṣya Janārdanī

"Mother please save me, help me, lead me." However, in meditation, you just say a *mantra* which simply burns the impurities in your heart. So, gradually all these billions of thoughts are burnt by the power of the seed letters in the *mantra* and we are in silence.

You have already listened to the cassette of the *Saraswati mantra* in which the *Saraswati mantra* is chanted five times followed by an equal period of silence. The silence part is the real meditation. When we chant the *mantra,* our mind is still working. In general we realize when our mind is working outwardly. Even when we go inside, our mind is still working, wandering here and there. But when we chant the *mantra* we must concentrate at one point. All the *chakras* are blocked by the past *karmas.* There is so much *karma* load. Gradually this load will be reduced by the power of the seed letters in the *mantra* because the seed letters are extremely powerful. Of course the *karma* load is not reduced in one day, fifteen days or one year. It doesn't happen immediately or instantly. It takes time. We must be patient. When the *karma* load is lessened, we begin to feel peace inside. If it is too much, and our nature is either *tamasic* or *rajasic*, we must work hard to reduce it. If we have a *sattvic* nature, it is okay, ninety percent okay, and if we have a *vishuddha sattvic* nature, the curtain of ignorance is very transparent.

In holy incarnations, there is no curtain at all. Why did Jesus meditate? Why did Buddha meditate? Why did Ramana Maharshi meditate? Why did all the holy persons meditate? Why did Amma meditate? Because they wanted to be models to this world. If I practice, I have the authority to say: "Son, you must do this too." If you ask me: "Amma can You do meditation," I can answer: "Yes, this is the path. You come and merge with your eternal Mother." This is the authorization. What do you think is the worth of the holy people in this world? They do not expect anything from this world.

So children be like an infant baby in Mother's hands. Infant babies have no thoughts. They are always in bliss with a smiling face because there are no thoughts at all in the infant baby's mind. She is always in a blissful state. Be like that. Practice forgiveness, compassion, dispassion, and discriminating knowledge. Pray to God for divinity and purity. Purify each and every cell in your body with *mantra*. Let no impurity remain even in one little cell. Purify yourself with *mantra*. Then the mortal body becomes immortal. Now it is a mortal body. When we meditate this mortal body becomes a temple for immortality:

Deho devālayaḥ jīvo Deva sanātanaḥ

This beautiful saying from the *Vedas* describes the body as a temple, *devalaya*. And our soul is divine. So divinity is in your self. Divinize all of your thoughts, meditate and purify your life with the divine fragrance of peace. Meditate and merge with the Eternal.

Texas is beautiful and sweet. I have so many beautiful flowers here. I will come back again. So many children in Dallas thirst for a meditation retreat. In India I have meditation retreats with ten hours of meditation a day and in some courses, fifteen hours also. In those meditation retreats only those who are able to sit for a long time participate. For beginners, we have just one hour, two hours, three hours or four hours in every course. If you wish, we can conduct a ten hour retreat here or in San Antonio or in any other beautiful place. In that retreat we will maintain complete, absolute silence. No talking. Silence in meditation is very powerful because silence is the language of Mother Divine. So learn that language. In silence we observe our life and our thoughts and realize: "O, my views are like this. I must work so hard. I have a lot of anger, I will remove that in meditation."

All these things are possible only in this human birth. So children, divinize this birth, purify this birth and achieve the destiny in this birth. That is Amma's only wish. I will come back again. Tomorrow I am leaving for San Antonio but I am always with you. Enjoy your Mother in your meditation in the form of peace. Mother is not this physical body, She is everywhere. So enjoy Her and keep Her in the secret place in your heart. Call out to Her in meditation and She will come and comfort you. You say "A-" and before you say "ma" I will come and comfort you. That is only Amma's responsibility to Her children. *Hari Om Tat Sat.*

[Amma sings some *bhajans* and then speaks in Telugu for the benefit of Telugu speaking devotees.]

Houston *14 April 1997*

ॐ

ALL DEVATAS ARE WITHIN DIVINE MOTHER

[This discourse is translated from Telugu. It is addressed to the Indians in the audience. It follows the previous discourse in English.]

Blessed Divine Souls!

Amma conveys her sincere and heartfelt love to you all. The Telugu speaking people here have been intensely desiring to hear Amma talk in Telugu and therefore, I will say a few words in Telugu.

The root cause for the creation of this infinite universe or cosmos is *Adi Para Shakti*. The infinite Brahma mayi has been compared to a great big fire pit. That big fire pit is emitting many sparks of fire, and these sparks of fire in due course of time, become the innumerable suns and planets in the countless galaxies. Recently many people have been researching the ancient Indian culture and its many unique *dharmas*. They have researched the *Gayatri mantra*. They have discovered in their investigation of a hundred and fifty years, the power and marvel of the *Gayatri mantra*. It has been proven by scientists and even videos have been taken to show that when one meditates on the *Gayatri mantra,* the power and brilliance of the sun's rays shine brightly around the meditator and give him the benefit of complete good health. It is through chanting of the *Gayatri mantra* that we absorb the morning rays of the sun. For example you will find that the energy of the sun is absorbed by the leaves, and when we are hungry and we eat those leaves, it is considered very beneficial. Similarly, this unique *shakti* is in the seed letters of the *Gayatri mantra* and when a person meditates on those seed letters, one's life becomes extraordinarily powerful. One rises above repulsive substances such as blood, bones and flesh and experiences a wonderful peace and blissful state of the soul by coming into the subtle body.

Adi Para Shakti is the Empress of a hundred thousand suns. She is the Mother of the ant as well as Brahma, the Creator. Whoever meditates on such a wonderful Mother goes to that state beyond birth and death, which is permanent and eternal. In the *Lalita Sahasranama* Lord Hayagriva, who is Lord Vishnu incarnate, is instructing Agastya Muni, the very incarnation of Lord Rudra, that when one chants the name:

Om Sri Lalitāmbikāyai namaḥ

All the sins accrued from many births from the beginning of time are immediately destroyed. In reality, when one meditates on the Divine Mother, all the desires are burnt, no desires are left. She removes all petty qualities and elevates one to the noblest state wherein one is willing to donate one's very life for others if necessary.

What does Mother give in return? She gives *kaivalya pada*, the state of oneness with the Divine. Therefore She is said to be Kaivalya pada dayini. She is also the giver of complete wisdom and knowledge of Truth—*Satya sampurna vijnana siddhida*. When She serves food in your dinner plate, She just doesn't make one or two dishes with the idea that you will eat something. A good mother serves the plate full of various dishes with great love, affection and responsibility. If you don't eat them, She will make another ten varieties so you will eat something. Such is mother's love. Therefore, this Divine Mother fills this dish called the heart with Truth and complete knowledge and wisdom.

Jnāna mosaga rādā, sujnāna mosaga rādā

This is a line from one of Thyagaraja's *kirtanas*. He says: "I am in great ignorance. Why don't you give me knowledge?" Realizing that She might give what he asked for, he quickly says: "Please give me wisdom and good knowledge. By mistake I asked for ordinary knowledge, but please give me good knowledge and wisdom. Give me the knowledge by which I can know You." See how beautiful this song is! These are not mere *kirtanas* or ordinary songs. It is as though he is talking to God in all purity. You also talk to God. Open your mouth and heart and talk to God. Shed your tears and weep in front of Mother and say: "Amma, I have failed to realize You in all my previous births. I came to You and asked You for all kinds of things but never realized anything about You."

This world is just a stage for dramas or plays. Many actors come and act their parts and leave. The millions of *jivas* are like the waves in the ocean. They come into existence like waves and then fall back into the ocean. The ocean, however, remains forever. Similarly all thc agcs like the *Krita, Treta* and *Kali yuga* have come and gone. They rise and fall like the waves in the ocean. Millions of beings come into existence and vanish like the bubbles in the waves of the ocean. However Janani, who is the ocean of *Chaitanya*, Consciousness, is Truth—eternal, wonderful and indivisible, infinite, unfathomable and incomprehensible—beyond human understanding. These physical eyes are not sufficient to see and understand this wonderful Truth. We have to open our eye of divine knowledge to know and understand the great brilliance of the light of Divine Mother which we describe as extraordinary, unique, indivisible, invincible and immutable. It is not something that can be seen by the external eyes.

Siva means auspiciousness and the form of Siva has millions of meanings. The pictures of the *linga* and Siva that we see do not simply mean He is Siva. It means He is

Mangala kara, bestower of auspiciousness, Gunatita, beyond qualities, Jnanatita, beyond knowledge, Vedatita, beyond the *Vedas*, and Sarvatita, beyond everything—eternal Truth and completely whole. Siva is fulfillment and wholeness. Therefore, we are praying to God to give us the power and ability to see both inwardly and outwardly, that best of the best Lights which is most auspicious. There is a *mantra* in the *Lalita Sahasranama:*

Śivāyai namaḥ Śiva Śaktyaikya rūpiṇyai namaḥ

Amma is also Siva in the form of *Para Shakti.* All these other forms are like small bubbles. Therefore, that Light is extraordinary and excellent, invincible, immutable and indivisible, without any deformaties. Sometimes a man has too much temper and other small negative qualities. However, Mother doesn't have any qualities, She is Gunatita, beyond qualities and beyond everything. She is in everything in this universe and yet She is not of it. Therefore, it is said in a *shloka:*

Girāmāhur Devīm Druhiṇa gṛhiṇīm Āgamavido
Hareḥ patnīm Padmām Hara sahacarīm Adri tanayām
Turīyā kāpi tvam duradhigama niḥ sīma mahimā
Mahā māyā viśwam bhramayasi Parabrahma mahiṣī

Srishti, creation, *sthiti,* preservation, and *laya,* destruction occur when the earth and all the universes are created. Mother, You have sent millions of Brahmas, Vishnus and Ishwaras and maintained the creation, preservation and destruction of all these universes. You are Panchakritya parayana—ever engaged in the five actions of creation, preservation, dissolution, *nigraha* (casting of illusion) and *anugraha* (bestowing of grace). *Tirodhana* is a beautiful word for dissolution, and means reabsorption. O Divine Mother, You are beyond all these—Nirguna Para Brahma svarupini—attributeless.

We who have studied the *Agamas* and the *Vedas*, in our innocence are limiting You by saying now and then that Mother is Lakshmi, Mother is Saraswati or Mother is *Devi*. *Devi* means divinity, beyond division. Nobody knows anything about You. You are the only one who knows about Yourself. Even Brahma does not know anything about You. He is really a small child in front of you.

Therefore, O Mother—You are

Samhāriṇī Rudra rūpā Tirodhāna karīśwarī

"When You take back the millions of beings You are in the form of Rudra."

Maheśwara mahākalpa mahā tāṇḍava sākṣinī

At the time of the destruction of the whole world at the end of a *kalpa,* time cycle, when all beings are destroyed, Mother is the only witness to the whole process of destruction. If we want to meditate on such a Mother who is Tirodhana karishwari, imagine how pure we must be! How can we do so when we have petty qualities like anger, impulsiveness and other such negative attributes? There are too many weeds in this garden which are emanating foul smells. *Sugandhim pushtivardhanam.* One has to have a longing to blossom that *Chaitanya kusuma*, the flower of consciousness, from which will emanate the fragrance of the soul. That kind of longing is called *tapana,* burning, *arti,* intense painful longing, *avedana,* beseeching, and is a form of *tapas*. This becomes meditation when we lose ourselves in the object of our longing, Divine Mother. We sometimes refer to it as "intense desire," but even that does not really convey the true meaning. The more intense your longing, the closer you will come to Mother.

If that longing is not intense, then your prayer will be superficial, not from the heart, and this has been going on for many lives. You pray, and then get angry and scold others, and shout at everybody. Thus we have been acting childishly and unwisely in various ways. You have to search carefully within. Write the name:

Om Śrī Lalitāmbikāyai namaḥ

Mother will make nectar flow from your heart. Chant the *Lalita Sahasranama* every day. The fruit of chanting the nine hundred and ninety-nine *mantras* out of the thousand *mantras* that are in it will come to you, and the last *mantra* will go toward world peace. Extraordinary and beyond description are the benefits of chanting this *Lalita Sahasranama.* Mother's *trishula* will always protect you from the millions of difficulties that you might have to face in life. It is because of your meditation on God that your life, instead of being restless, is at least as peaceful as it is now, because Mother has desired to make your heart Her temple and reside there. I will tolerate any amount of impurities but meditate on me with a pure heart.

Sacred souls! Let us get rid of these petty and mean qualities permanently for the sake of knowledge of the Soul, wisdom and discriminating knowledge. You read a *mantra* in the *Lalita Sahasranama:*

Prajnāna ghana rūpini

Consider a sugar candy. It is sweet inside and out—all through. It is not sweet inside and bitter outside. Similarly, *srishti*, this world which is Mother's creation—*atma jagat,* the world of the soul, and *jiva jagat*, the world of the being—are all very sweet. We do not have the correct viewfinder.

For example, when a small child is crying, we buy him glasses for a dollar. With these he cannot see the galaxies or the planets. They can only be used to magnify small letters into big letters. In order to see the planets we have to go to an observatory and see them with the help of an appropriate lens. We cannot see them with glasses bought for a dollar. Similarly, we cannot measure God's divinity with a small intellect and mind. It would be like measuring the depth of the sea with a thread or measuring the height of the Himalayas with a small ruler. In order to know Divinity no amount of intellect is sufficient.

Knowledge of the Self can be obtained only when we set aside our ego just as we set aside our shoes before entering the temple. In order to obtain this extraordinary knowledge of the Soul one has to practice humility. True knowledge gives one humility, and where there is humility there is eternal purity and discriminating knowledge wherein wisdom shines. In order to know Mother who is Prajnana ghana rupini, if there is even a trace of ignorance, it is not possible to understand Her.

Atma jnana, knowledge of the Soul, is full of nectar. In order to obtain this *Brahma jnana siddhi*, one has to rise to a very high elevation through meditation:

Dhyāna dhyāṭr dhyeya rūpa
Dharmādharma vivarjitā

One has to cross both *dharma* and *adharma.* The act of meditation, the meditator and the object of meditation, all have to become one. This is called *yoga*. It is very difficult. We are so separated when we are meditating. While we are chanting the *mantra*, the mind is wandering elsewhere and we are meditating on something else. We do not have the connection. You sometimes phone Amma. No matter how many times you dial you do not get the connection because you do not have the right code. If you find out the correct number and dial, you will get the connection immediately. It does not matter if the line is busy you will definitely get the connection one day.

Similarly we have been chanting the *mantra* for many years. Nobody is picking up the phone at the other end. Nobody is answering "Hello" even once because we are calling superficially. Call wholeheartedly either early in the morning or some time in the night. You cannot observe any strict regulations in this country. So as far as possible keep all strict regulations in your heart and with a pure mind open your heart wide and welcome Mother into it. Pray, "Mother, no matter how ignorant I may be or how bad I may be, You are not a bad Mother. I may have killed a cow, or a woman or a brahmin, You are the only one who has a heart big enough to forgive me. Nobody else in this world can forgive me. I may have knowingly or unknowingly committed a lot of sins in my previous lives, but please forgive me and protect me and lovingly take me close to You, Mother. For whether you may bless me, love me, caress me or punish me, blame me or reproach me, I will never leave your lotus feet.

"The great *pundits* of the *Agamas and Nigamas* mistakenly call You Saraswati, the wife of Brahma. Others call You Hari patnim, Hara sahacharim, the consort of Vishnu, Maha Lakshmi. And some others call You Parvati, the daughter of Parvata Raja. Mother, nobody knows You. Saraswati gives knowledge, Lakshmi gives wealth and Devi gives *shakti.* You are of the form of Tripura sundari in which all these three are combined. You are the power of all these three combined, without form and name." It is mentioned thus in the *Lalita Sahasranama*:

Nāma rūpa vivarjitā
Dharmādharma vivarjitā
Nirbhedā Nirākārā Bheda nāshini
Moha nāshini Kāma nāshini Krodha nāshini

She destroys all the qualities of *moha,* attachment and delusion, *kama,* desire, and *krodha,* anger, when you worship Her. What does She give in return? The state of *kaivalya,* oneness wih the Divine. Where does She take you? This body is Siva and the soul within is Shakti. She unites Siva with Shakti, opens the universal lotus, the *sahasrara,* and gives one the ability to worship Her with all the universal flowers. Amma does not want your faded flowers. You must offer Her those flowers of the soul that never fade. You should offer your entire life to Mother as *naivedya.* You must make your heart like lighted camphor and wave that burning flame as *arati* to Mother.

Amma sings beautifully:

Bhavet pūjā pūjā tava caraṇayor yā viracitām...

"I am sitting all the way back and not in the front among all those people like Brahma, Vishnu and Maheshwara, who are performing *puja* at Your lotus feet. However, please give me also a part in that worship of Your sacred feet, Amma."

You should pray thus in all humility and devotion to Mother. You have come so far away from your country. However, the whole world belongs to Mother. She is not partial. Mother has only one eye and that is the *agni netra*, the eye of fire. She has a *chandra netra,* a *surya netra* and the third is the *agni netra.* In this *agni netra*, Brahma is sitting somewhere like a small mustard seed. All the *devatas* in this whole wide world are within the form of Devi. We cannot even imagine the cosmic form of Divine Mother. It is beyond description. All the universes are revolving in Her like dust particles of *vibhuti.* And the Earth is a small speck somewhere in that ray of dust particles. From this point of view we are very insignificant, present somewhere in our country and hardly visible! Yet we are so madly entangled in our ego. When we reduce our ego we see this infinite vast world as Devi and exclaim:

Devī viśva vigrahā Bhāvanā mātra santuṣta hṛdayā

Devi is very pleased by your devotional feeling. If you get the thought, "I should see Mother in a beautiful silk sari in the temple today." Mother will simply hear your prayer and grant your wish by accepting the sari you give as *prasada* and wearing it. There is no doubt about this. She will not deny even your smallest wish. She will definitely grant your every wish. She does not have the power to say "no" to you. She will grant all your wishes, each and every one of them, whatever you ask. But you should ask Her for the appropriate thing and reach the highest state. You have a long way to go. You have to reach the state of *kaivalya* and *Brahma jnana sthiti.* It is said beautifully in the *Vedas:*

Duradhi gama niḥ sīma mahimā

It is a very beautiful expression: "The cosmos and all the innumerable millions of universes that you see in the infinite sky are simply held by Her in Her fist." She has immense affection for mankind on this Earth. She is called Malini, the one who loves human beings in all sincerity. She is also called Manonmani for Her children are singing Her praises in this world. Therefore, She has an inexplicable connection with this world.

What kind of birth did Brahma give to Valmiki? But what did Mother do to him? She made him a great poet. And what kind of birth did Brahma give to Vishvamitra? He was born a king, but he was living in great ignorance and had a bad temper. Once he started meditating on Divine Mother, She gave him the knowledge of *Brahman* and made him the *Guru* of Rama, the Lord incarnate. See to what an exalted state She took him! So, meditating on the feet of Divine Mother is never futile. She will shower on you, with both Her hands, eternal, permanent, unique, immeasurable *aishwarya*, glory!

A blind man unknowingly goes to a diamond mine, and there someone tells the people present to take as many diamonds as they want. And people are taking as many diamonds as they please, but the blind man decides he won't take anything. Someone nearby puts some diamonds in his hand too. At this the blind man thinks he is being ridiculed and insulted by the stones put in his hand, and throws them away. There are many who have come to this world to distribute such diamonds. Don't be like the blind man and throw them away.

Cultivate invaluable qualities like *tyaga,* renunciation, sacrifice, knowledge, love, truth and peace. Adorned with these beautiful qualities, live your life peacefully. You can either live in frustration feeling that you are missing something or lacking something like some people do or, live in contentment feeling that you have everything, like some others. No matter how much they have, some people live with a feeling of frustration. And then there are those who don't really have anything but live with a feeling of extraordinary contentment. Why? Because the Lord has burnt all their desires within. There is no wealth greater than contentment.

Contentment is a great virtue and opens the gates of a vast empire. If there is no contentment then we live in darkness. Time passes by and we reach the end of our lives. Then we take another birth. Who is going to tell us all these things again? Will we be educated or not, what kind of cultural values will we have, and what kind of atmosphere will we be in? We should not lose this opportunity, an opportunity we lost in innumerable lives before. What is the point of losing the opportunity even now? We need knowledge of the Soul and true devotion.

"Amma, I cannot understand You even after reading the four *Vedas*. Did anybody understand You after reading the

Agama or *Nigama shastras?* O Para Brahma mayi! Only when You command through Your grace that Your child should attain the knowledge of the Self, only then in a moment will I gain the knowledge of *Brahman.* You will make me sit in meditation in pure solitude in complete peace, and you will remove all the six enemies from my heart." She will remove all these small weeds and allow the tree of consciousness to grow tall and reach the sky and merge in universal peace.

Therefore, sacred divine souls! In order that you should desire universal peace, your Mother, Saraswati has given you birth in the most sacred land, India. You must have worshipped Divine Mother for many lives with golden flowers, and as a result taken birth in that holy land. Due to the merit of your good and sacred deeds you have acquired an education. The whole world belongs to us and you may have served all humankind. However, everyone belongs to some place with its inherent cultures. And you have come from a land that is extraordinary. There is no better *karma bhumi, jnana bhumi* or *tyaga bhumi.*

No matter how much you search, you will not find such a land anywhere in the world. It is a land with the wealth of the knowledge of the Soul and is compared to the heart filled with nectar. The honey from the flower of the knowledge of the *Vedas* is overflowing to the entire world. It is your responsibility to attain the wealth of that knowledge of the Self, pray to Divine Mother, become contented, and distribute that love, peace and service to your fellow beings in the whole world. This is your duty as a human being. If you all assume this responsibility in your heart, then no power in this world can do anything to you. If you hold Mother's power in your heart, every other power in this world is comparatively small and cannot do anything to you.

Divine blissful souls, Mother, as your birth mother from innumerable births, wishes that you should sit in that exalted state on the lion throne of righteousness. Our children should not roam in the streets of darkness—in the alleys of anger and lust and other immoral qualities.

Hari Om Tat Sat

Houston *14 April 1997*

ॐ

MOTHER IS THE EVER-BLOOMING FLOWER OF CONSCIOUSNESS

Swamiji: *Jai Karunamayi!*

Just now Amma was speaking in Her own language, Telugu, that is, Her physical language—I'm sorry! Actually this year's tour started in Dallas. There Amma was giving discourses completely in Telugu because most of the people were Telugu-speaking, most of them being from India. However, over here you have the rare opportunity to listen to Amma's discourse directly in English. But as many of the Telugu-speaking people here have expressed a desire to hear Amma's voice in Telugu, Amma has blessed them today and spoken in Telugu. The rest of you want to know and understand Her speech. To translate the language is hard, and to translate the feelings of Amma is even harder because in translation the feeling and the meaning sometimes changes as we are always in a lower level of consciousness.

Telugu is one of the four languages of South India. The others are: Tamil, Kannada and Malayalam. The Telugu language is thought to be a very sweet language and as Amma was saying now, it is a musical language, more musical than Sanskrit. It is the elder sister of Sanskrit, so most of the words used in Telugu are common to Sanskrit. The sound of Telugu words is soothing and it gives rest to our mind also. Some of you have experienced this here. Even though you do not understand the language, you must have understood the vibrations of the sounds of this language.

Amma: Mother is not partial to any language. Mother is Saraswati. There is only one language, the language of the heart. Your pet knows your love. Your pet's language is the heart's language. There is no other language between you and your pet. Language is very powerful, but silence is the most powerful language. Be silent daily for at least one or two hours. When it comes to love, there are no language differences. Speaking is different.

Swamiji: *Jai Karunamayi!* Many devotees who have come have brought notebooks to be blessed by Amma so that they can begin to write the *likhita japa* of Divine Mother's name, "Om Sri Lalitambika." Amma will be blessing each book by writing the first name, after which you can start the *likhita japa.* Before that, I would like to tell you the difference between *japa* and *dhyana.* In *japa* we have the consciousness of what we are doing.

Dhyānam nirviṣayam manaḥ

"*Dhyana* is freeing the mind from all thoughts." You must not have consciousness at all. For this we need a lot of practice. To write this *japa* properly, you must not just take the book and go on writing till the pages are finished. Each *mantra* must be written with full concentration. That is very important. And the vibration will be high when you do this. This is because, according to Amma's wishes, these books will be installed in the great temple which is being built in Amma's *ashram* in Penusila in Andhra Pradesh, in Southern India. A big *stupa,* a pillar as big as the temple, is being built in the meditation hall, where already thousands and thousands of books have been installed. The deity will be installed on the foundation of all these *likhita japa* books. So all these books will be in the meditation hall where a thousand people can sit and do meditation. And Amma's view is that each and everyone's vibration of *dhyana* on this *mantra* has to be in that *stupa.* Therefore you have to write this *japa* with full concentration. *Likhita japa* means "written *japa.*"

You might ask one more question, "What should we do with the books after we finish them?" You can just mail the books to the Indian address on the card we have given you. Mail it to the address for the Bangalore *ashram.*

[Amma requests Swamiji to relate the experience of a devotee who had undertaken a pilgrimage to Mt. Kailasa. Amma mentions that many people have spiritual experiences there. They can hear the sound of Mother's divine bangles and the sound of Her anklets when they lie down near the Manasarovara lake. The lake is golden, has pure water with no pollution at all. Manasarovara is no doubt Parvati, She says. From Mt. Kailasa, we can hear the sound of *Omkara.* So people never touch the sacred Kailasa mountain. They just have its *darshan* and do the fifty three miles *parikrama.*]

Swamiji [describing the journey to Mt. Kailasa]**:** One has to walk for 800 miles—not on a plain road but on a mountainous path—going up and down….

Amma: Without food…

Swamiji: …until one reaches an altitude of 25,000 feet above sea level. So on one day pilgrims will climb one thousand feet, rest there and then go on. As the oxygen becomes thinner, after a week or so they will be on multivitamin tablets only, with no food at all. They cannot carry anything. They cannot carry their clothes or belongings because they become heavy as they reach higher altitudes. Some of Amma's devotees have gone there, but first the government has to give permission after they approve their physical fitness. Amma says if Lord Siva wills, He gives us the permission. If Lord Siva thinks that you can come, only then you can go. People go in batches of thirty and there are nearly fifteen batches every year.

One of Amma's devotees went three years ago. This was before he became a devotee of Amma's. He is a very pious man, does regular meditation and is always inward.

Amma: He does the *Gayatri mantra* meditation.

Swamiji: One day as they were climbing, after journeying for a week or so, they had to cross different ridges of mountains and in one place there was a ridge of only one foot to cross. If one were to slip there, one would fall nearly a thousand feet to the lower level. As the devotee was crossing that point—remember, at that time he had not yet come to Mother—he slipped and was about to fall. At that time, he said, a small girl about eleven or twelve years old appeared, caught hold of his hand and prevented him from falling down. He was not able to thank the girl. He just watched her as she led the way in front of him. He was about to ask her something but she kept walking in front of him and he followed. After some time she disappeared, and he was left wondering who that girl might have been. He thought that perhaps she belonged to the mountain area, as some mountain people lived there and she may have spotted him and come to help him.

After the journey to Manasarovara and Kailasa, the devotee returned to India. One day while in Bangalore, he saw an article about Mother in a magazine and he came to Mother to get his child initiated with the *Saraswati bijakshara mantra*. There were thousands and thousands of people waiting eagerly for the *Saraswati bijakshara*. This was during Navaratri, when Amma was inscribing the *bijakshara* on everyone's tongue. The devotee came to the doorstep of the main hall, and as he saw Mother, he was shocked. He was completely taken aback and was unable to speak. He was in a sort of unconscious state and he sat down. Many people thought he had fainted and they gave him some water. Afterwards they asked him, "What happened to you? You are not feeling well?" He replied, "I had been to Kailasa and Manasarovara, and on the way I had slipped. A small girl suddenly appeared and she took my hand and helped me. And the same face which I saw that day is the face of Amma here. It was none other than Amma only who came and helped me and saved me. And that was the greatest experience!" And he said that he had not seen Amma before. But he said, "I still remember and it is imprinted on my mind that it is none other than the same Mother in the form of a young girl of eleven or twelve years."

In the *shastras* it is said that Devi appears in different forms, and one of them is the *Kaumari rupa*, that is, a young girl of ten to twelve years. That is the form in which the devotee saw Amma before coming to Her. That is why Amma always says that even if you don't come to me, my blessings will always be there with you. And that was the greatest blessing and experience of the devotee, which I shared with you all today. *Jai Karunamayi!*

Amma: So come back to Mother's sweet home, the real Kailasa. Texas is not our place. We have a separate home. Kailasa is our home.

Swamiji: We have a video film about Manasarovara and Kailasa which we will bring next time. The devotees who have gone there have filmed it, but not professionally, as one cannot carry big cameras. The film was taken with a small camera, and although the quality is not good, you can still have a glimpse of Kailasa and Manasarovara.

Amma: Amma is always at the front door,

Mokṣa dvārā kavāṭa pāṭanakarī

She is always waiting for Her children. O my babies, come, come, come!

Swamiji: Amma gives us an example here. Suppose you are coming from a different country, you will need a passport to enter this country. You have to pass customs and immigration and you have to show your passport wherever needed. And even when you come out and are walking alone on the road, the police may stop you and ask for your identification; then also you have to show your passport and establish that you belong to a different country. [Amma laughs] And when you come to your home, even there you may be watched. There may be guards there to whom you will have to show your identity. To every person you have to prove your identity. [Amma laughs and exclaims, "Pathetic!"] But when you come to your real home, your Mother will be there ready to open the door. She never asks for your passport. She knows you.

Devotee: Last year at the East Coast meditation retreat in upstate New York there were about fifty of us. We meditated for about three days with Amma, for about five hours a day—not all at one time. We meditated for an hour at a time with breaks in between. On the last day we had meditated for about five-and-a-half hours. Amma had us sit in two concentric circles for our last meditation. She had already told us that She was very pleased with our meditation. We meditated for about two hours. Some of the devotees attending had never meditated for more than ten minutes before the retreat, but they had the desire to come and through the grace of Amma they were able to sit and meditate for that period of time.

When we finished the final meditation. I looked up and Swamiji was there doing *pranam* to Amma and he was staying for a little longer than usual. So I got my glasses and looked to see what was happening and there was a mound of *vibhuti* covering Amma's feet. This is the sacred ash that Amma puts on our forehead. The *vibhuti* had materialized while we were doing our meditation. Of course, all of a sudden people began to realize what had happened and they converged and began to take a bit for themselves. Afterwards Amma told us that Lord Siva had been very pleased with our meditation and that the *vibhuti* was the blessing of Lord Siva. *Jai Karunamayi!*

****

Amma's Discourse:

Om śaraṇāgata dīnārta paritrāṇa parāyane
Sarvasyārti hare Devī Nārāyanī namostute

Embodiment of Divine Souls, Amma's Most Beloved Children,

I have not come to you as a spiritual master. I have not come to you as a *guru* or Divine Mother. I have come to you all the way as your own near and dear mother. My children, you are already on the beautiful, divine spiritual path. This is the right path. Where there is *dharma,* righteousness, there only is divinity. Where there is divinity, there only is peace. So we need peace. It is not available in the external world. Peace is only found within.

Seeing God in beautiful idols in temples is one stage. It is a very good stage because in this *Kali yuga* we forget all these spiritual things. We are afraid and we have a lot of negativity. So, seeing God in temples and having faith in God is one stage. Seeing God in holy people and in good things is another stage. Seeing divinity in oneself and in others—that is a beautiful state. That is spiritual consciousness—seeing divinity everywhere; not only in the good, but also in the bad—that is the highest stage. That is the real essence of spirituality.

Children, you are already in your path. There are innumerable paths in this world, innumerable religions. But Truth is only one. If our path is devotional, *bhakti yoga,* or if it is the path of knowledge, *jnana yoga,* or *dhyana yoga* or *nishkama karma yoga*, the goal is the same. When our little self is one hundred percent less, then only *yoga* starts. In selfless service, if our self disappears one hundred percent, our service is wonderful to this universe. That is the *karma yoga* mentioned in the *Bhagavad Gita*. So we are already on the path.

But why this anger in our heart? Why again do we have lust, greed, and these little, little things in our heart? For so many years—twenty, thirty, or fifty years, we have been chanting the *Vishnu Sahasranama*, the *Lalita Sahasranama*, the *Bhagavad Gita*, and performing spiritual activities. Yet we have some curtains—anger, lust, greed, hatred and jealousy. These are little, little weeds. There is a beautiful divine plant in our heart. That is the cosmic consciousness. When we elevate ourselves to the highest peak of purity, to desirelessness, this consciousness touches the cosmos. We belong to each and every religion in this world. We belong to this universe. The animal kingdom, bird kingdom, and everything else is ours only. But we get stuck in some little, little points: "Oh, this is my religion. Only my religion is good. Only my feeling is good." Really, your feeling is very good and sweet, but it is our responsibility to give respect to other religions also.

The sun is only one but its rays are innumerable. There are billions upon billions of rays. God and Truth are only one. The paths are many. So why do we quarrel, particularly in spirituality? Why do we argue, "Do not go there, do not see her, do not enter the temple, do not enter this mosque." By doing so we bind ourselves to a mortal frame and to our mind, because we are in this limited frame.

So children, only in this spiritual path we have that wisdom. Wisdom is so beautiful. It beautifies our entire life so that we may attain God-Realization. You know, the main aim of human life is Self-Realization. Seeing divinity in one's heart and in everything good and bad is the highest *turiya* state in spirituality.

India has given the beautiful *Sanatana Dharma* to the entire universe. In *Sanatana Dharma* there is a beautiful saying,

Vasudhaika kuṭumba

Just now we chanted a beautiful *mantra*,

Lokāḥ samastāḥ sukhino bhavantu

"May the entire universe always be in peace and prosperity." We wish all this for the entire universe. That is liberation. So we need that liberation—liberation from our anger. Anger is a little weed. It controls the cosmic tree in our heart. Lust, greed, hatred, jealousy, and pride are also little, little weeds. These six weeds we must immediately remove from our heart, which is a beautiful garden.We must elevate ourselves to the highest peak of *samadhi*. That is Realization. That is the essence of spirituality.

Since innumerable births we have been searching for this reality. Reality is not outside; it is always inside. Peace is always inside. So we need liberation from these lowly natures and elevation to the highest peak of *dharma*. Where there is *dharma*, there only is real wisdom. If we do not have wisdom in our life, and if any desire remains in this birth, then again we take one more birth. This is like a *chakra—janana marana chakra*. Mother resides in the *Sri Chakra*; children reside in the *janana marana chakra*. Mother is wearing the *trishul*; the children are wearing the *trigunas*, not the *trishul*. We should have liberation from these negativities such as anger. Anger is not sweet, it is bitter. In the *Bhagavad Gita*, there is a *shloka*,

Krodhāt bhavati sammohaḥ

"If there is anger, that is the main entrance for *naraka,* hell." Where there is peace, that is the entrance for liberation, the main gateway for wisdom.

So children, meditate and pray to God with tears. The prayer must not come from the lips. It must always come from the bottom of our heart. From the bottom of our heart. Wake up early in the morning and pray to God with a pure heart, without any desire. Desire is the impurity of the mind, the force of motion of our mind. Desire creates so many problems. Desirelessness is the highest peak of purity. Purity is the gateway for wisdom So where purity and inner beauty, *anta sveccha,* exist, we have wisdom in our life. We have limited ourselves to a small part. When this energy spreads (*vyapaka*), as the nature of our *atma* is *vyapaka*, it spreads through the entire universe. Now it is like a small atom in our heart, enclosed by the little, little, little weeds. Just vacuum all those weeds from the heart and have liberation—liberation from anger, liberation from lust, liberation from greed, liberation from jealously. Jealousy is like jaundice to our mind—it is not sweet. We are the soul; we are not this body. This body is like a dress, a dress for our soul.

So only those who have spiritual elevation in their lives are able to open their third eye and see divinity everywhere. They are always in that Supreme Consciousness, that is, bliss and peace. They have this experience, "O, I myself am wisdom, I myself am Truth, I myself am past, present and future." You yourself are time and you yourself are attributeless. And you yourself are the entire cosmos. The whole cosmos belongs to you only, to your soul. You are bliss! The *Vedas* and all religions belong to you. Why are we stuck like a little cassette and are so limited here, thinking, "O, only this is my path, I never go and visit any *gurus,* I don't like to go to the temple." We limit ourselves.

Spirituality leads you from this mortal frame to immortality, to the permanent peace, the permanent bliss that is like a hidden treasure in our hearts. So open the heart and invite divinity. Kill the ego and pray to God for purification. You know that meditations and all those things are just for remodeling our life, remodeling our life to divinity, for our upliftment towards divinity. Meditation gives purification and a lot of inner beauty to our life. Where there is inner beauty, there we have all the divine attributes, such as compassion, kindness, equal vision, wisdom, truth, peace, and bliss. We have all these divine attributes, *sugunas,* just like gems and jewels in our heart. Wear these jewels. For a spiritual aspirant these jewels such as kindness, compassion and real devotion, are very much needed—not the show of devotion.

Have one hundred percent faith. Achieve your destiny in this birth itself. Achieve that destiny and realize what is good and what is bad. Search the inner reality inside first. Seeing divinity inside is good, that is a divine virtue. Honesty is the greatest wisdom. If we have real truth and we pray to God with true devotion, we will have all these divine attributes in our heart and gradually be elevated to the attributeless state because divinity is only oneness. There is no second.

Ekamevadvitīyam Brahma
Nanyad asti akincanaḥ
Satyam jnānam anantam

You know all that. So we will just summarize the little points. One is faith—have one hundred percent faith, discriminating faith. Without faith, even if we pray for hundreds and hundreds of years there is no meaning in our spirituality. Faith is the main basis. Where there is faith there is everything—more and more real devotion in our heart. Where there is no faith, any religion, country, or personality is gradually ruined because faith is the main power. Faith develops will power, faith gives immense strength and real knowledge. So have faith, discriminating faith.

Develop your dispassion more and more, and meditate and pray to God. If you like *bhakti yoga*, proceed on that path. If you like meditation, you proceed on that path. If you like singing, sing some *bhajans* or songs. In music there is nectar, but silence is the language of God. There are innumerable languages. Mother Saraswati is not partial to only Sanskrit. If it is the language of the birds or animals, or the language of the ocean or wind—She likes every language in this universe. But because Her language is absolute silence, we must learn that language too. In silence only we learn so many things. If we are restless, walking here and there and wandering in this world, we will not learn anything.

So children, silence is the beautiful language of the Divine. Learn that language. Wake up early in the morning, at least by five o'clock. Pray for fifteen to twenty minutes. Meditate. Meditate on the Self—Truth. Truth develops inner beauty so that we have spiritual consciousness and we enjoy peace and bliss in our Self. Then we are able to see divinity everywhere in the universe. So peace is not available by just going and sitting in Himalayan caves. It is not possible. We must conquer the enemies. Who is the enemy of peace? Our desire. Our desire is the first enemy of our peace. So reduce the unnecessary desires and have a good desire, that is, Realization. Realization of the Self is to see divinity in bad also. Then we have forgiveness and the beautiful flowers will bloom in our heart.

It is mentioned in the *Lalita Sahasranama*:

Caitanya kusuma ārādhyā
Caitanya kusuma priyā

"Mother is like the beautiful ever-blooming flower—the flower of spiritual consciousness." That is the tenth gate in our body in the *brahmakupa*, the universal lotus. So open all these *chakras*. All the inner flowers are blooming because of cosmic love and cosmic consciousness. We have *Brahmic* awareness. We enjoy the silence and bliss in our life. Our life becomes so sweet. There are no words in any language to describe that state. That is only by our experience.

So, children, send this ego problem away permanently. The main problem is innumerable births of "I," "me," and "mine." This is our only problem. So immediately send this problem from your heart and open the gate. Ask Mother to grant a divine grand life. A divine grand life means only peace. Where there is peace, there only is divinity. Where there is divinity there only is *Sanatana Dharma*. Be seated in that seat of *dharma*. Do not walk in those little, little paths of anger, lust, greed and jealously. Those are slippery paths, not good paths. No good fragrance at all. For births together, since billions and billions and billions of births, we have been on these slippery paths. The path that is so beautiful, indescribable—that is only the absolute truth, benediction, wisdom. So oneness is important. That is the essence of spirituality.

What is the essence of human life, children? What is the essence of our human life? The essence of our human life is selfless service. We must give our service to this universe, but we should never display it. We must always be behind the curtain and give our service one hundred percent to mankind. That is our responsibility, because you take so much from nature. You never repay anything to Mother Nature.

If you love Mother Nature, you will become wise. It is also one of our responsibilities to love this entire nature—

the animal kingdom, the bird kingdom and the entire universe. You are everything. Everything belongs to your soul only. If we have that *Brahmic* awareness, we can never hate anyone in this world. We will have a lot of cosmic love in our hearts. That is the highest state of spirituality. So Mother wishes that Her children will earn that highest state. Give your selfless service. Be humble. Humility is a jewel for a seeker. Humility is the enemy of egoism. Develop humility and send egoism away. Permanently send away egoism in this birth.

We have three stages of the mind. In the stage of *tamas—tamasic* food, *tamasic* words, *tamasic* thinking—we never listen to anyone else's words, even if it is good for us. Because of our *tamasic* nature we have many faults. So *tamasic* food and habits and excessive sleep are not good. The spiritual consciousness is also working in *tamas,* but only a quarter percent.

Rajas also can be very, very dangerous to society. Commanding and forcing others, imposing our will on others, and expecting people to do things according to our wishes, this is *rajas*. We tell people, "You must be like this or like that." We cannot give wisdom to others. How pathetic it is! So a *rajasic* nature is more dangerous than a *tamasic* one.

In *sattva* we have spirituality, humility, inner beauty, devotion, knowledge, all these good qualities. And we can develop our spirituality more and more if we meditate, pray, sing, worship, and have *darshan* of holy people. Just one dust particle of theirs is enough to give us elevation. Even thousands and thousands of sittings of meditation are not equal to one particle of dust from a holy person. So in *sattva* we have humility, spirituality, real devotion, and we have faith, discriminative knowledge, and all these good qualities. Gradually we elevate ourselves from *sattva* to *vishuddha sattva*.

Vishuddha sattva is the place of the *vishuddha chakra.* In the heart *chakra* we have all these good natures—we are pure, we never tell lies, we never cheat others, we never injure others' feelings, including their religious feelings, and we have a lot of respect towards everyone in the world. So gradually when you are elevated to the *vishuddha chakra,* you are in pure consciousness, you are in silence, you have peace, you have bliss, and you have awareness. You are in the consciousness of *Brahman.* And your third eye, your eye of wisdom, is open here in the *ajna chakra.* [Amma points to the forehead]. The entire cosmos is in between your two eyebrows. You feel that little Mother Earth is a very tiny particle compared to the cosmos, and where am I? Oh, that is a very beautiful state! So stage by stage, stage by stage, you are elevated. It does not happen in one day but by gradual practice.

To practice spirituality, intense desire is needed and all the divine attributes, the jewels, are very important. Children, you already have all those. Elevate yourself more and more and more and more and be always in wisdom, be always in Truth, be always in *Omkara*, be always in oneness, nonduality. There is no secondness, duality, in this universe. Only oneness. So remove these curtains, these black curtains between your eyes and your heart. Your entire life is covered with these curtains of illusion. So remove these curtains immediately. Send away egoism permanently from your life. Egoism is the main problem. Birth is a long play. This is a play of forty years, fifty years, seventy years, or ninety years. In this play we are always assuming a role. Be a spectator in this play. A spectator enjoys the play more than an actor. So enjoy this play, this cosmic play. Stop your part and balance your mind.

Meditation and spirituality control our emotions. Sometimes we have so much emotion for unnecessary little,

little things. We do not have a balanced state of mind because there is no meditation and no purity. So if we meditate we can enjoy the balanced state. We will have equal vision. We will love every religion, everyone, even if they have committed sins. We will have that understanding, the right understanding. We will have knowledge. We will love this entire nature. We will go beyond the body, mind and intellect, and we will see divinity in everything in this universe. That is spirituality. That is *Sanatana Dharma.*

Sanatana Dharma is not for Indians only. Mother is not partial to anyone. Divine Mother Parashakti is

Sanātanī Ārya Ārādhya Devī
Akhaṇḍa Caitanya Brahma svarūpiṇī
Koṭi koṭi yoginī gaṇa sevitā
Akhilāṇḍa koṭi brahmaṇḍa nāyakī
Ādī madhyānta rahitā
Kānti dhuta japāvalī

Sṛṣṭi kartrī Brahma rūpā
Goptrī Govinda rūpiṇī
Samhāriṇī Rudra rūpā
Tirodhāna karīśwarī

All these forms are only Mother's form. Mother is *Omkara.* She is the Absolute. Our main aim is to attain Realization at least in this birth. So many billions of births we have failed, failed, failed. We are stuck in little, little points—in anger, in lust, in greed, in hatred—little points. Really these are not big points.

There is a great reason for this life. What is that reason? If we have real knowledge, if we have awareness in our heart, immediately we will start our eternal journey with a definite aim—to attain bliss. So, children, be like an infant baby in Mother's arms. The one- or two-day-old infant baby always closes her eyes and smiles in her sleep. When her mother touches her she is so happy. When anyone else touches her, she immediately senses the other's presence and she cries. She doesn't like others' vibrations. She only likes her mother's vibration. So always be in that bliss, children. Do not invite the little things any more—send them away permanently from your heart, and beautify your heart with all these divine attributes.

Forgiveness is the greatest penance.

Kṣamā tapas kṣamā yogam
Kṣamā jnānam kṣamā sarvam

Where there is forgiveness there is everything. When we have cruelty in our hearts we are not beautiful. Along with physical beauty, inner beauty, *anta saundaryam* is also important. Children, you already have all those good qualities, so elevate yourself more and more and attain God-Realization in this birth at least. Stop this *janana marana chakra*—the cycle of birth and death and again rebirth. This is a cycle. Stop this birth and death cycle. Achieve the destiny of the *bindusthana* in the *Sri Chakra*. That is your abode. Come back to your Mother's sweet home. Enjoy divinity always—in yourself and everywhere in this universe. God is not only in one particular place, He is everywhere. So have that experience and enjoy bliss, peace, and oneness in this birth.

Meditation purifies our life; it purifies each and every cell of our body. It gives us self-confidence, self respect, willpower, balance of mind, and gradually, attributelessness. First we need all these. So, children, whatever your religion may be—that is not the question. All religions lead to one goal only—that goal is only bliss, peace. The question is not about which religion is good and which religion is bad. Every religion emphasizes Truth and wisdom. Have wisdom at least in spirituality. We do not have wisdom in our life—in our office, our family, our country, the universe. We have rules and regulations everywhere. For a little happiness we work so much, suffer so much and we lose everything. Only spirituality, only Truth supports your entire life. You will develop strong willpower in your life. Develop that more and more, and if any problem comes to you, it will not touch your heart. You will be stable and forgiving and always in that spiritual consciousness. This is so beautiful.

So Truth is our main aim. To attain this Truth we must have purity. Purity is the gateway for wisdom. Where there is purity, there only is honesty. Where there is honesty, there we have all these beautiful divine flowers blooming in our heart: the root *chakra,* the *svadhisthana chakra,* the *manipura chakra,* the *anahata chakra,* the *vishuddhi chakra,* the *ajna chakra*, and finally the tenth gate, the universal lotus, the *sahasrara kamala.* That is your seat. Come back to your Mother's sweet home—*Omkara.* You are in a hostel, a temporary hostel. We are searching for happiness here, but really there is no happiness in these limited things. For a tiny bit of happiness we are working and working and working and our entire life is just wasted. Happiness is always inside. It is in the form of bliss. So search for that bliss, have willpower, be always in wisdom. Try to understand reality and attain God-Realization in this birth. This is Amma's only wish for Her children.

Children, never injure the religious feelings of others. If your friends have a particular faith, give respect. That is our responsibility. Go to all holy people, have their *darshan* and get their blessings. If they are really enlightened, you will have a good blessing. If they are not enlightened, also you get blessings. Your salutations go to the Absolute only. So there is no problem.

Do not criticize anyone. Criticism, hurting, and using bad words—that is the pollution of our tongue. After taking the holy *tirtha* and repeating *mantras*, we criticize people. Is it good? It is not good. And with angry words, we hurt only our own people, our own family members. Is it good? So control the anger, gradually control this weed and then remove this weed. Whenever you have anger go to another room. Do not talk to them. If people have hurt you ten times, forgive them. Love them. Because you are on the spiritual path, you have devotion and such qualities in your life. If you continue hurting people hundreds of times, what is the meaning of your spirituality? Never come down from that highest peak to the lower level. That is a different level. Because people do not understand, they have anger. Anger is one nature. That is a weed, just a little weed which covers the cosmic tree. So immediately burn all these weeds with a laser beam, which is the *mantra*. Chant the *Narayana mantra,* the *Om mantra,* the *Siva mantra,* or whatever *mantra* you have.

The power of the seed letters in the *mantra* cannot be described. They remove the ignorance, illusion, and dark forces in our life and give enlightenment to the seeker. This also depends upon your *sadhana*. Your *sadhana* is your best friend in this world. Listen to your friend's words. If your *sadhana* is without any interruption, you will always have good feelings, and you will have some message from your pure heart telling you what to do and where to go. You will always get messages from your heart, from your soul. So listen to your heart. Always listen to your heart. Be always in pure consciousness. Be always in wisdom. Be always in divinity. Divinize your thoughts.

In the *Rig Veda* many years ago, our thoughts have been mentioned. Now we have so many polluted thoughts—negative thoughts, very poisonous thoughts. Because of our poisonous thoughts we have polluted this Earth more than atomic pollution and all other kinds of pollutions. Those pollutions are only one percent. Our negative thinking is millions of times greater than this atomic pollution. "Let noble thoughts come to us from every side," is a beautiful saying in the *Rig Veda*. Always have noble thoughts—they beautify our entire life. We should divinize our thoughts, which will then beautify our lives with peace, forgiveness, equal vision, discriminative knowledge, discriminating faith, true devotion, and humility. Decorate your life with all these beautiful ornaments and be attributeless. In meditation only it is possible. So you know all those things.

Once more Amma is just summarizing those points with Her children on this beautiful evening. It is so beautiful here, it seems to be like Tirumala with the *murtis*—here in this special, temple atmosphere with pure vibrations. So, children, take a vow that from now on we will never invite these negative qualities into our hearts. Send them away permanently. Have peace, more peace and experience the real bliss in this birth. That is Amma's wish towards Her children. *Hari Om Tat Sat.*

Once again we will meditate for universal peace for five minutes. Daily try to repeat the *mantra* twenty-four times.

[Amma recites the *Mrityunjaya mantra* and then the *Saraswati mantra* with devotees.]

This *Saraswati mantra* is for pure thoughts, good words, pure feelings, immense knowledge, spiritual inspiration, and good education. So this *mantra* gives a lot of inspiration in our life. The *Saraswati mantra* purifies our words, our life and gives a lot of inner beauty.

Om Ayīm Śrīm Hrīm Saraswatī Devyai namaḥ
Om śānti, śānti śāntiḥ

San Antonio *15 April 1997*

ॐ

SRI RAMA'S SACRIFICE

Embodiments of Divine Souls,

The lighting of the stars illuminates the whole universe. So, from a special star, Rama descended to bless this entire universe. He purified each and every part of India by His *pada yatra,* travelling through India on foot. This is so beautiful. Sri Rama first blessed Dasharatha and his family. For innumerable births Dasharatha and Kaushalya had prayed to God, and were very pure souls. So Rama—Sri Ramachandra Prabhu—descended to this great Dasharatha's family. But He was in their home for five years only.

At the age of five, He went to Vasishtha Maharshi's *gurukula* for education, and stayed there till He was sixteen or eighteen. So Vasishtha Maharshi and his wife enjoyed His presence for longer than His own parents.

The life of Sri Rama is beautiful. Rama was full of compassion and kindness—all the sixty four divine attributes were manifested together in Sri Rama. This is even mentioned in the *Ramayana* through the words of a demon named Maricha. He was a *rakshasa,* but he said about Rama:

Rāmaḥ vigraha dharmaḥ

"O, Rama is the very embodiment of *dharma.*" We never find all the divine attributes assembled in one place, only in the *Rama avatara.* He sacrificed everything, not for His own family, but for the entire universe.

When an incarnation descends to this world, His purpose is not confined to one country or one family. God is for everyone—just as the sun is for everyone and the moon is for everyone. The fire, air, sky—all the elements are the subtle form of the divine body of these pure incarnations. Whenever they descend in any form, they give fulfillment to this entire universe—that is the beauty of divinity. So we can see purity, unconditional love, compassion, decency, dignity, wisdom, truth and all these beautiful divine qualities in them. But they are beyond these attributes. They are really beyond these attributes. They are always in their natural state, which is beyond *dharma.*

So children, on this auspicious day of *Rama Navami*, fill your heart with love for Sri Rama, and pray to Rama for elevation—liberation from anger, liberation from greed, liberation from jealousy, liberation from mean things in the heart. Selfishness, restlessness, and all these things are not sweet, not good. So elevate from these little things and achieve the ultimate destiny in this birth.

Let me relate an incident to you: One of Amma's sons came and asked Amma, "How can we control our anger, our mind and our thoughts? How is it possible to do this in our daily life?" Yes, it is possible but only through continuous practice. You have to train the mind. It depends upon the training you give your mind. At first wild animals such as elephants and horses do not obey us. But through constant training, they listen to our words and do whatever we wish. In the same way, we have to train the mind. We can control our mind gradually by practicing righteousness, by meditation, by singing *bhajans*, chanting divine names, and all these things.

Pranayama is the key to control the mind. Without *pranayama*, meditation is meaningless. *Pranayama* means *kriya yoga*, that is, doing some breathing exercises to regulate the *prana* and control the thoughts in meditation. In recent research, scientists have found that from childhood to the sixtieth year, twenty five thousand million thoughts arise spontaneously in the mind of a human being. These thoughts may be positive thoughts, bad thoughts, good thoughts, spiritual thoughts, normal thoughts, unnecessary thoughts—so many kinds of thoughts.

How can we control these thoughts? Every thought becomes an action. If we want to do this *puja* for Amma, that is a good thought, so it is all right if it becomes an action. But if it is a bad thought, if we want to scold others, abuse others, what about that thought? Can we continue with that thought? Our mind becomes so poisoned when we continue with that kind of thought. So immediately burn that thought with the pure divine name, by mentally chanting God's name, or by *japa,* or meditation with your *mantra. Mantra* has the power to burn all the impurities inside and gives mental peace, balance and equal vision in our life. So only spirituality can give us wisdom. If there is no wisdom at all in spirituality, it is a waste. So children, elevate more and more.

Many people repeat the *Gayatri mantra.* During *pranayama* take a deep breath into the left nostril while repeating the *Gayatri mantra* or *Om mantra.* Then close both nostrils and again repeat the *Gayatri mantra* once. This one repetition of the *Gayatri mantra* with the breath held inside is equal to a hundred and eight repetitions. One hundred and eight such rounds of *pranayama* with the *Gayatri mantra* equals one hundred and eight multiplied by one hundred and eight—over ten thousand repetitions of the *Gayatri mantra.*

Thyagaraja chanted the *Gayatri* mantra one *lakh* times daily. It is impossible to chant the *Gayatri mantra* one *lakh* times in twenty-four hours—it is never possible. Yet, Thyagaraja completed twenty-four *lakh* repetitions of the *Gayatri mantra* with *pranayama.* This is the way the ancient *rishis* practiced the *Gayatri mantra* combined with breath control, and they were able to control their minds immediately.

We must focus our mind between the two eyebrows—this is the place of Saraswati, Goddess of Knowledge, our third eye place. What happens when we concentrate on the *ajna chakra?* When the rays of the sun are concentrated by passing through a lens, they burn paper in a few minutes. In the same way, when you meditate at the *ajna chakra* with the power of *mantra*, the cosmic energy comes from divinity through the lens of the third eye, and burns all the layers of the dust of thoughts covering the *chakras*. Gradually all the *chakras* begin to bloom inside, energy is released from all these *chakras*, and we have a beautiful blooming of cosmic flowers, divine qualities, in our life. Then there is no anger at all. Gradually our thoughts are burned by the purification of meditation.

So meditation remodels our life from humanity to divinity. In *mantra japa* we repeat the *mantra* continuously, but *mantra* meditation is different. First close your eyes, focus on the *ajna chakra,* and begin by saying *Om* nine times, followed by *pranayama* five times. *Pranayama* can be done without the *mantra,* but it is good to repeat your *mantra* during *pranayama.* It is difficult to repeat the whole *Gayatri mantra* while holding the breath inside. It needs a lot of practice to combine the *Gayatri mantra* with *pranayama*, and the process should be learned from a *guru.*

When you meditate, repeat your *mantra—Om mantra, Om namah Sivaya mantra,* whatever it may be—five times mentally, and then sit in silence. You can concentrate between the eyebrows or on the heart *chakra.* While we repeat the *mantra,* the mind is still working. The real meditation is in complete silence—without even the *mantra:*

Dhyānam nirviṣayam manaḥ

"Freeing the mind from thoughts is true meditation."

At present we are in the grip of our thoughts, so we are full of frustration, anxiety and restlessness. When there is silence, and there are no thoughts at all, we are so peaceful, we are so happy.

We have an immense load of *karma*, the load of thoughts. Just calculate: twenty five thousand million thoughts into billions and billions of births! Can you imagine how much thought-load is inside? When we sit in spiritual activity—any activity such as singing *bhajans* or anything—immediately the poison comes out of our mind. When the *devas* and *danavas* did the *Kshira Sagar manthana*, the poison came out first, the nectar later. All the snakes of our thoughts come from this anthill of the mind. Send them away, burn them permanently. So watch your mind—"Oh, how am I? Do I hate others, scold others, abuse others?" If you are doing these things, try to control yourself. Watch your heart. Watch your life, watch your deeds, watch your words, watch your self.

Enquiry should be about ourselves—we should never find faults in others, we should never abuse others or injure anyone's feelings. We must try our level best to achieve our destiny, salvation, and for this we need to purify our life more and more by our own spiritual practices. We can follow *jnana yoga*, the path of knowledge and self-enquiry, no problem. *Dhyana yoga,* the path of meditation is also beautiful. *Bhakti yoga, karma yoga*—all *yogas* lead to the same destination.

Yoga means a combination of several things. When the three rivers, the Ganga, Yamuna and Saraswati meet, it is called *yoga*. In *ayurveda*, the Indian system of medicine, the combination of several herbs is called *yoga*. Sometimes many good planets come into one line—that is also called *yoga*. Sri Rama descended to this world during such a *yoga* of stars in order to establish *dharma* on Earth for mankind. According to the *Vedas*:

Manuṣyatvam mumukṣatvam mahā puruṣatvam

"In the heart of a mortal, or *manushyatvam,* when there arises *mumukshatvam,* an intense desire for liberation, then man attains through *sadhana, maha purushatvam,* the status of a great soul." The vision, the thoughts, the love of *maha purushas,* everything is elixir. So *yoga* purifies your life with beautiful spiritual love—whether you follow *karma yoga, bhakti yoga, dhyana yoga,* or *jnana yoga*—and leads you to the final destination. Kill this anger and send egoism permanently from the heart.

If anyone says something negative to you, can you bear it? You will also respond in a negative way because of your ego problem. So pray to Mother, for She is your true mother. She has the responsibility; She will never leave you. Understand your problem, reduce your ego, and gradually burn it completely. Send it permanently from the heart and make your life beautiful with peace, with bliss, with tranquility, and oneness with God. Now you are separate from Amma. But you and your Amma are only one—that is the conclusion of all spirituality. So enjoy this bliss, enjoy this bliss, at least in this birth. Now already forty years, fifty years are gone. Only a few pages remain in the diary of life—five pages, ten pages, or forty pages. So at least fill these remaining pages with peace.

Life is a bundle of golden coins. You have already wasted sixty or seventy coins, but use the remaining five or six coins well. Do not waste them. In this *Kali yuga*, there is so much negativity. Why? Because that is the nature of this *yuga*—spirituality is only one percent. All the religious and holy persons are working, but spirituality is still only one percent, and negativity is ninety-nine percent. That is why there is no balance or moral harmony in this world. If there is fifty percent of spirituality and fifty percent of negativity, it will be balanced.

So, children, pray to Mother Divine for liberation from these limited qualities, this restlessness and anxiety. Why do we have them? Because of our desires. Why these desires? Because of ego. Why this ego? Because of our selfishness. When we practice real spirituality we will have selflessness instead of selfishness, and peace instead of anger. In the place of lust we will have self-control and in the place of greed we will have compassion, discrimination and strong determination. In the place of jealousy, we will have love—cosmic love.

Cosmic love alone can conquer this entire universe. So start developing cosmic love immediately. Cultivate *dharma*. Cultivate compassion, dispassion and oneness with God, liberation. That is the conclusion of *Sanatana Dharma* and of all spirituality. We need salvation in this life, but if even one desire remains in our heart, even one thought remains in our mind, we will be born again. Stop this *chakra*, this eternal cycle of birth and death, and merge with the universal personality—that is your destiny. Have a definite aim. Have a definite aim.

[Amma continues in Telugu]

Swamiji [translating]**:** *Jai Karunamayi!* The following is the essence of Amma's message in Telugu. This is a summary. Today is very auspicious, because it is *Sri Rama Navami*. Many of you, all the Indians, know how this festival is celebrated throughout India. And in Andhra Pradesh in Bhadrachala, we perform the wedding ceremony for Lord Sri Rama and Sita Devi on this day every year. One may ask why these Gods have to be married every year. It is not like an ordinary wedding ceremony; it is for *vishva kalyana.* In Sanskrit the word *kalyana* means a wedding and also welfare. This *kalyana,* the wedding of Rama and Sita is performed for *vishva kalyana,* for the welfare of all humanity and for the whole universe.

Sri Rama and Sita Devi are not ordinary human beings, just a man and a woman. They are *prakriti* and *purusha,* who have descended to this Earth at different times as Lakshmi and Narayana, as Siva and Parvati, and as Rama and Sita. They are the main source of energy, and have come down to this Earth with different names and forms to elevate all humanity. That is the main purpose for which they have incarnated on Earth. The *Rama Avatara* is a complete one. It is a *purna avatara*, the absolute and perfect *avatara*, because Rama was the ideal embodiment of humanism. Valmiki has said that Rama is the true human being.

Why is Rama said to be a *purna avatara?* In His *dashavataras,* ten incarnations, Maha Vishnu appeared in many different forms—as a fish, a reptile, an animal, a man-lion, a dwarf, etc. But this *avatara* of Rama was the complete one, with all the qualities an ideal human must have. God always likes to come very close to man, because He wishes to draw people to Himself. So He takes a human form and comes closer and closer to men.

Hanumana was one of the greatest disciples, and one of the greatest *bhaktas.* He was the embodiment of selfless service. We should try to be like Hanumana. He was very fortunate because he was the only disciple of the Divine Mother, Sita Devi. When Sita Devi asked Hanumana, "Who is Rama?" Hanumana replied, "He is not *Dasharatha putra,* the son of Dasharatha." Hanumana was in higher consciousness, and he knew Rama to be beyond human form. For example, when we look at a plant, we see only a beautiful plant, not the pot. In the same way, Hanumana saw Rama as primal Energy, Absolute Consciousness, which had descended to Earth in the form of Rama to elevate all humanity.

Rama had come to accomplish the task of blessing, awakening and elevating the inner *ahalya.* When God comes to Earth, He doesn't forget the task for which He has come, not even the smallest one. At the ordinary level, our view is very limited. Even though we see God, we are not able to understand the divine qualities and the Consciousness of God. This is due to our egoism. When Rama took form, he blessed many people. He blessed his family, He blessed the people of Ayodhya, and then the people in the forest also, and not only that, He blessed all the great *rishis.* That is why *avataras* come to this Earth—they always come to accomplish some purpose.

Sri Rama blessed not only the people but also the Earth. He blessed the mountains, the rivers and the seas, and all the animals, too. What did He not bless? When He came to Shabari, He blessed her and gave her *moksha,* salvation. When Rama came to her, she was in a state of higher consciousness. She did not ask Rama what had happened to Sita. She knew, and it was Shabari who directed Rama to go in the right direction to find Sita. She was not on the material plane as we are. That is why she never asked what had happened to Sita. So we must not be on this lower level at all. We should take the example of Shabari, and elevate ourselves to her level.

Amma also said, "Children, do not drink the juice of worldliness, drink the elixir of *Rama nama.*" Then Amma sang a very melodious and beautiful song,

Pibare Rama rasam

Shuka Rishi, Saunaka Rishi, Kaushika Rishi, and Vishvamitra Rishi drank this juice, this nectar. They were like honeybees, drenched in that nectar, intoxicated by the name of Rama. So we should also be like them.

Valmiki was elevated and came to the level of higher consciousness because of the blessings of the Divine Mother, Saraswati Devi, even though Brahma the Creator, had created him as a robber. This means that it is enough to have the blessings of Divine Mother. And speaking about Sita Devi, She had unconditional love towards all Her children, and that is why She came to Valmiki. Even though Valmiki has praised Sri Rama in *Ramayana*, it was not Rama who came to Valmiki; it was the Mother who came. And She stayed in Valmiki's *ashram* for many years.

Finally, we have to remove our immoral qualities, which are like flowers without fragrance, and cultivate and bloom the beautiful flowers that have a good aroma. These are all the divine *gunas*—truth and benediction and contentment and humility. These fragrant flowers are the ones we have to cultivate and bloom in our heart.

On this auspicious occasion of *Rama Navami,* the *Ramayana* teaches us how to lead a good family life, whereas the *Mahabharata* teaches us how to live in society. That is the main difference between the *Ramayana* and the *Mahabharata*. We have to take the message from both. Amma is saying that we have to mold ourselves according to the *Ramayana* for good family values, and also maintain correct societal values. In order to have a peaceful society, peace must start from the home. If we are not peaceful we cannot give peace to society.

The relationship between the husband and wife is very delicate. It is not just a physical relationship; it has to be an internal one, with a lot of love and affection. Great saints like Adi Shankaracharya and Vivekananda and others led a very, very pure life, and they could walk alone easily in this world. But we are not able to go through life alone, and so God has graced us with a form of energy, the wife. And for the wife, it has been the grace of God to have a good husband.

Many people think that in order to lead a spiritual life, one has to renounce completely, and wear the *kashaya,* the orange robes of a renunciate. Instead, we should lead the life of a good householder. Everyone cannot become a *sannyasi,* so with this understanding we should lead a householder's life and ultimately reach the Supreme. So do not hurt each other, and live together with delicate feelings, and sensitive understanding.

Finally, if we have immoral qualities, we are really like a dead person. Even though we are alive our life is useless. So we must give them all up, elevate ourselves and cultivate peace, *shanti*.

If we lead a very true, a very pure life, even though we give up the body, we will live forever in the hearts of others.

You have come to this Earth, and the Earth and society have done a lot for you. You too must do some good for society and the Earth during your life span. *Jai Karunamayi!*

Amma:

Śrī Rāma jaya Rāma jaya jaya Rāma

Swamiji: Now there will be *pada puja* for Amma's divine lotus feet, and after this Amma will be inscribing the *Maha Saraswati bijakshara mantra* on the tongues of the students who have come here to be initiated in the *Maha Saraswati* *mantra*. All that you have to do after you get this *mantra* inscribed is to chant it 108 times every day:

Om Ayīm Śrīm Hrīm Saraswatī Devyai namaḥ

This is very important. You should do this after your bath, and it will take only five or six minutes. This *mantra* enriches your memory and concentration power, and it gives you the highest knowledge. And after the initiation in the *Maha Saraswati mantra,* Amma is going to bless the devotees here with the healing *vibhuti*, each and every one. The *Mrityunjaya mantra*, as Amma was saying yesterday, is the greatest healing *mantra* of the *Vedas.* Amma has blessed the *vibhuti* with Her divine hands, and She will be healing each and every one with it after the program is over. *Jai Karunamayi!*

Now we will have the *pada puja*. Today on this most auspicious *Rama Navami* day, this *dampati,* couple, is very fortunate to do the *pada puja* for Amma's divine lotus feet. And before starting the *puja* I would like to share an incident that happened just a few days before we came to America. In India, on a Sunday, we had twelve hours of meditation in Amma's *ashram* in Bangalore. About one hundred to one hundred and fifty people participated in the twelve-hour meditation course. And throughout the day, right from early in the morning, from *Brahmi muhurta*, 3:30 a.m., till 9:00 at night, everyone was doing meditation in rounds of one to one-and-a-half hours duration. During the last round of meditation, Amma was also sitting with the devotees, and after the meditation was over, everyone was overjoyed and overwhelmed to see nectar, the divine *amrita,* flowing from Amma's lotus feet. This was the rarest opportunity and the greatest blessing for everyone present. Some of the devotees from Bangalore were there, as well as an American devotee who witnessed this. The

American devotee had a camera, and so was able to photograph this incident.

Today is a very auspicious day, and this couple is really blessed to do *pada puja* to Amma's divine lotus feet, which overflow with divine nectar. Let us all imagine that we are also offering that *puja,* because they are performing it on behalf of all of us. And Amma is *Bhavana matra santushta,* She is satisfied even by the feeling of devotion in our heart. So imagine that we are also doing the *puja* and let us participate in this sacred worship.

[Swamiji chants several *mantras.* These are followed by *Sri Vijayeswari Panchakam,* an exquisite *stotra* of five verses honoring Amma, which flows into an even more beautiful *Sri Vijayeswari Ashtakam,* a lyrical and moving composition of eight verses dedicated to Amma which deeply touches the heart. Next, the *Sri Suktam* is recited, followed by *Sri Karunamayi Ashtottara,* the hundred and eight divine names of our compassionate Amma. The program ends with individual blessings for all present].

San Antonio *16 April 1997*

ॐ

UTILIZE YOUR ENERGY IN A POSITIVE WAY

Embodiments of Divine Souls, Amma's Most Beloved Children,

During my last tour, in so many places I had an opportunity to speak in churches. I was so happy, because everywhere I feel everyone's heart is very open. People have patience and right understanding about so many religions. All religions are paths to the same goal, Truth. Really, Truth is absolute. Truth is a hundred percent pure wisdom. Some meditate on the Truth in the form of *Omkara*, others in the form of Jesus, Buddha, so many aspects. So have faith in your *Guru* more and more. Give your respect to your *Guru* more and more, offer your heart lotus—the flower of consciousness—to your *Guru*, and give respect to all the great souls. All true *gurus* are only one. The rays are innumerable, but there is only one sun in the solar system. Children, we meditate only on the Truth. So have respect, more respect, more and more respect towards your *Guru*, and give the same respect to every religion and all *gurus* also. That is our humility and humanity.

Today we will talk about energy. There are two types of energies in our life, one positive and the other negative. Spirit, *atman*, is beyond both these energies. If the mind is working in *tamas* and *rajas*, our energy is bound by negativity. We will have negative energy. All our energy is wasted when the mind is limited to *tamasic* and *rajasic* tendencies. We have so much energy, but when the mind is limited in this way, we never utilize that energy in a positive way.

So many people know about *chakra* meditation. We have *chakras* in the body. In *chakra* meditation there is a beautiful focused movement of this energy. When we say *Omkara* once, all the *chakras* in our entire body are stimulated by the power of that seed letter. Gradually after some years, we begin to have awareness in our hearts—*Brahmic* awareness. With this *Brahmic* awareness, our negative energies, the *tamasic* and *rajasic* tendencies of the mind, gradually disappear by the power of meditation.

Meditation remodels our life and elevates us to divinity. So meditation is nothing but purification, inner purification. Gradually we begin to control our anger, lust, greediness, jealousy and hatred. These are the limited *tamasic* natures of our mind. Before the Spirit, our mind and intellect are spellbound, powerless. Spirit is absolute. You are the Soul, not this body. This body is a dress for the beautiful, self-illuminated Soul. When you achieve the fourth stage, *turiya*, you experience in meditation: "O, I am not this body!" So how can we achieve that stage? That is the question. How can we achieve this? Can we control the anger, and all these things in our life? Can we control our mind, our *tamasic* nature, and our *rajasic* nature? In these two natures, pure consciousness is working negatively. Even in our body, in the right hand we have positive force, in the left hand we have negative force. So whatever we take and give, we must give with positivity, and take also from others only with a positive feeling.

The body itself is the greatest place of energy. The soul and spirit are inside the body. Without that spirit, there is no life at all. This spirit is really wasted by our limited mind. The mind is working through all these six natures. These are the *arishadvargas*. You know all about these negative natures. Because of these weeds we never attain peace in our life. We have no liberation from these little natures. When we have liberation from these negative qualities of anger, lust, greed, hatred, jealousy, we have so much peace. We enjoy peace; we enjoy a balanced state of mind, equal vision and real wisdom; and we understand Reality, and the entire universe also, first from inside.

Only he who has this intense desire towards the Soul will be able to understand the inner reality. He will enjoy the play of God: "O, this is only God's play. This is a beautiful play." So how can we achieve that state? By constant practice of meditation. Meditation balances our mind. It reduces the restlessness of our ego, ignorance and all the dark forces. It develops the virtues, the divine attributes, and gradually the buds within us bloom. These buds are inside our body. These divine attributes are in the form of little seeds in our heart. Gradually we have selflessness and we have peace of mind. We never abuse people, never criticize people under any circumstances. If others have caused injury to people—even if they have injured us—we never injure the feelings of others—in religion or in daily life. This is possible because you are an elevated soul. You have all the good natures and good qualities in your heart. That is forgiveness.

Forgiveness is so beautiful. Where there is forgiveness we have tolerance, patience, courage, dispassion, discriminative knowledge and real dedication towards any work. Every kind of work is also a *yoga,* not only meditation. All work is a form of worship. So we have that elevation and expansion. We expand and become full of cosmic, divine love.

So, children, practice meditation daily. Whatever meditation you do, have faith in your *Guru*. Whenever you are initiated, that is like starting a new birth. All these innumerable births are like human buses, which have stops. With each bus you start a new journey to eternal bliss. So initiation is a new birth. Your *Guru* shows you a good path. That path is permanent. The real treasure is the abode of peace and divinity. It never perishes. We always enjoy that divinity and the fragrance of peace in our life. When we see divinity in our life, then that divinity is everywhere in the universe: "O, I myself am the Soul, and the entire universe is also part of the Divine Soul." There is a full stop to this long play, the innumerable births of this long play. This has not happened accidentally or miraculously. Innumerable births filled with prayers have given you the gift of this human life.

So utilize this life, children, and develop all those divine attributes. The bulbs, seed bulbs, are inside. These little weeds cover all the bulbs and we have no peace and dispassion or discriminative knowledge. Sometimes we lose all these things and instead we have anger, restlessness, and we are selfish. We are so thirsty for meaningless things. Our thirst, our hunger must be always only towards the Divine. Divinity is only one, although the paths are so many. Through innumerable billions and billions of births also, your question need not be, "What is my path?" There is a permanent aim and destiny for you. That destiny is absolute peace. So achieve that destiny. That is the essence of humanity and spiritual life.

Practice meditation daily in the early morning. Why in the morning? We have rest for five hours, eight hours in the night. After this long rest our mind is so fresh, and with our fresh mind we pray to God with tears, from the bottom of our heart, "Give me purity, O God, give me wisdom, give me real liberation from all these natures of my mind. Control my negativity." Negativity is always in the form of *tamasic* and *rajasic* behavior.

If we have a *sattvic* nature, our life is so beautiful, marvelous; and we never curse other people; we never cheat any person in this world; we never expect anything from anyone if we do any service also. We are very humble, noble, and our life is full of the fragrance of *sattva*. In *sattva*, energy is working in the form of positivity. Yet spirit and soul are beyond even *sattva*. So reduce these natures, *tamas* and *rajas,* and tune the *sattva* more and more. Develop and elevate, expand and achieve the destiny of divinity as a definite aim. If we have not that definite aim, again our life is meaningless. From the age of five to sixty, for over a period of fifty five years, we have spontaneously in our mind twenty five thousand million thoughts—positive, negative, ordinary, spiritual, meaningless, useless—so many thoughts. Meditation is freeing the mind from thoughts.

Dhyānam nirviśayam manaḥ

Freeing the mind from good thoughts also, that is meditation. So how is it possible? Imagine all the ants coming out from an anthill. Gradually that anthill becomes empty. When we meditate, all these thoughts—the poisonous thoughts, normal thoughts, negative thoughts, good thoughts, highly spiritual thoughts—come out from the source, from the anthill, and after some time this anthill becomes calm. So send them away permanently from our heart through meditation.

Meditation is a ladder from mortality to immortality. This is one world and that is a separate world. So be always in that world. That world is inside. The external is unhappy, full of misery. You know all those things more than Amma. So be always in happiness. Be always in Truth. Be always in honesty. Honesty is the greatest wisdom.

I saw a billboard, a beautiful sign which said: "This world is yours." Really, this entire universe belongs to your soul only. In spiritual terms we express this differently. This entire world consisting of the animal kingdom, bird kingdom, rivers, oceans, humanity, everything belongs to your soul only. Your soul is absolute. The nature of Soul is peace. Soul is happiness—boundless happiness. And every soul is everywhere. Soul is never bound by a little frame. This body frame is just like a dress for our soul. So your soul is limitless truth and wisdom—attributeless.

When we meditate we are in our natural state, that is, peace. Now we are so unhappy because we are not in our natural state. When we elevate to our natural state, our happiness can never be destroyed under any circumstances. True happiness is boundless and it is a real treasure—the treasure of a *yogi.* So be a *yogi. Yogi* means one who has control of his mind. We have no control of our mind; we are on a low level. So control your mind. Control this wild horse and ride on that horse. Limit all these little, little things. Gradually send all these snakes from the anthill and be always in beautiful silence. That is the language of the Divine.

When we achieve that state, already fifty years, forty years, thirty years are over. Now our body is not able to sit in meditation for longer than half an hour. *Padmasana* is the best posture to stimulate our nervous system. In *padmasana* we have a lot of concentration and our energy has direct tracking to the *sahasrara kamala,* the thousand-petal lotus. From the root *chakra* to the entire nervous system, all the energy is beautifully tracked. When we say *Om* just one time, it reaches the *sahasrara.*

So have inner vision, develop the inner beauty, understand the value of silence and do not break that silence under any circumstances. Here Amma is not referring to verbal silence. Amma means mental silence, the thoughtless state. So you ask, "Amma how can we silence our mind?" By praying to God mentally. Concentrate on a particular *chakra*—the heart *chakra* or throat *chakra.* All these dark forces just burn by our concentration and we develop immense strength and immense concentration. Our will power develops more and more, and we enjoy meditation as part of our life. Enjoyment simply means we have peace. All of these qualities like jealousy and lust come from our mind. Once we have peace of mind, we develop a balanced state of mind and gradually we want to sit more and more and more in meditation and see God not only in the body but also in this entire cosmos. That is the highest state of spirituality.

So children, have a beautiful awareness in your spiritual life. You already have that awareness. Develop the intense desire a hundred percent. Have a definite aim and send egoism and the little natures permanently away. Tune into the *sattva* energy more, reduce the *tamas* and *rajas,* beautify your heart and divinize your thoughts with beautiful divine attributes. Have compassion, forgiveness, and dispassion. Discriminative knowledge is very important, and mental renunciation—not physical renunciation. Mental renunciation is much more important than physical renunciation. So renounce all these selfish natures and have the good aim of realizing the Self. The main aim of human life is to realize the Truth. Have wisdom in life.

So how can we achieve that state? Now already seventy years, eighty years have passed away. So very little time is remaining in our life. We have twenty-four hours in a day. Spend one hour in the morning. Use the other twenty-three hours for your other activities. Spend one hour for God. Spend it for yourself, for your elevation. Attain God-Realization at least in this birth. So open the third eye. The third eye means knowledge, divine knowledge. We have knowledge about so many things in this world. That knowledge is not enough to attain God-Realization, because before the Spirit our knowledge is mute, our mind is spellbound. Soul is very, very powerful. It is the self-illumination of billions and billions of rays of sunlight. In front of that divinity we are spellbound, in silence.

So reduce this limiting anger, jealousy, greed, selfishness, lust, and all these things. Send them permanently away. Say to yourself, "Oh, it is not good for me. I will remove all these weeds from my life because I want wisdom and liberation from these weeds." So pray to God with tears, "O Mother! Give me wisdom! Give me liberation! Please accept my prayer—whether it is one or five minutes long—and grant me a grand life." And you know that a grand life means wisdom.

Where there is no wisdom, there is no Truth. Where there is no truth there is no peace. Where there is no peace there is no divinity. So these are connections with divinity. Where there is discriminative knowledge we have faith. Where we have faith we have real understanding, we have inner vision. Only he who has this vision will be able to understand this entire universe: "Oh, this entire universe is nothing but my Self only. It is my Self that I love in all of nature. I love only my Self. I love everyone in this world. There is no secondness. Only oneness is here in this world." That is the spiritual feeling in that highest elevation.

Be elevated to the highest peak of purity. Our main enemies are our egoism and our desires. We can counter these enemies with the beautiful virtues of humility and real devotion. So where there is true devotion and humility, we have correct understanding and knowledge about the Divine immediately—not after seventy five or eighty years. We enjoy our entire life in peace, in permanent peace, which is the most beautiful, greatest treasure. It is hidden in our life.

So elevate to this highest peak, children! You are already on a good path. Continue, continue your path.

Examine your progress: "How is my heart? Am I selfish? Do I have any boundaries to my heart?" Because we are bound by our limited intellect, we like only a very limited number of persons. If we have that elevation we understand that this entire cosmos is only ours. We never limit ourselves to a particular frame. If we have selfishness, our viewfinder is very, very tiny. If there is no selfishness at all, we are without bounds, without attributes. We are everywhere in this universe with our subtle body. Spirit is not visible with this naked eye because of this subtle form, this very subtle form.

Children, we are the greatest Spirit in this body cage. Meditation elevates the human life from the physical body to the mental body and from the mental body to the intellectual body. From these three cages we are elevated to the spiritual body, the subtle body. That is the effort we have to make to come back to our sweet home. This is not our home. This is a place of so many diseases, unhappiness, miseries, so many questions and suspicions—always crying, craving for something. We are working, working, working harder than machines for a very, very, very, little, tiny happiness. We are so tired.

Last time I had more than 5000 requests from this country, "Amma, try to build a Peace Village in India. We want to spend our entire life in that Peace Village leading a simple and high-thinking life. We want to stop making a living. We are so tired of this life. We want to realize that wisdom. We want to meditate." So the building of the Peace Village is in progress now.

Everyone in this entire universe wants only peace. Who talks with us affectionately, freely in this world? Who has the time? Everyone is hurrying, hurrying, running, running after work, running after money. Everyone has so many desires. So, children, give your boundless love to this universe. Elevate yourself more and more and more and more and expand your heart, your soul and work along with the spirit. Think: "This is my responsibility—to love this universe." Reach that highest state through meditation.

Meditation remodels our life. If the home is not proper, you remodel the home. We have beautiful flower vases and furniture. In the same way, exchange a beautiful heart for this little heart which is there now. Remove all these *tamasic* and *rajasic* natures, and in their place keep a beautiful peace and immense will power. Our strength must not be the strength of money and power. It must be the strength of wisdom only. It must be always the strength of wisdom only. Where there is faith you have immense strength in your life.

So have faith, pure faith, a hundred percent faith, not even ninety-nine point nine percent faith. That faith is your strength. Where there is faith, you have a lot of will power and mental strength: "O, I have God! God, save me!" So you solve your problems with the grace of God. Gradually you are elevated more and more with faith, and one day you attain God-Realization. This does not happen miraculously or accidentally but by the intense practice of meditation, together with our burning desire.

Intense desire is important. Sometimes our *bhakti* is only on the surface. We sing some *bhajans*. We are restless and we watch the time. If we have no time we stop meditation and all spiritual activity also. If you just pray to God sincerely only for one fraction of second, from outside the meditation room even, that fraction of a second of real prayer is enough. If you sit eight or nine hours in prayer, but you are restless during that prayer, really, it is meaningless. Physically we are there but mentally we are not in prayer at all. Mentally, if we truly pray even for one second also, immediately it reaches the Absolute.

You have the knowledge; think what is good. One second of prayer is enough. If you have no time and you are in a hurry to go to work or somewhere else, okay. Just pray for one second before going outside. Pray for only one second or half a second, but that prayer must be from the bottom of your heart. Prayer purifies our life. Prayer gives immense strength. Prayer gives more and more and more and more peace. Prayer gives us much happiness. All the misery and unhappiness inside disappears by the power of real prayer.

So devotion must be real devotion. Do not show off your devotion under any circumstances. Pray with real devotion, pray for more and more devotion, for Realization of the real Truth in this birth, and to put a stop to the cycle of births in this birth itself. If one desire is remaining in our heart, again we will have one more birth. Do not expect more and more births. So imagine children, what about the twenty five thousand millions of thoughts and innumerable billions of previous births? Calculate how much meditation and prayer is needed, and how much help of God is needed in this birth.

You are already on the good path of spirituality. So you do not have such a *karma* load. Children, it is a good way, a very good way. In the beginning, on the path of spirituality, there are so many thorns, slippery places, and ups and downs. But after some time, the way is strewn with the fragrance of rose petals. In general life, in the beginning we have colorful flowers; life is very colorful. But after starting the journey, everything is emptiness. No doubt. Everywhere our life is so colorful in this entire universe. But inside, without spirituality, there is only one hundred percent emptiness. There is no destiny at all. There is no definite aim at all. So we have emptiness and feel emptiness.

"What is my destiny?" people often ask. So many people want to commit suicide because they do not know their destiny at all. What can we do? We can have the aim to attain the Truth, Realization. We must give service to the universe. Living on this Earth is a boon from God. Utilize this boon; give selfless service to this universe. Give your service to nature. Mother Nature gives you so much. You never repay anything to your Mother. You must pay something—at least one percent if not a hundred percent. So that is the responsibility of humanity. When you love nature you will become so wise.

Have *satsang* with the Divine and in the presence of divine people. You will be elevated, even more than through your meditation. They will give you the essence of love, and this elevates you to the highest peaks by their presence, touch and love, among other things. So go everywhere. Give more and more respect to all holy people and have their *darshan,* have their blessings and have contentment in your life.

Contentment is the greatest treasure. Contentment is the greatest happiness. When we have contentment, we feel our life is so smooth and we enjoy so much. Contentment is a jewel for a *yogi*. Silence, contentment, compassion, dispassion, real mental renunciation—these are the ornaments of a true spiritual aspirant. This does not belong to a particular religion. Truth is absolute for everyone. So children, go accordingly on your spiritual path. Have a particular aim and destiny in your life and attain God-Realization. Our body is a limited frame, a mortal frame. Merge in the immortal. That is the aim; that is the essence.

The spirit and essence of our human life is selfless service. It is mentioned in the *Bhagavad Gita* very beautifully. But how many people understand the selfless service explained in the *Bhagavad Gita?* It is very easy to say, "Be like this and do like this." But in practice it is a hundred percent difficult. So have real mental renunciation. That mental renunciation will give you real *bhakti,* real devotion.

We have to understand spirituality and wear the real ornaments of Truth, purity, knowledge, love, dispassion and all these things. When these divine virtues are in our life, we will feel contentment. These are the main pillars for contentment. How can we get contentment in our life? By gaining knowledge, divine love and Truth. With contentment gradually comes elevation. From our mind, body, and limited intellectual cages we attain Spirit in this birth. This depends upon our practice of meditation.

Meditation is not a blind belief. So many people think, "Oh, meditation is an escape from life!" In reality, it is no escape. It can never be so. The meditator works with a thousand hands in this universe because Spirit is working through his body. This is not the power of man. Humans have only two hands, while the Spirit has the power of a thousand hands, millions of hands, more than a million hands. Working through Spirit is very powerful. Working through Spirit is speedier than manual work. All human natures are spellbound before Spirit when it is working in the body. So this body is the temple for the Spirit.

Deho devālayaḥ jīvo Deva sanātana

Every soul is *sanatana*, divine. The body is a temple for God. This was mentioned innumerable *yugas* ago in the *Vedas*. Seeing divinity everywhere is the highest level of spirituality. Seeing divinity only in particular places is limited. We limit ourselves to particular things. Seeing divinity everywhere is limitless. That is our destiny. Attain that God-Realization in this birth.

Have forgiveness, kindness, and compassion. You may feel, "I have little compassion." Develop your compassion billions and billions of times, more and then some more. Will power is based on our devotion and our faith. Have faith, more faith, and purify each and every cell of your body with pure devotion. Always mentally pray to God for purification, for real wisdom: "Oh God! Grant me a grand life of wisdom. Now I have no liberation. I still have anger and these limited natures in my heart. When will I get all those great virtues of forgiveness, equal vision, inner beauty? When will I attain these positive natures? Please grant me a grand life of honesty."

Where there is honesty and Truth, that is the main entrance gate for true wisdom. So, children, be always in that wisdom. Be a practical person, not just one filled with the passive knowledge from books and lectures. That is not enough. Practice the knowledge you have gained—give your selfless service to humanity, develop your cosmic love more and more, and love all of nature more than anything. Be boundless and try to observe silence mentally.

Verbal silence is also good because we commit so many mistakes with our tongue alone. This is very poisonous. We are always abusing others, telling lies and speaking useless words. If our words were just like rose petals and jasmine flowers, the fragrance of our words would cover the entire universe with truth like the *tulasi,* the sweet basil—they would be sweeter than honey.

Gradually when you elevate yourself through meditation, you attain *vishuddha sattva* with one hundred percent purity. This is very beautiful. In this *vishuddha sattva* we have no desires. We are in the highest peak of desirelessness. It is very beautiful. Desire is the main force behind our emotions. It is impurity of the mind. Desire leads us to hell. Only true devotion, desirelessness, and your thrust towards God or Realization leads you to the Absolute. So understand reality. You have the knowledge.

Divine Mother already gave you the knowledge. You have the intellectual power.

Use that power and elevate yourself more and more, and attain peace in this birth. We have peace of mind sometimes but it is not permanent. Sometimes we enjoy peace also in the presence of *satsangs.* In meditation, sometimes we are so restless because of the thoughts which come spontaneously from our heart. If the thoughts are negative, we are especially restless. So send all these snakes from this anthill, burn all these enemies permanently and have a grand life, good life, and peaceful life. At least we need peace of mind. Peace is not available anywhere in this universe. It is only in your Self. If you feel peace in holy presence, in prayers, in meditations, that is also temporary. Have permanent peace. This permanent peace is attained by God-Realization only.

Practice silence daily for half an hour. Saraswati burns our negativity and gives the seeker real knowledge. She opens the seeker's heart and gradually his faith is developed more and more and more. With that faith he develops a lot of will power, and gains immense strength in his life. With this will power he opens the gates of wisdom and attains Realization. This is very easy to describe in words, but difficult in practice. So be a practical seeker.

Your faith is your greatest protection. If you have faith you have everything. If you lose your faith in your God you lose everything. The one who loses faith loses everything. The one who has faith has everything. The one who has Truth in his life has a hundred percent contentment and inner joy. So enjoy the joy and peace inside your life and attain real Spirit in this birth. That is your Mother's only wish for Her babies.

Now we will chant the *Saraswati mantra* for purification of our thoughts. We always want good thoughts, positive thoughts and noble thoughts. The power of the *mantra* burns all the impurities in our heart because of the seed letters in this *mantra*. If you wish you can meditate on that *mantra* also.

Swamiji: The *bijakshara Om* consists of three different sounds—that is, the sound "a," or *akara,* the sound "u," or *ukara* and the sound "m," or *makara.* When we start chanting this *mantra,* the *akara* travels from the tips of our feet to the abdomen; from there, the *ukara* travels up the spine. Finally the *makara* travels all the way up to the *sahasrara.* It is very important to keep our lips closed when chanting this latter sound. We must close our mouth and lips so that the *makara* is pronounced inside only. Then the vibrations are very great and it stimulates our entire nervous system.

There is a certain way in which we have to chant this *Pranava mantra*, the *Om mantra.* We must chant it neither very long nor very short. There is a certain rhythm to chant this *mantra*—it must be in a medium way. And whenever we chant this *mantra,* we must have the inner feeling. We should not just go on repeating the *mantra*—it must come from the bottom of our heart. We must have the feeling that the energy is entering into our body.

The other *mantra* which Amma has taught today is the *Maha Mrityunjaya mantra.* It is the essence of the *Vedas.* And this *mantra* also, when we chant it, must be chanted very slowly and very gently. We must not be in a hurry to chant this *mantra* also, because the *mantra* has the greatest power to give us a lot of energy. It also removes all the blockages in the *chakras.* That is why we have to very carefully learn this *mantra* and pronounce it in the right way. We have to take it deep into our heart and only then do we chant it, very slowly.

To chant this healing *Maha Mrityunjaya mantra,* three things are very important. First is the rhythm, the exact rhythm of how Amma has chanted just now. We have to copy Her exactly. Second is the voice. We have to chant it very softly, not with a harsh voice. Third is pronunciation. It has to be as it is in Sanskrit. If we follow these rules, we will get immense strength and this *mantra* will be the greatest protection for us whatever the situation; you will even be saved from accidents. So very powerful is this *mantra,* it envelops you with a protection always all around you!

There have been innumerable cases of patients in a state of coma, the unconscious state. When four or five people sit around him and chant this *mantra*, just by the vibrations of this powerful *mantra,* even a patient who has been unconscious for a long period of time wakes up. He gets immense strength and energy from the vibrations of this great *mantra.* This *mantra* gives mental peace, and if you want to chant it, you can do so.

Jai Karunamayi. Amma will give blessings now. Please come forward one at a time.

San Antonio *16 April 1997*

ॐ

THE POWER OF THE MANTRA

Swamiji: Amma has said many times that even if one has been initiated by another *Guru* or has been practicing another *mantra*, one can also practice the *Saraswati mantra* meditation. The *Saraswati mantra* is not new, it is ancient and universal just like the *Vedas* and the *Bhagavad Gita,* and does not belong to any organization or *Guru.* Just as the *Bhagavad Gita* is universal and anyone can read it and take its essence, likewise, the *Saraswati mantra* is a universal *mantra* which is known to enrich one's memory and concentration. It also gives energy.

This great *bijakshari mantra* contains three most powerful *bijaksharas*, namely, *Ayim, Srim* and *Hrim.* When meditated upon, it removes all the blockages in the *chakras* and confers true knowledge. Yesterday Amma was speaking about this. We must have true knowledge. Until we get true knowledge, we will not have the power of discrimination. Whatever meditations you have been doing, do not stop them; you can continue them along with this *mantra*.

Apart from the *Saraswati mantra,* Amma has taught us the *Maha Mrityunjaya mantra* which is the healing *mantra,* and is the essence of the *Vedas.* This particular *mantra* is so powerful that its vibrations remove any illness we may have. Amma emphasizes that apart from our physical ailments it is very important to remove our mental ailments. This powerful *mantra*, the *Maha Mrityunjaya mantra,* has the power to remove all mental ailments. It is like a shield which protects you so that there will always be an aura of energy around you and no negative force can enter your mind or body. This universal *mantra* from the *Vedas* was not created by any *rishi* or *Guru.*

These two *mantras* are the two great blessings and boons which Amma has been giving to the entire world—all that is in the *Vedas*. So these are the two fruits Amma has bestowed upon you, and now you can all do the meditation of *Saraswati mantra,* and for healing you now have the *Mrityunjaya mantra.* Some people have expressed doubts and raised questions about whether or not they can use these *mantras*, that is why Amma asked me to give you this brief explanation. *Jai Karunamayi!*

[Amma speaks in Telugu]

Swamiji: *Jai Karunamayi!* Amma wants me to tell you that She is going to sing a melodious Telugu song, but before She sings it She wants you all to know it's meaning. It is a song to the Divine Mother and was composed by Amma Herself. In this song it is very clearly described how a devotee talks to the Divine Mother from the depths of his heart:

"O Divine Mother, I have completely surrendered to Your lotus feet. I have no one else in this world. You are the Empress of the whole universe. That is why I have not gone anywhere else but I have come to You for refuge. I have completely surrendered myself to You. Manidwipa is Your abode and You reside in the *bindu* of the *Sri Chakra.* Your home is a great palace studded with beautiful gems."

Many of you know about the *Sri Chakra* or *Sri Yantra,* which has nine triangles. It is a representation of the Divine. You can see the *Sri Chakra* in the *Lalita Sahasranama* book here.

In this song Amma describes Mother: "You always reside in the *bindu,* the dot in the center of the inverted triangle, O Maheshwari." Maheshwari means "Great

Empress," and is another name for the Divine Mother —there are thousands and thousands of divine names for the Divine Mother, and Maheshwari is one of them. "You have been there from the beginning of this universe and You have been observing the cycle of creation and destruction many, many times. You have been watching this play, whereas we have been coming into this world and acting in it." We have been entangled in *maya,* the illusion of *samsara.*

"Your *rupa,* Your form, is to be worshipped. When one sees You, one automatically closes one's eyes and bows down. Your *shakti* is unexplainable, it is beyond words. O Maha Devi, You are Maha Lakshmi, the Goddess of Wealth, You are Maha pataka nashini, the destroyer of all the sins which we have committed. You are Maha buddhi, the intellect of all intellects. You are Maha siddhi, the bestower of all the divine virtues on a *sadhaka.* You are Maha Tripurasundari and Maha Yoga yogeshwari—You are the greatest *yogi* of all the *yogeshwaras*." A *yogeshwara* is a master of *yoga.*

In the *Bhagavad Gita*, Lord Krishna has been addressed as Maha Yogeshwara. Here, Divine Mother is Maha Yogeshwari. She is the greatest, beyond even Lord Krishna. This is the essence of the song. In my explanation I was limited by the words of the English language. Now you can listen to this song and appreciate its beauty better with an understannding of its meaning. That is why Amma wanted me to explain it to you before singing it. *Jai Karunamayi!*

Amma's Discourse:

Amma's Most Beloved Children, My Immortal Babies,

Prayer must always come from the bottom of the heart, not just from the lips. Mother is always in the temple of your heart. So if your prayer comes from the bottom of your heart, it reaches Mother immediately and She feels so happy listening to your prayer or *mantra,* or any other form of worship you offer.

Surrender, surrender, surrender! Be one with Amma, one with Amma, one with Mother! That is the essence of prayer. You and your Mother are One—the very same. This is said in *Sanatana Dharma* and is also written in the *Bible*: "I and my Father are One." This was said in *Sanatana Dharma* many thousands of years ago in the *Vedas.* The essence of the *Rig Veda* is, "You and your Mother are One." You are nothing but Mother's flesh, blood, bones and soul.

Meditation and devotion elevate you to the highest peak of inner silence and you can enjoy the real silence and bliss inside. So my immortal babies, pray to Mother every day. Prayer purifies our entire life—our hearts, our thoughts—and removes all our negativities.

In this song, there are several special *ragas.* There are innumerable *ragas* in Indian classical music. All the compositions of Thyagaraja, known as *kirtanas*, are in Telugu. Sanskrit is called the divine language. In Telugu, ninety-nine point nine percent of the words are derived from Sanskrit only. Telugu is a musical language, a very beautiful language. There are so many words for "beautiful" such as "*shobha,*" "*saundarya,*" and "*shobhayamana,*" —maybe a hundred words which all mean "beautiful." In English there is only one word, "beautiful." Telugu is called a musical language because of all the compositions of Thyagaraja and Shyama Shastri. These renowned music composers have sung *kirtanas* only in this language.

In this song there are many *ragas* such as *Megha ranjani, Chakravaka, Kalyani, and Mohana.* When one listens to these *ragas,* the heart melts and is filled with compassion. Our negative tendencies gradually disappear—such is the power of *ragas*. In addition, many *ragas* destroy illness in the human body. This has been shown by recent research. Many scholars have done research in music, or *nada yoga,* the science of sound. Now in the West—in London and in the U.S.—many people are learning about the power of *nada yoga. Nada yoga* purifies the body, but correct pronunciation is very important because the meaning of a letter or word changes when it is pronounced in a different way.

In the *Bhagavad Gita* there are seven hundred *shlokas.* In the *Devi Mahatmyam* or the *Chandi Sapta Shati* there are also seven hundred *shlokas.* In the very powerful *Narayani Stuti Nama Stotras,* all the *devatas* pray to Mother Divine because Mother is the Supreme Personality, Adi Para Shakti. They pray, "O Mother, You are Energy, You are the Mother of all Mothers. You are the Mother of Lakshmi, Saraswati, Brahma, Ishwara—You are the Mother of everyone. So there are no words to describe You. Mother, forgive me even though I have committed millions of mistakes. You have a kind heart, I know that. My Mother, only my Mother, will excuse me in spite of all my countless bad deeds. Only She has the heart to forgive me. She has that kind of forgiveness in Her heart. Tender loving Mother, so beautiful!"

Yā Devī sarva bhūteṣu matṛ rūpeṇa samsthitā
Namas tasyai namas tasyai namas tasyai
namo namah
Yā Devī sarva bhūteṣu śakti rūpeṇa samsthitā
Namas tasyai namas tasyai namas tasyai
namo namaḥ
Yā Devī sarva bhūteṣu dayā rūpeṇa samsthitā
Namas tasyai namas tasyai namas tasyai
namo namaḥ

Yā Devī sarva bhūteṣu kṣamā rūpeṇa samsthitā
Namas tasyai namas tasyai namas tasyai
namo namaḥ
Yā Devī sarva bhūteṣu jāti rūpeṇa samsthitā
Namas tasyai namas tasyai namas tasyai
namo namaḥ
Ya Devi sarva bhūteṣu cetanetyabhidhīyate
Namas tasyai namas tasyai namas tasyai
namo namaḥ
Sarva bādhā praśamanīm trailokyam
cākhilāṇḍeśwarīm
Namas tasyai namas tasyai namas tasyai
namo namaḥ

Rogān aśeṣān apahamsi tuṣṭām
Ruṣṭātu kāmān sakalān abhīṣṭān
Tvām āṣṛtānām na vipannarāṇām
Tvām āṣṛtā hyāśrayatām prayānti

Etat te vadanam saumyam locana traya
bhuṣitam
Pātu naḥ sarva bhutebhyo Kātyāyanī
namostute

Ninne madi nammiti Amma... Amma...
Ninne madi nammiti nikanna mākevarammā
Akhilāṇḍa koti brahmāṇḍa nāyakī
Amma... Amma...
Ninne madi nammiti Amma... Amma...

Embodiment of Divine Souls, Amma's most beautiful beloved children, start the day with cosmic love; fill the day with cosmic love. Before going to bed summarize the events of the day and all your activities during the day. Before going to sleep meditate for ten to fifteen minutes, even five minutes, or just for one minute. Think about whether you injured anyone's feelings, so that you do not make the same mistake again. Clean the *chakras* inside and have awareness—*Brahmic* awareness. In general we have devotion. We may repeat *Om namah Sivaya* ten thousand times. Ten thousand times of audible repetition of *Om namah Sivaya* is equal to one mental *japa.* A thousand mental *japas* are equal to one meditation on *Om namah Sivaya.*

Nada is the *namah Sivaya nama.* All sounds—devotional sounds, the sound of the *Vedas,* the sound of *Om* and all the seed letters—every sound, the essence of all sounds, is contained in the *nada,* the *nakara,* the sound "na" in *namah Sivaya.* The essence of billions and billions of *mantras* is in *makara,* the sound "ma" in *namah Sivaya.* All the *stotras—Om Ya Devi sarva bhuteshu* and innumerable others—are in the *sikara,* the sound "si" in *namah Sivaya.* The essence of all *stotras* is *sikara.* The essence of all four *Vedas* is *vakara,* the sound "va" in *namah Sivaya.* You know the four *Vedas*—the *Rig Veda,* about Mother Nature, *Yajur Veda,* with so many *mantras, Sama Veda* about balance in life and *Atharva Veda* about contentment. The last seed letter in *namah Sivaya, yakara,* the sound "ya" is the essence of all *yajnas. Om* is benediction, indestructible power. It is omnipresent, omniscient and omnipotent. So *Omkara* is the final bliss. This is the essence of all the five seed letters in *Om namah Sivaya..* You know the meaning.

When you meditate on that *mantra*, you attain God-Realization—you attain *samadhi.* Without dispassion, there is no *samadhi.* Without *samadhi*, there is no Realization. Without Realization of the Self, there is no meaning to life. You may ask, "Amma, we are in *maya,* this world is in *maya.* So how can we have all the divine attributes? How can we meditate? Is Realization possible in this world of *maya*?" Really, *maya* is subtle, very subtle.

Maya is in two forms: One is "I," "me," "my" and leads to egoism; the second is *mamakara*—attachments, bondages. So we must meditate daily. We have twenty-four hours in a day. Spend twenty-three hours for this materialistic world, but spend at least one hour a day in spiritual activities, half an hour in the morning and half an hour in the evening. If you have no time in the evening, then do your spiritual practice early in the morning. Constant practice is called *sadhana.* Without the cultivation of *dharma,* truth, it is really very hard to do spiritual practice. But it is possible. Always ask Mother for right understanding and knowledge.

Say to Mother, "Amma, in innumerable births I have been asking for little, little things, for meaningless things. Now I pray to You for a grand life, a life of divine knowledge."

A grand life is so beautiful! In that grand life, we have so much inner beauty. In that inner beauty, we have contentment. We can get so much contentment only in spirituality, not in this materialistic world. We can never attain the highest state of contentment in materialistic things. If you have one million, you will want one million more, so there is no contentment at all. There is no fulfillment in this world of *maya.* So try to understand the reality and have mental detachment. Yesterday also Amma stressed mental renunciation—not physical renunciation. Mental renunciation is very important for a spiritual aspirant. Without mental renunciation our life is childish, like that of an eight year old—very childish, with no discriminative knowledge. Mental renunciation develops inner purity, detachment, forgiveness, compassion, dispassion, and discipline. Without discipline there is no spirituality at all. Discipline is the very foundation of spirituality.

We must spend at least one hour out of twenty-four in spiritual practices for developing inner peace, contentment, forgiveness and a balanced mind. Even if you are not able to obtain God-Realization it is okay. But you get inner peace and a balanced mind only through meditation. When we chant a thousand divine names verbally, it is equivalent to one mental *namah Sivaya japa*. One thousand times of mental *japa* is equivalent to one sitting of meditation. And you should also understand the meaning of the *mantra*. Without knowing the meaning of the *mantra,* just repeating it mechanically is not so good. So first you should understand the meaning of the *mantra* and then gradually practice chanting it.

So many people sow seeds—fruit seeds and flower seeds. But when we store the seeds for some years before planting them, what happens? They do not grow because there is no life in them, they are lifeless. In the same way when you get the *mantra* from the *Guru,* the very next day onwards you should begin to meditate using the *mantra.* Only then, after four years of continuous practice, the seed, or the life in that *mantra,* sprouts and becomes a big tree. There may be many obstacles during the first four years, but after that you will enjoy meditating on the Self. You will have one hundred percent contentment, peace, and bliss in your life, and you will experience the divine fragrance, which is beyond beautiful. Beautiful is limited and "beyond beautiful" is difficult to explain. So taste the bliss, children, taste the bliss and experience it!

Constant practice with no interruptions is called *sadhana.* So practice *mantra* meditation every day early in the morning, from five to six o'clock. Practice *mantra* and meditation before going to work, and start the day with full cosmic divine love. Fill the entire day with cosmic love, and end the day with love, and have contentment. Only in meditation will you get lasting contentment. Gradually all the divine inner qualities bloom in your heart—forgiveness, detachment, discipline and silence. Where there is silence, there only will be inwardness. Without inwardness we cannot expect meditation because we are always in physical consciousness, entangled in physical things. Where there is no inwardness we cannot expect dispassion or *samadhi.* Without dispassion there is no *samadhi.* Without *samadhi* there is no Realization.

This human life is the result of innumerable births of prayer and is a gift, a boon from God. There are so many additional boons such as singing, which is also Saraswati's grace, writing, the arts, and so on. Meditation is the greatest art of remodeling life in order to develop a beautiful attachment to divinity. So meditation is modeling—there are no words to explain it. Look at the picture of Lord Siva. It gives so much inspiration to meditators. Lord Siva, who is in Mount Kailasa, is always in meditation, He is always inside, in the universe within. So taste your Self, eternal bliss, in absolute silence. The power is indestructible power. The state of *samadhi,* the state of bliss and silence, cannot be described or explained. Only those who have inward vision are able to understand the Reality—the true essence of life.

There is a beautiful four-pillar support for this human life—compassion, cosmic love, divine knowledge and dispassion. These are the four pillars that support our lives. And the main entrance for this life is.... What is the main entrance gate for our life, babies? Selfless service! Selfless service towards all beings in the world is the greatest *yoga* to merge with the Eternal. So, selfless service is the entrance gate to divine life. Open that gate, children, open that gate! Selfless service beautifies our life and fills it with divine fragrance, blooming all our *chakras* with selfless thoughts. Enjoy infinite peace and inner joy. Be always in the state of higher consciousness.

So meditate daily for at least one hour and never give up the practice. You can spend twenty-three hours in worldly activities and spend only one hour in spiritual practice, but the practice, the devotion, must be one hundred percent pure and not a show. Cry for Mother with pure devotion. Pray for knowledge, "Mother, I surrender to You. I surrender to You one hundred percent. Grant me peace and bliss. Make my mind silent. Remove all thoughts from my mind—bad thoughts, good thoughts, noble thoughts, all thoughts—and make me thoughtless. Grant me the grand life of divine knowledge; I want to enjoy the bliss in this birth. In innumerable births I have been an actor, acting in your play. You have always been in front of me, but I have not had the eyes to see You or even see myself, because of ignorance and *maya,* illusion. Even when my eyes are open, I am blind—physically and mentally blind. O Mother! Please grant me the grand life of divine knowledge."

In general a devotee with a little elevation in spirituality has the vision to see divinity in churches, temples and mosques and in all good people. He who has devotion in his heart, respects all religions and sees divinity not only in his religion but also in other religions. The mature, elevated souls, the divine souls have equal vision, balanced vision for everything in the universe, "The good and bad in every religion belong to my soul only. Mother Earth, the oceans, the animal kingdom, bird kingdom, the cosmos, time, all religions, all paths, good, bad, everything belongs to my soul only. And I have indestructible power and infinite joy. Time is my supreme Self—not my egoistic self—everything is my Self' They have this highest vision and highest status. They enjoy divinity everywhere.

Children, come to that highest peak which is your Mother's abode—*Omkara.* Come back to your Mother's sweet home, children! This world is a hostel. In this hostel you have fear, you are restless and you have very little happiness. You are working very, very hard and your entire life is restless with jealousies, etc.

So immortal children, divine children, you are *Shuddha Brahman*—pure *Brahman*—your Self is divine; you are not limited to this body cage; you are not this limited mind and limited intellect. You are beyond all these. Your Self is bliss, your Self is wisdom. Be always in wisdom. In spirituality only we have wisdom. So children, have one hundred percent wisdom.

If you wish to go and visit a place of Buddhism, Zoroastrism or Sikhism, do so freely. Have every holy person's *darshan,* take their blessings, love them and give them more respect than you give to Amma. If you give one percent respect to Amma, give a million percent to them. I am your mom, I never expect respect from you. You are nothing but my flesh, blood and soul—this is my real feeling towards you. You can even go to a small *sadhu*, but give your hundred percent, thousand percent, million percent respect to him and get his blessings.

Open your heart, and have *Brahmic* awareness. It is so beautiful. Without that awareness, life is really meaningless. You are very childish, just running after worldly things. You are in worldly intoxication and are never fulfilled. You have that fulfillment only in Truth. Truth alone can stand without any support in this world. The *Saraswati mantra* is Truth, hundred percent Truth. So chant the *Saraswati mantra*. The *Bhagavad Gita* is universal and so beautiful. The *Mrityunjaya mantra* has the essence of the *Yajur Veda*. In the *Yajur Veda,* the eighteenth *mantra* is the *Maha Mrityunjaya mantra*. This is a boon from Siva to this Universe. This is not anyone's creation. No one invented this *mantra,* it is from Maha Rudra:

Om namaste astu Bhagavan Viśveśvarāya
Mahādevāya Trayambakāya Tripurāntakāya

Trikāgni Kālāya Kālāgni Rudrāya
Nilakanthāya Mṛtyunjayāya
Sarveśvarāya Sadāśivāya
Śriman Mahādevāya namaḥ

Om namo Bhagavate Rudrāya

Om Trayambakaṃ yajāmahe
Sugandhim puṣti vardhanam
Urvārukamiva bandhanāt
Mṛtyor mukṣīya māmṛtāt

Om namaḥ Śambhave ca Mayobhave ca
Namaḥ Śankarāya ca Mayaskarāya ca
Namaḥ Śivāya ca Śivatarāya ca
Sriman Mahādevāya namaḥ
Om namo Bhagavate Rudrāya

These *mantra*s flow continuously like a river with innumerable *bijaksharas*. The *Maha Mrityunjaya mantra* is the essence of *Rudra parayana.* Everyone has the wisdom to chant the *Maha Mrityunjaya mantra* which is also for divine knowledge and spiritual elevation. We always have anger, jealously, hatred and we are so tired of these negative energies. The power of the *Mrityunjaya mantra* flows around you and protects you from all the negative energies of the universe and positive energies are attracted by you. The holy and divine people, good souls, pure souls and good-hearted children—all these souls attract the power of the *Maha Mrityunjaya mantra.* All injuries inside the heart—not only from this birth, but also from innumerable births—are cured by the *Maha Mrityunjaya mantra.* This is the boon of Lord Siva from Mount Kailasa.

Mahādeva Śiva Śambho
Māra koṭi sundara Prabho
Sarveśwara Karuṇākara mūrtim
Sāma gāna priya Veda mūrtim
Parameśwara Gangādhara mūrtim

Patita pāvanā Paśupate
Mahādeva Siva Śambho

So the *Mrityunjaya mantra* is the boon of Lord Siva. Whenever you have time, chant the *mantra.* You can chant it even while driving. Siva knows all your problems in this life—your restlessness, fast pace of life, lack of time, and all these issues. Forgiveness is Siva, kindness is Siva, compassion is Siva. Siva is more than all these, beyond all these—beyond beautiful, beyond compassion and beyond attributes. He is attributeless.

So children, develop all the divine attributes inside. Practice meditation daily. Meditation removes all the curtains of negativity and ignorance from our hearts, from our eyes, so that we have more and more devotion. Devotion is the main base. Without devotion there is no faith. Do not have blind faith, just chanting or praying, but have hundred percent discriminating faith. Have dispassion. When we have dispassion we can have discriminative knowledge. With this knowledge all the inner flowers bloom—the beautiful flowers of noble thoughts—leading to pure words and good deeds. When you do meditation or practice spirituality your presence purifies the whole universe.

Be always in your own path. Amma never disturbs anyone from their path. If a little plant is in its little pot, and you remove it to another pot, the little plant becomes tired, and wilts. So I never remove any plant from its own path. Why are you like these bonsai plants? Amma wants all Her plants to grow quickly and touch the cosmos. That is Amma's only wish.

Why get entangled in this *maya*? This "I," "me," and "my" egoism? Egoism is because of *maya,* illusion. It is subtle. There are two forms of *maya*. One is egoism and the other is attachment. Attachment is bondage, so cultivate mental detachment, mental renunciation. Be in your dress, be in your home and meditate and expand yourself, elevate yourself more and more and touch the cosmos. Unseen Amma's arms embrace the whole cosmos. Where is this Earth? It is a tiny speck of holy ash. Unseen Holy Mother's arms embrace the entire universe. So children, you are already in Mother's lap. Why do you have fear? It is because of duality. When you meditate, by the power of meditation, the power of devotion, and the power of your *mantra* you begin to understand, "I am not the body, I am the soul."

There are no words to describe the power of *mantra*. The chanting of your *mantra* and the power of your meditation creates so much energy around you that no negativity can approach you. It may be the *namah Sivaya mantra* or *Namo Narayana mantra* or *Hare Rama* or any *mantra*. So have hundred percent faith in your *mantra*. First know the meaning of the *mantra*. *Mantra* initiation is a new birth. When your *Guru* initiates you, start practcing the *mantra* immediately. *Mantra* is a subtle form of Mother Divine. All *mantras* belong to Mother only. There are innumerable *mantras* and it doesn't matter which *mantra* you have…

Can I sing that in Sanskrit?

Sarva mantrātmike sarva yantrātmike
Sarva tantrātmike sarva yogātmike
Sarva jnānātmike sarva sarvātmike
Sarva rūpātmike sarva śaktyātmike
Sarva mokṣātmike
Sarva svarūpe hé Jagan Mātṛke
Pāhimām Devī namo tubhyām
namo namaḥ

All religions and all *mantras* belong to Divine Mother, the Supreme Personality, Para Shakti, Adi Para Shakti, Lalitambika. In the *Lalita Sahasranama* it is mentioned:

Śivāyai namaḥ

"Mother Herself is Siva."

Śiva Śaktyaika rūpiṇyai namaḥ

"Siva is one part of Her body, and She is merged with the entire cosmos."

Lalitāmbikāyai namaḥ

Mother's heart is so tender—so tender that there is no comparison for Mother's heart. Beyond compassion, beyond inner beauty, beyond attributes—that is Lalitambika. Lalitambika means very soft and tender with indescribable inner beauty. She loves so much. Mother has so much responsibility towards this world and towards Her children. Even now if you commit a thousand mistakes, Mother has compassion. The word "compassion" does not properly describe Her—She is beyond compassion.

So children, Mother, with Her thousand hands, is in your heart. Your heart is the greatest temple for Mother. So clean your heart, remove the weeds of anger, lust, greed, jealousy or any others that are in your heart. Clear all the weeds, cultivate righteousness, develop inner beauty and purity by your devotion. If your path is Buddhism, it is okay. Buddhism is also Mother, Buddha is also Mother.

Ya Devī sarva bhuteṣu
Buddhi rūpeṇa samsthitā
Namastasyai namastasyai
Namastasyai namo namaḥ

Buddhi means the divine intellect. *Namastasyai*—my salutations to this body, the inner body and the main source of energy. Four *namaskaras!* This is beautiful—beyond beautiful! The first *namaste* is for this temple, our body; the second *namaste* is for the soul in this temple; the third *namaste* is for this entire universe, and the fourth *namaste* is for the Supreme. How beautiful this *mantra* is! *Shakti rupena*—energy is in so many forms, in fire, air, all the elements, in everything. So open your third eye and have the divine vision. Divinity is not visible to the naked eye. Open your third eye, open your third eye!

Surrender, surrender, surrender to Mother! Love Mother more than anything in this world. Mother doesn't expect anything from Her children—only love, true love. Devotion is really pure love. Pure love is devotion. Have pure love, hundred percent love. Now we have love towards so many things and only one percent love towards Mother. So there is no balance. Children, have hundred percent love for Mother. Children, what does Mother expect from you? Mother doesn't expect anything from you. She is:

Annapūrṇāyai namaḥ
Sadā pūrṇayai namaḥ

Only Mother gives all fulfillment in this universe. So pray to Mother for real knowledge, a grand life and supreme bliss. And meditate daily with your *mantra.* If you do not have a *mantra*, you can meditate with the *Saraswati mantra*. The seed letters of the *Saraswati mantra* are very powerful. *Omkara* opens the crown *chakra* instantly; the third eye is immediately opened by *Ayim;* the *vishuddhi chakra* is opened by *Srim*; and the main source of energy, our heart *chakra* is opened by *Hrim.* The entire *Saraswati mantra* gives self illumination You have oneness with Mother and you begin to feel, "I am the soul, I am peace, I myself am time, I myself am Truth, I myself am wisdom and I myself am everything. The *Vedas,* this Earth, humanity and all the religions belong to the Self only."

There is no difference between any of the things in the world. You experience oneness in your life. That is the main aim of human life.

So no more tears! Give up all your problems to Amma. She will immediately burn them all. She wants to elevate Her children to the highest peak of peace. What is the enemy for our peace? Desire is the enemy of our peace.

Desire—so many desires! Desire is the impurity of our mind. Reduce your desires—unnecessary desires, unwanted desires, bad desires. Have good desires and finally have only one desire—the desire for Realization.

Have dispassion, compassion, equal vision, balance of mind and real spiritual wisdom. If your *Guru* is a true *Guru,* He must give you wisdom. Go everywhere and get everyone's blessings. Be always in wisdom. Never limit yourself to a particular path. Every path belongs to your *Guru* only. See your *Guru* everywhere. That is wisdom. The sun is one, the moon is one, Earth is one, air is one, fire is one, the entire mankind is one. Love is one, hunger is one and anger is one. Everything is only one. And all real *Gurus* are only one. All holy people are only one. Truth is only one. Truth may be expressed in different words in different languages in Russia or China or India or the USA. But Truth is always only one.

Children, have wisdom. Be always in Truth. Have cheerfulness in your heart. Cheerfulness is the best asset for a spiritual aspirant. Always be cheerful. A cheerful word heals many inner injuries. Amma gives a little love to this universe, but you elevate yourself more and more—a billion times more than Karunamayi—and give your cosmic love and compassion to this entire universe. There is so much pain wherever you go. Try to remove the pain with a cheerful word and love. Love mankind. Have wisdom and with that wisdom become attributeless.

Even divine attributes are very limited. Your Self is not limited to these divine attributes. So do not confine yourself to that little pond. I will never hurt you; I will always love you. Even if you commit billions of mistakes, I will still love you. That is my responsibility towards my children. But I want my children to elevate and expand themselves and have discriminative divine knowledge and more and more wisdom in their spiritual life. I want them to understand the Truth and experience Reality at least in this birth. That is Amma's only wish. Why are we continuously wasting our time in this worldly intoxication? There is no meaning in this at all. Understand the Reality with true knowledge. Have true knowledge.

Pray to Mother with faith, have truthfulness in your heart, and pray for more purification.

Meditation is the greatest art of remodeling yourself. Achieve the destiny of divinity. Meditation is a beautiful art. You know so many arts in this world, learn this art also. Remodel your life. Purify your life. Have truth in your heart and attain Realization in this life.

Sometimes when we are tired, we fall asleep during meditation and think we have attained *samadhi.* Do not mistake sleep for *samadhi.* In *samadhi* the bliss is unexplainable.

In any religion, holy people will only show the path, they will not explain about bliss. So understand the difference between the state of sleep and the blissful state. Have right understanding about meditation. Ask your *Guru* about your *mantra*, about your path and about all your doubts, and continue your *sadhana* without any interruption.

Have a tender heart. If anyone scolds you, remember this beautiful story from the life of Buddha: One disciple abused and scolded Buddha very badly. If I have a flower in my hand that I want to give to a lady, and she refuses to accept it, what happens to the flower? It stays in my hand. If she does not accept this flower it remains with me only. In the same way if anyone scolds or criticizes you, do not accept the words, just like the woman who did not accept the flower. Where would all the scoldings and abuses go? They would remain with the person who spoke them. Do not accept the abuses, but forgive and love those who abuse. Why? Because you are a meditator. You are an elevated soul. You have devotion. You are more evolved than an abuser. Forgiveness is divine. Always be in that elixir. That is Amma's wish.

In many places children are abused. Never abuse children, not even small children. Love them and give them your compassion. I love nature only one percent. You, I love billions of times more. Do not abuse anybody's children. Give your compassion, your kindness, your cosmic love to all children in the world. That is my only request to my children. My children, give this gift, this *dakshina,* to Amma. Love every child. Have equal vision. Give your compassion and give your kindness to all beings in this world.

Four pillars—compassion, wisdom, Truth and divine love—support our life. The gateway to the temple of divinity is selfless service. Selfless service towards all beings is the greatest *yoga* to merge with the Eternal. Mother is not the physical Mother. Mother is the eternal Mother. If you really want to merge with your eternal Mother, open your heart, open your doors of selfless service and give your cosmic love to all mankind. That is Amma's only wish.

Elevate yourself; never speak ill of anyone, utter no negative words. We have committed so many mistakes with our tongue, millions of mistakes. So purify the tongue with the *Saraswati mantra*. When Saraswati is with us, we can never abuse anyone in the world. So this is the lesson—if I abuse anyone, the abuse or scolding remains with me.

Have forgiveness in your heart, have kindness, compassion and all the good attributes. Virtues beautify your entire life. Jesus, at the last moment, while being crucified, asked God to forgive his persecutors and give them wisdom. That was Jesus! Go beyond Jesus, children! Go beyond Amma, children! That is Amma's wish.

Can you be like Jesus if anyone tries to take your life? He was so compassionate—he was beyond compassion. He prayed for the life of the two thieves. They were robbers, very low level people, but Jesus never scolded them. He loved them because He was their Father and felt responsible for their welfare. He forgave them and prayed to God to give them peace.

So be at that level, children, never go to a lower level. Stay at the level of the Spirit. If our mind is working in *tamas* and *rajas*, that is, at a low level, we abuse and curse. Our attachments are limited to our family and we are very limited, no doubt. If we have *sattva*, we are limitless, we have love and compassion, kindness, equal vision, inner beauty and all those divine attributes. Go beyond divine knowledge and see divinity in everything, everywhere, in every religion, in good and bad also, in this whole universe. That is the highest peak of spirituality. Be always in that wisdom. Be always in that greatest state of Spirit. Before the Spirit, the mind, intellect, even the *Vedas* are powerless. So taste that Spirit. Elevate yourself to that level. That is Amma's only wish.

Hari Om Tat Sat

Santa Fe *19 April 1997*

ॐ

THE GREATNESS OF THE SARASWATI AND MRITYUNJAYA MANTRAS

Swamiji: I welcome you all on this pleasant evening to be in the presence of our Divine Mother, Karunamayi Bhagavati Sri Sri Sri Vijayeswari Devi. Just now we meditated a few minutes for world peace. Yesterday when speaking about meditation Amma was saying that meditation is nothing but purification of the mind. In these few minutes of meditation, we meditated with the *Maha Saraswati mantra*. Amma has asked me to mention some points before She gives Her discourse on the *Maha Saraswati mantra*.

As you know, Maha Saraswati is the Goddess of learning, knowledge and thoughts. In India we have seen the great *rishis*, the great saints like Valmiki, praying and meditating on Maha Saraswati. Valmiki attained immense knowledge by chanting this powerful *mantra*, the *mantra* which we have just chanted and meditated upon:

Om Ayīm Śrīm Hrīm Saraswatī Devyai namaḥ

These are most powerful *bijaksharas* or seed letters. They are the condensed forms of the energy of Maha Saraswati. When we chant the first *bijakshara*, *Ayim*, which represents Maha Saraswati, we get immense knowledge, the whole nervous system is activated and our mind is enriched with memory and concentration power. Just one meditation on the *Maha Saraswati mantra*, just the single *bijakshara, Ayim,* blesses us with true knowledge. That is why the renowned sage Valmiki was able to write the greatest epic in the world, the *Ramayana*, as you all know.

Similarly Vyasa Maharshi, one of the greatest of all sages, has written innumerable scriptures. The most notable of these is the other great epic, the *Mahabharata*, which contains the *Bhagavad Gita*, the universal message which Lord Krishna has given to the entire world. And apart from that he wrote the *Puranas* and the *Upanishads*. He also condensed and gave mankind the *Dasha Upanishads*, the ten *Upanishads*, which have now been published so that everyone can understand the *Upanishads* easily. Vyasa Maharshi's great ability to write commentaries on all these great works was acquired by the grace of Maha Saraswati. He achieved this by the worship and meditation of the powerful *Ayim bijakshara,* with which we have just meditated.

The *Saraswati mantra* has three *bijaksharas*, namely, *Ayim*, *Srim*, and *Hrim*. *Ayim* represents Saraswati, the Goddess of learning; *Srim* represents Maha Lakshmi, the Goddess of fortune and wealth; and *Hrim*, the most powerful *bijakshara* in this *mantra*, represents Shakti. It is the greatest energy. So in this *Maha Saraswati mantra*, we have a combination of the highest knowledge, the greatest wealth, and the most concentrated energy.

Yesterday Amma was speaking about how wealth does not just mean material wealth. We must be rich in the wealth of contentment, happiness, humility and many, many moral qualities. We must be wealthy in all the moral qualities, not only in material wealth.

The great Rishi Yajnavalkya composed and wrote the *Brihadaranyaka Upanishad*, one of the greatest of the ten *Upanishads*. And Bharadwaja Maharshi, one of the greatest saints of India, wrote the *Vaimanika Shastra,* in which he has explained very clearly, how to build an airplane. This science was known in ancient times, although it has been rediscovered recently. The *rishis* were able to attain the highest knowledge by praying to the Goddess of learning, Saraswati.

These three *bijaksharas* give us so much knowledge, and that is why Amma says that whatever belief you may have, whichever path you may be on, do not worry about that. This *Saraswati mantra* is universal. One who has performed good deeds in his life will be able to chant this *mantra* and will be elevated from the lowest levels to the highest consciousness or blissful state. Whatever your belief may be, whatever *mantra* you may be using, or whatever meditation you may be doing, once again Amma says that this *Saraswati mantra* is as universal as the *Bhagavad Gita*, the *Koran* and the *Bible*. Anyone can read these books and take the message from them. In the same way, this *mantra* is so unique and universal that anyone can chant it, or meditate on it and attain the greatest knowledge, wealth and energy.

These three *bijaksharas* in the *mantra* also stimulate our nervous system. You may ask how it is possible that just by repeating these sounds, these *bijaksharas*, we can get a benefit and what that benefit could be. When you chant these *bijaksharas* in the right way, with the correct pronunciation, the whole nervous system gets stimulated. Your mind begins to turn inward as you go on practicing the *Saraswati mantra*—so very powerful is this *mantra!*

The *Saraswati mantra* is the *mantra* of sound, because Saraswati has been praised as Nadabrahma mayi. If there is no *nada*, if there is no sound in this world, in this creation, there is no meaning at all. When you go to the ocean, you can hear the sound of the ocean; you can hear the sound of the wind. Even if your mind is troubled, when you hear some music, your mind goes inward and you reach a tranquil state. The sound of musical instruments has this effect. All the languages which we speak belong to Maha Saraswati only. And if a kind word is spoken when someone is unhappy or in misery, just a kind word can make that person happy. All this depends upon sound.

Without sound, this world has no meaning. That is why all sounds are the sounds of Maha Saraswati Devi only. This *mantra* has a positive sound and is the subtle form of the energy of Maha Saraswati. That is why when we meditate on this *mantra*, whatever we speak will always be positive, not negative. Also, whatever we hear, we will take only in a positive manner and not in a negative way.

And still speaking about the *Maha Saraswati mantra*, as I have said earlier, *Ayim* is Saraswati, *Srim* is Maha Lakshmi, *Hrim* is *Shakti* and the *Om bijakshara* with which we begin every *mantra*, is Adi Para Shakti. Adi Para Shakti is the Supreme Divine Mother who with all Her divine radiance and luminous energy gives *darshan* to Her devotees on *Vijayadashami* day. That is the most auspicious day after the nine days of *Navaratri*, also called *Dashehra*. On that day, Divine Mother gave Her *darshan* to the people. That is why She has been praised as Lalita Parameshwari. So when we chant this *mantra*, we get the energy and blessings of the most Supreme Divine Mother, Lalita Parameshwari. Lalita means very tender, full of kindness, above kindness and beyond tenderness also.

When we speak about the *Ayim bijakshara* or the tenderness of Lalita Parameshwari, we can understand them just by looking at our Divine Mother, Karunamayi. Just being in Her presence we are blessed—even though we may not go and speak with Her. Her kind look, Her beaming smile and Her very presence emanate tenderness and kindness, filling us with peace. If we have the heart, and if we have the inner beauty we will feel this. In Her presence we can experience perfect tranquillity, limitless and boundless as the ocean. Just sitting in the presence of Amma is the greatest healing.

Yesterday it was announced that there would be healings and many people wanted to come and receive healing from Amma. Today the healings started at 9 o'clock and continued right up to 4 o'clock. Actually, the appointments were only till 12 o'clock, but a lot of people came and wanted to be blessed. Most of those who came for healing did not have any physical ailments; they wanted some inspirational words and blessings from Mother. What I feel is, sitting in Amma's divine presence is itself the greatest healing, because just a ray of Her grace is enough to heal all mental agony, misery, anxiety, depression and frustration. This is because Amma is the embodiment of love and kindness, and in Her presence there are no questions at all, just absolute silence.

We have seen that whenever we sit in Her presence, some people come and offer something to Amma. Whatever they give to Amma can be seen, but what Amma gives to us is not seen by the naked eye, it can only be experienced. The love, affection and compassion which Mother showers on all of us has to be felt—it cannot be described or explained. Many people have experienced this and have given their view of how they feel when they are in Amma's presence, because Amma is the embodiment of purity. She is also the embodiment of love and the embodiment of compassion.

That is why, when we are in the presence of the great souls, our doubts are cleared. Just by a ray of their grace, and by being in their presence, all our doubts vanish. Many people have this experience. They often say that they had some questions which they wanted to ask Amma, but in Her discourse, all their questions were answered. This is because Amma knows what is in our hearts. And that is why Amma's message is always universal. Whether you are a small child or the oldest person present, everyone gets the message. Each of us thinks that Her message is for him only because Amma's discourse goes directly into the heart and melts even the hardest of hearts.

I have seen that whenever Amma speaks, the whole world becomes silent. This is because, as you all know, Amma is praised as the embodiment, the incarnation of Saraswati Devi. But many people around the world say that Amma is the embodiment of the Divine Mother and some say that She is the embodiment of Maha Lakshmi. I think we are limited by our knowledge when we try to depict Amma this way, because we don't know the nature of Mother. But Amma Herself always says: "I have not come to you as a God, and I have not come to you as a *Guru* or as a preacher or teacher. I like to be always with you as your near and dear Mother." That is why Amma calls you Her children. It is not possible for everyone to do so. We cannot say: "Come babies," and "come children." She is the universal Mother and that is why She is able to embrace the whole world.

As Amma says, it is not the whole world, it is the whole cosmos—Her unseen arms are embracing the whole cosmos. That is why Amma is able to travel the whole world and give Her motherly affection, love and compassion to all humanity.

[Amma speaks in Telugu]

Swamiji: *Jai Karunamayi!* Amma has asked me to tell you a few more things regarding this *Maha Saraswati mantra*, because some of you have asked Amma how to start doing this *Maha Saraswati mantra* meditation. Apart from your meditations, you can start the *Maha Saraswati mantra* meditation by playing the cassette as we have done just now. Take the vibrations of the *mantra* inside, and repeat this *mantra* internally, not verbally. You have to repeat it mentally. After hearing this *mantra* five times you will hear only the instrumental music. This is the real state of meditation, because we have to go beyond the *mantra* also.

In the initial stages, it may be hard for some of you to sit in meditation without any *mantra*. That is why you need this powerful *mantra*, the *Saraswati bijakshara mantra,* for it activates the whole nervous system and puts the mind on one track. It controls the mind and helps it to go inward. During the period of silence, that is, while only the instrumental music is playing, you have to sit silently concentrating in-between your eyebrows. If you are distracted, after two minutes you will hear the *mantra* being chanted again on the cassette. After five repetitions, once again you have to withdraw the mind.

If your mind is in absolute silence, it is not necessary to chant the *mantra*, because you are already in *sattva.* However, if the mind is still wandering here and there, in *tamas* and *rajas*, you need to repeat the *mantra* mentally. The *mantra* automatically leads the mind within as you listen to it. This is the way to start the process of meditation. Initially you can listen to the cassette for fifteen minutes and then slowly and gradually you can increase the time of meditation. This is how Amma has taught us to meditate with the *Saraswati mantra*. If at all you have any questions about this meditation, you can write them down and give them to us, and in tomorrow's discourse, Amma will clear your doubts. *Jai Karunamayi!*

Amma's Discourse:

Embodiment of Divine Souls, Amma's Most Beloved Children,

This morning during the healing session so many children asked about the *Saraswati mantra*—how to meditate on the *Saraswati mantra* and what is the significance of the *Saraswati mantra*. We have knowledge about this world, we are educated and know how to behave in this world—we have good manners and all those things. Saraswati means the divine elevation in our life which reveals itself in our words and in our behavior. Saraswati purifies our words; they become like pearls, rose petals, jasmine petals and more sweet than elixir. In general, where there is education there is knowledge. Everyone respects those who are highly educated. Doctors, engineers, and scientists are praised as *Saraswati putras,* children of Saraswati. Artists such as dancers, painters, sculptors, and singers have the first seat of honor wherever they go. Everyone enjoys all the arts—literature, music, sculpture and painting.

Saraswati shares Her riches with everyone in this world. Lakshmi on the other hand—can anyone carry dollars openly in their hands and walk on the road? People do not do this. Lakshmi is always inside the pocket. Saraswati shares. Knowledge is for everyone. The sun is for everyone; the moon is for everyone; air, fire and all the five elements are equal for everyone. Everyone has a right to *dharma*, everyone has a right to enjoy and learn the arts such as music and so on.

Saraswati means divine knowledge, the knowledge of the Self. This knowledge was known ages and ages ago in *Sanatana Divya Dharma*. The sound of the word *dharma* is so sweet. It is translated in English as "righteousness." This is an approximate meaning, but not the appropriate word for *dharma*. For instance, if you were to call a flower a plant, it would be incorrect. A plant has many aspects such as the leaves, the stem, and other parts, which a flower does not. In the same way, *dharma* encompasses peace, tranquillity, benediction, attributelessness, inner silence, equal vision, tender devotion—there are no words to explain the state of *dharma*. It is divine knowledge and compassion. It is beyond compassion, beyond kindness, beyond everything—that is *dharma*. So Amma wishes all

Her children, this entire universe, to be always in that highest peak of *dharma*. Then we will have inner richness and inner beauty in our life.

Physical beauty is not important, inner beauty is much more important than physical beauty. When our life is enriched by the grand Truth, the fulfillment of knowledge, and by contentment, we have so much peace and we enjoy divinity from the beginning of our life to the very end. Our entire journey in this world, this limited time in our eternal journey, is forty, seventy, eighty or ninety years. All these years we have been unhappy, frustrated and anxious. You know more about all these things than Amma—the daily problems, frustrations, unhappiness and tears. So many children are crying and are burning inside like lava, with so much pain. Sometimes they even injure themselves, because such are the problems in this world.

This is *maya*, but how can we understand this *maya?* Only with knowledge. So children, have awareness —*Brahmic* awareness—in your life. By practicing meditation you achieve *Brahmic* awareness and all the dark forces, the dark curtains covering our eyes, our heart and our entire life are removed by meditation. Meditation remodels your entire life to purity and you develop a connection with immortality.

All my little, little cute birds, all the birds are in the cage—the body cage. We give great importance to the little ego in this world. Kill this limited ego, burn the limited feelings with divine knowledge, and elevate and expand yourself to the highest purity of divine desirelessness.

Because of thoughts, we have desires. So these desires are working in three viewfinders. When our mind is working at the lowest level of *tamas*, our thoughts and deeds are also according to the *tamasic* nature. When our thinking is in the *rajasic* mode, we have so much pride and we never listen to anyone's words. We have no humility in our hearts. We hurt and injure others' feelings, not just in worldly matters but with regard to spiritual beliefs also. It is really very sad.

In the *Rig Veda* there is a beautiful saying: "Let noble thoughts come to us from every side." Always have noble thoughts, not selfish thoughts, *tamasic* thoughts, *rajasic* thoughts, and not even *sattvic* thoughts. Go beyond *sattva* also—always have noble thoughts. We always think: "This is only mine," "that is different from me," "you do not belong to me." This is the limited egotistic "I" feeling. When you elevate and expand your soul and touch the cosmos in meditation, your thinking and behavior are entirely different. That is, you realize that all paths and faiths belong to you only; your soul is pure—pure consciousness; you are attributeless, divisionless, *avinashi*, indestructible. You are *sarva vyapaka,* omnipresent, *sarva shaktimana,* omnipotent, *sarvajna,* omniscient, and *Omkara*. Your self is divine. Your self is not the body, mind or limited intellect. You are beyond all these things; you yourself are Divine Mother. This body is a temple for divinity.

Embodiments of Divine Souls, my most beloved children, elevate, elevate, elevate! Expand your soul, and go beyond the egotistic self—"I," "me," "mine." Understand the difference between the real and the unreal, and achieve the goal of Self-Realization. That is the main aim of human life. Gradually practice meditation and continue with whatever belief you have. Proceed with your *sadhana,* meditation and other spiritual activities without any interruption. Give respect to all the beliefs in this world. Believe in all the paths and see your *Guru* everywhere in the universe, not only in the good, not only in holy persons, but also in the bad. Then only will you become a highly elevated spiritual soul.

SMVA Trust
21 Baldwin Hills Road
Millwood, NY
10546

Credit Card Donation to SMVA Trust

(After filling out, please place in donation envelope.)

I would like to donate to SMVA Trust. Please charge my credit card (*check one box*)

☐ once every month   ☐ once every year   ☐ one time only

for the amount of (*check one amount*)

$20___ $50___ $100___ $500___   Other $____________

Credit Card (circle one)   VISA   MasterCard   American Express   Diners Club

Credit card number ______________________________ Expiration date ______________

PLEASE PRINT CLEARLY

Print your name as it appears on the card ______________________________

PLEASE PRINT CLEARLY

Print email ______________________ Tel number with area code ______________

Please sign your name ______________________________ Today's date ______________

Thank you very much for your generous donation.

God is first—divinity, our divine Self is first. Worldly things are second. Our little self, the limited egotistic self, is last, absolutely last. Do not give much prominence to the ego, the "I, me, mine." Give first prominence to divinity only, that is Self. When you come to me, I put the dot on your forehead, *"Om Shanti praptir astu!" Shanti* means peace. Peace does not mean peace just for this one moment, which is temporary peace. Real peace, permanent peace, is the true treasure hidden in our lives. It is a natural part of us. When you meditate you achieve permanent peace, you enjoy the fragrance of peace throughout your entire life—from the beginning to the end.

In India since ancient times, from the time of the *Ramayana,* children have been given *mantra* initiation in their seventh year. At that age children are able to understand the difference between good and bad in the world. The great sages would initiate them into the *Gayatri mantra*, *Saraswati mantra*, and *Om mantra.* From that day onward they stressed that these boys and girls should meditate on their *mantra*. The hearts of children are so pure, very pure, because they have not touched money and they know nothing about the pollution of this world. From the time of their seventh year they meditate on the *Gayatri mantra*, the *Saraswati mantra*, the *Siva mantra*, the *Narayana mantra*, the *Om mantra*, or any other *mantra*. From the age of seven to fourteen they develop a little maturity, because of the power of the seed letters in the *mantra*.

Both in Telugu and Sanskrit, there are fifty four seed letters. Each and every seed letter has its own power. The combination of the seed letters causes so many miracles in our life. Even if the heart is like a stone, it soon becomes soft when we chant the seed letters of *mantras* such as *Om*, *Rama* etc. Gradually we become more and more tender, above and beyond tenderness. We have inner beauty and all the divine attributes gradually bloom in our heart—kindness, devotion, wisdom, purity, truth. All these bloom in our heart, in our Mansarovara—the pure lake in our heart.

Children between the ages of seven and fourteen are really not able to meditate well, but the seed begins to sprout in their heart. From the ages of fourteen to twenty one they are under the control of their parents. They lead a very restricted life, following the directions given by their parents. The parents insist that they study hard, get good educational qualifications such as a doctor's degree, engineering degree, etc. If necessary, the parents force their children to study, because they have a long-term view of the future. They stress these values very strongly because they want their children to have a good life, a great life. So these boys and girls have humility and devotion because they meditate with the *mantra.* They complete their education, and at the same time, they have humility, wisdom, truth, devotion, and are one hundred percent pure souls. Thus society is filled with beautiful people of wisdom. Such are the expectations we have for our children. Society is beautified when wisdom blooms in its children.

My immortal children, Amma expects from Her children the same qualities, the same highest divine attributes. In spirituality everything is "beyond." So there is no question of, "I belong to this country, you belong to that country." In the *Vedas*, there is a very high concept, that the entire universe is only one—V*asudhaika kutumbam*. We are all part of a very small family—a little, little, family. India is a small room, like a *puja* room, the U.K. is another room, the U.S. is another room, Australia and Japan are also small rooms, all in one small home. We are all in one house; we are all the same. Whether a light is in a small mud lamp, in a silver lamp, or in a gold lamp, the light is the same. It does not matter in which garden the rose flower blooms, the flower is the same. Everywhere, a rose is a rose.

Wherever the soul may be, whether it is in the U.S.A. or U.K., in London or in Japan, your soul is divine. You are divine. So children, why this ignorance, why this illusion? *Maya* is very subtle; it is not visible to the naked eye. If we have divine vision, the eye of knowledge in our life, we are able to understand this subtle *maya*. Our ignorance is due to selfishness—being limited to this body, this mind: "I am very intellectual, I know the *Vedas,"* and all those things. The *Vedas* belong only to this limited Earth. Divinity, spirituality is beyond the Earth, beyond the five elements, beyond religions, beyond everything. All paths belong to you only. The entire mankind belongs to your soul only.

O children, elevate yourselves to the highest peak of tranquillity! You must elevate and expand your soul. Meditate, meditate, meditate, meditate! Surrender, surrender, surrender to God! And ask God: "Grant me a grand inner life. Send all these limited immoral natures away from me and elevate me to purity. Purify each and every cell of my body." That is possible in devotion only. Without devotion, just having only general knowledge is a very dry feeling, children. Do not give lip service to *Vedanta.* Lip-*Vedanta* is not sweet; lip service is also not sweet. When we have inner richness, we never even speak about the Truth. We are beyond the Truth. And Truth alone can stand without any support in this world. You are the support for this entire universe. You do not need any support from this universe. So be always in your real Self. That is Amma's only expectation from you.

O my babies, embodiments of divinity, embodiments of purity, embodiments of the universal consciousness, children, wake up from this long dream and elevate yourselves, expand yourselves to the Ultimate. All these faiths are only different paths that lead to the same destination. The destination is only one—oneness. Oneness is the destiny. So do not criticize anyone. Never injure the feelings of your friends or your spiritual companions. Let them have their own beliefs. Show respect—that is your responsibility to mankind. Have your own belief, proceed in your path, and maintain inner richness in your life. Attain *dharma*, cultivate truth, cultivate compassion, cultivate all the divine attributes in your life and achieve the main goal, that is, pure silence.

Shanti, shanti, shantiḥ: Shanti means no birth, and no death—beyond birth and death, beyond thoughts, beyond everything. There is no lust, no anger, no other negative qualities, nothing in that highest state. So children, that is your soul. When will you achieve this purity? It is in your hands. Practice, practice, elevate, expand. Without discriminative knowledge, our life is very childish. Have discriminative knowledge, cultivate dispassion and have divinity. Without self-discipline there is no spirituality.

Wake up early in the morning every day, start the day with meditation or with rituals or prayer, whatever you wish. Start the day with your spiritual practice, and cultivate *dharma*, cultivate *dharma*. Be always in *dharma*. *Dharma* means righteousness. Cultivate truth, then you will be able to understand the real and unreal in your life. You will taste true bliss. What can we drink in this universe except ordinary juices? Drink the elixir of bliss, dwell in bliss. Have peace, more peace and achieve the divine peace—eternal tranquillity. All this is possible for you through your true devotion and meditation.

Meditation is nothing but purification of our life—inner purification, development and remodeling. It is the greatest art of remodeling our life. You have a permanent contact with divinity. This *jiva,* the limited soul, enters into the *purna*, *akhanda*, or complete and indivisible oneness of divinity and merges with the Eternal. So children, from this universe to the highest level of immortality, meditation is just like a ladder. Meditate on whatever *mantra* you have. If you like to meditate on the *Saraswati mantra*, use that *mantra.*

Why this *mantra* meditation? This is because from childhood to the fiftieth or sixtieth year, twenty five thousand million thoughts come spontaneously to the mind. Some of these thoughts are unnatural, useless thoughts. Sometimes we have good thoughts, positive thoughts, pure thoughts and sometimes very emotional thoughts. We trouble other people with our thoughts: "Do this, do this according to my wish." When other people are stressed out because of us, we become a big negative force in society. Really, it is very bad. This is the nature of *rajasic* people. So be wise with people, do not pressure your children, your husband, wife, father or mother. If they like something, do it according to their wish. Why do we need to stress people? That is not good. *Sattvic* people never pressure others.

So from childhood to the sixtieth year, all these innumerable thoughts come from your mind spontaneously, unconsciously. Particularly at the time when you sit in meditation, so many thoughts, like poisonous snakes—thousands and thousands of poisonous snakes—come from the mind. So, how can we destroy all those poisonous snakes? Imagine the body to be like an anthill. All these poisonous snakes come out of the anthill in meditation and go away. This is possible because of the powerful seed letters in *Sri Rama*, or the *Om mantra* or any other *mantra*. These seed letters are very, very powerful for they burn all thoughts. Thought is very powerful; thought is nothing but our desire. Desire is the pollution of our mind, the motive force of our mind. Because of our desires we have so many problems in this world. So, understand the nature of desire and reduce your desires.

That is the essence of spirituality in this universe. So children, have faith in your path—one hundred percent faith, discriminating faith, in God's name, in your *mantra,* and in your *Guru.* If you are not able to have respect for your *Guru*, if you are not able to see divinity in your *Guru*, all your spirituality is of no use. Have faith in your belief and have contentment. This is a natural treasure in your life. Develop more and more peace, for peace will fill your whole life with fragrance. If you attain Realization on the last day, one day before physical death, what is the use? Throughout life you have been crying, craving for something. Achieving it on the last day is of no use. Attain the boon of peace and fill your entire life with the divine fragrance of permanent peace.

At this moment we are in peace, and all in one mood, the *sattva* mood, and we are listening to some good things. But we do not practice these things. Lip *Vedanta* is very easy, but to control anger, desire, lust, greed—all the immoral qualities in our nature—is very difficult. Still, it is possible by the regular practice of meditation or other spiritual activities. So children, be a true devotee of God. Have truthfulness in your heart and be sincere in your spirituality.

Sometimes we are not serious about our spiritual practices. We are very casual, writing *mantras* fast, etc. That is not good. We have twenty-four hours' time per day—spend twenty-three hours in worldly matters, and just one hour in cleaning the inner heart. So much vacuuming is needed inside. Give the opportunity to Amma. She wants to vacuum the entire universe with Her big arms. Why is there this dust in my babies' heart? This is not good—this anger. Because of anger, we are limited to a lower level. If we remove the dust from our heart, we will be elevated very high, very high. There is no beauty in anger. There is beauty only in peace. Peace is revealed in our face, in our words, in our heart, in our actions, in our whole life. The fragrance of peace is very silent—there are no words to describe peace.

Oneness is the essence of all spirituality. Ages and ages ago, *Sanatana Dharma*, the Path of Righteousness, the great *dharma*, called out to the entire universe, "O, embodiments of the Divine, my children, come to my lap. Unseen Amma's arms embrace this entire cosmos, not just this universe. Embrace the real spirituality in your life. Be truthful and pure, have contentment and attain God-Realization in this life." This is the message from the highest peak of the cosmos. So children, elevate yourselves!

Amma loves Her children. A mother is always playing with her baby. The baby is also always playing and playing and playing. When will this baby study and become a good, educated person in this world? Do not be always in this first class, the zero class of A, B, C, D. Small children just learn A and B and they get very tired, so they go to sleep. When they wake up they eat some candies and repeat A, B. This is one birth, this birth is finished. Again in the next birth we start in the same class—still the anger is there, the greed is there. All the immoral qualities in our nature are there. We never finish learning our ABCs. We keep repeating A, B, C, D over and over again. No, no more! Mother expects Her children to reach the highest peak as *paramahamsas*. If this baby is continuously playing in Amma's lap, when will she get an education and be elevated? And when will she attain the destiny of her life?

You need Knowledge as well as love. It is only through *jnana,* knowledge, and *bhakti,* devotion that you will experience *samadhi.* When you meditate in absolute silence without any thoughts, you can reach *samadhi* in eleven seconds! Sometimes, early in the morning, at three o'clock, when you wake up and meditate, you fall asleep. Do not mistake that sleepy state for *samadhi.* The state of *samadhi* has to be experienced—there are no words to describe that blissful state. So children, practice, practice meditation and achieve oneness—oneness with Mother Divine.

Immortal children, merge with your immortal Mother. You are already on the spiritual path. Don't get held back by any negativity. Come fast and merge with Mother, merge with peace and fill your entire life with the fragrance of peace. Without dispassion there is no *samadhi.* Without *samadhi* there is no salvation. So, how can we attain salvation? By the regular practice of *dharma*, righteousness, and true meditation. So attain God-Realization at least in this birth. Innumerable births have been wasted in just eating, talking, walking, and other useless activities in this long play. Be a spectator in this play. Don't merge more and more into this play. Be a spectator. A spectator enjoys the play more than an actor does.

Enjoy this play of God. See divinity everywhere, in each and every particle of this universe, in the whole cosmos. That universe is a festival for us to enjoy. Normally we have festivals only on special days such as Christmas, New Year's Day, *Sankranti*, *Vijayadashami*, *Sivaratri* or *Navaratri*. For a spiritual aspirant every minute is a festival, because he enjoys peace in each and every cell of his body, every moment in his life, everywhere in this universe! So every moment is a festival for him. Children, always enjoy divinity like that only. That is Amma's expectation. Go beyond all the holy persons, go beyond Jesus, go beyond Ramana Maharshi, go beyond

Ramakrishna Paramahamsa, go beyond everything and achieve the highest destiny, Self-Realization! Amma wants to see all Her babies on the highest peak of spirituality, that is Amma's wish babies!

Let us now talk about the *Maha Mrityunjaya mantra*, the great healing *mantra* from the *Atharva Veda*. It is the eighteenth *mantra* in the third canto. It is an extremely powerful combination of seed letters. We must be very careful to pronounce Sanskrit *mantras* correctly, as the correct pronunciation is essential for a *mantra* to be effective.

Om Trayambakam yajāmahe
Sugandhim puṣti vardhanam

Trayambakam means the entire power, oneness, the oneness of divinity. *Sugandhim:* the fragrance of divinity is only peace. *Pushti vardhanam:* Divinity is fulfillment. So there is a hundred percent fulfillment in divinity—*pushti vardhanam.*

Urvā rukamiva bandhanāt
Mṛtyor mukṣīya mamṛtāt

There is a special cucumber in India, and perhaps here also, that never falls from the vine even when the vine dries up. It is always attached to its vine, the mother vine. The devotee prays, "Even if I have committed millions of sins, and even after hearing all this talk about spirituality, if I still continue to make mistakes, O Mother Divine, O my Mother, You alone have the kindness of heart to forgive all my sins and mistakes. Only You can elevate me to the highest peak of purity. I cling to you like the cucumber to the vine."

That is Divine Mother. Mother never finds faults with Her children. So this *mantra* gives a direct connection to Mother like a direct-dial number. We have so many phone numbers—some of them are personal. Amma has given you Her personal phone number and asked you to dial it. You may not get the connection immediately, but you must continue dialing and one day, in prayer, you will talk with God! In meditation God talks with you. You receive vibrations and messages from divinity—that is the difference between prayer and meditation. In prayer, we talk to God, "O God, grant me this, grant me that, grant me a rich life, grant me a grand inner life full of peace," and all those things. But in meditation God talks to you, "O do not go now; do this; love them, do not criticize them; this is not good for you." You get all these messages so that you can live well in this world.

This body is the temple of God. "Only divinity is working in my life," that is your feeling in devotion. Devotion is so sweet and tender. In devotion, the highest peak is *advaita. Advaita* means "no duality," only oneness. There is no egoism in devotion—it is so sweet. So children, if you like the path of *bhakti,* proceed in that path. If you like meditation, proceed in *dhyana yoga,* the path of meditation. If you like *karma yoga*, the path of selfless service, proceed in that path; you have the wisdom. If you like *jnana yoga*, the path of self-inquiry, that is also good. All paths lead to one main goal—the goal of oneness. So you have the wisdom. Choose your path, proceed in your own path, and attain oneness at least in this birth. That is Amma's only wish for Her immortal children.

Be always in tranquility, be always in peace, be always in wisdom, be always in truthfulness. Have one hundred percent faith in God, and cultivate pure devotion. Faith is the main foundation for your life. Have knowledge, change your vision. Have divine knowledge and see divinity everywhere in this universe. That is the highest peak of spirituality. Cultivate more and more compassion. Go beyond compassion, have forgiveness in your heart and if anyone scolds or abuses you, do not give the same to others—love them.

Last year and the year before last, I received more than a thousand letters from the West—particularly from the U.S.A.—from students, children, and others. Those letters are amazing. They open their hearts to Amma, and reveal all the pain in their heart because of the abuse they have suffered. Do not abuse children. Children are like little flowers; they are very sweet. They do not have jealousies, they are not egotistic like adults; they are very tender. So all these homeless children, abused children, are in deep mental depression, and they meditate on the *Saraswati mantra*. They have very little peace but gradually, through *Saraswati mantra* meditation, they gain more peace. They elevate themselves and after six or seven months, they write to Amma about all their problems and pain. They say, "In Your discourses please tell people not to abuse children." So this is Amma's request to all Her immortal babies: "Children, never abuse small children. Give your love to this entire universe, even to the bad also." That is my only request and prayer to my children. Do not abuse children; do not abuse children under any circumstances.

Give your love; give your affection to the senior citizens of this country also. I have so many letters from senior citizens of this country. They are in a helpless condition: "We are human beings, we have a mind, we have a heart," they say. So help them, be kind to them.

The heart is beyond the mind, and spirituality and divinity are beyond the heart also. So be a real spiritual uplifter and give your true love and affection wherever there is need in this universe. Go to the senior citizens' homes, but do not show pity for anyone. Who are you to show pity? Give your real love to all, that is your responsibility towards this universe. So my babies, I expect my children never to abuse anyone and if you see someone being abusive, try to explain to him or her in a sensitive way that this is not good.

If you are a true friend, tell your friend the reality. That is the responsibility of a real friend. If it is a casual friendship, you need not bother about all these things; but if your friendship is permanent and true, you have the responsibility to say to them, "O, do not behave like this, do not injure anyone's feelings." This is how friends should help and guide each other, so that society becomes healthy. If everyone is crying and burning mentally due to problems, where is the happiness? No matter how colorful life may be outside, if there is only hollowness and emptiness inside, what is the use?

So fill this emptiness with your cosmic love and give your love and whatever else you have in your life. Do not think twice. If anyone needs you, willingly give even your life right away. Have this kind of dedication, children. From now on, we must change our views. All these years we have held other views, but now we should change and rise to the very highest peak of nobility. "Let noble thoughts come to us from every side." Always have noble thoughts! You are the giver; you are not the taker, because you are the embodiment of divinity! O my babies, that is the only expectation Amma has of Her immortal children.

So chant the *Maha Mrityunjaya mantra* regularly. In life you are so tired because of so many pains and problems. Since ancient times in India, our *Sanatana Dharma* has taught us to chant the *Maha Mrityunjaya mantra* at the time of any crisis in the home, such as the death of a father, mother, or child, or when there is any other problem which pains the heart. There is a ten day period of mourning when all the friends and relatives come and comfort the family. After that we have a big ceremony, the death ceremony, on the eleventh day. On that day, all the *vedic pundits* chant many *mantras*, the essence of which is contained in the *Maha Mrityunjaya mantra*. After grieving over the loss of your father or mother or any loved one for ten days, it is now time to stop grieving and continue with life. During this time the family members have stayed home in mourning, and their minds are so tired from the pain. The seed letters of the *Maha Mrityunjaya mantra* help to lessen and remove this pain from the heart and mind.

Sometimes we record some points on a cassette. When we have another important message, we erase the old message and record the new one. In the same way, through innumerable births we record so many things in our heart—pain, pleasure, and countless unnecessary things. We can erase that cassette and record a new message of immortality, tranquillity and oneness in the form of the seed letters of the *Maha Mrityunjaya mantra*. This *mantra* is the subtle form of divinity. Sometimes people think, "What is there in a *mantra*?" O, never think like that about *mantra*. *Mantra* is very, very powerful. There is no way to completely describe *mantra*. *Mantra* ties you to divinity, makes your heart a temple for divinity, and burns all the innumerable bad deeds, bad *karmas* from your life. *Mantra* elevates your soul to the highest peak of peace. It gives you a connection to immortality—that is the essence of *mantra*.

Every seeker prays, "I want a connection with divinity. I am always entangled in mortal feelings, so give me the immortal connection to my Soul. Elevate me from the body-mind consciousness to the highest level of Supreme Consciousness." *Mantra* gives this connection.

We must be careful to pronounce the Sanskrit *mantras* in the correct way. Also, every *mantra* has a rhythm.

If a patient is in a state of coma in the hospital, and we play the *Maha Mrityunjaya mantra* cassette, the vibrations are transferred to the patient's body, and gradually after a day or two, the patient comes out of his coma. This is because the vibrations of the *Maha Mrityunjaya mantra*, the healing *mantra*, come directly from the cosmos. The powerful seed letters of this great *mantra* heal even the inner, unseen injuries and elevate the soul to the highest bliss. You get immense strength and willpower by chanting it and gradually all the emotions are controlled. Thus we develop a balanced state of mind, without which there is no devotion.

By practicing the *Maha Mrityunjaya mantra* we develop a balanced state of mind, true devotion, a pure heart, strong will power and wisdom. So try to chant this *mantra*. This *mantra* is not for meditation. It heals not only the physical body, but also all inner injuries and prevents the negative energies of others from entering us. There are many kinds of energies in this world—some positive, some a hundred percent negative. We get so tired from the negative energies from other people. The powerful seed letters of the *Maha Mrityunjaya mantra* prevent the negative energy from affecting us. So this *mantra* is not for meditation.

Try to chant or sing this *mantra* twenty-four times daily, whenever you have time—even while you are driving, or gardening, or cooking. If you chant this *mantra* while cooking, all the food becomes elixir, so sweet. All the vibrations change. So always sing divine names and be absorbed in the consciousness of true devotion in your heart. This will lead you to salvation.

Hari Om Tat Sat

Los Angeles *24 April 1997*

ॐ

YOU ARE THE ESSENCE OF BRAHMAN!

[This discourse is addressed to the Indians in the audience.]

Divine Blissful Souls of Bharata,

When a wave falls into the ocean, what do we call that wave? We do not call it a wave any more; we call it the ocean. *Yugas* and *kalpas* rise and fall like waves in the ocean. The infinite Divine Consciousness is indivisible and complete *Para Brahman*—beyond the *Vedas*, beyond speech, beyond knowledge, beyond truth, beyond everything—non-dual and eternal. You are that *Brahman*. You are Infinite.

You have inexhaustible love in your heart. What can anything do to you? The treasury of universal knowledge is placed safely within you. If one were able to unlock the door of ego and cultivate knowledge with humility, one would experience his own natural state of oneness in all the four states of consciousness—*jagrat, svapna, sushupti* and *turiya.* The word "natural" means our true nature. On awakening to the unique experience of oneness that is natural to us, we reign supreme as *shuddhatma,* pure soul—*Brahman.*

But Divine Consciousness has been praised as *Duradhigama nissima mahima*—of infinite glory, and difficult to attain.

We cannot understand *Brahman* by merely reading the *Vedas* or by performing some rituals. Those who open the doors to Truth through *sadhana,* experience *Brahman* as unique, non-dual and beyond speech. Divine blissful souls of India! Shine in your supreme natural state, and give your love to the world, for it has become a place of sorrow. The world is in dire need of your service. Your Mother has done very little in this regard. How much can one travel and for how long can one meet people? You must share with your fellow humans the basic teachings of *Sanatana Dharma*—all-embracing universal love and infinite knowledge.

You all know how *Divali* is celebrated in our country. The rich people in big houses celebrate *Divali* by wearing beautiful new clothes and have their houses brightly lit up. However, in the nearby huts you find small children who get to fire just a few crackers. They will be crying for more crackers. From where can their parents get more, for they have small jobs and do not earn much. *Divali* is a festival that gives a lot of joy to a few, but brings hopelessness to many. Only the rich can celebrate it with a lot of lights—*Divali* is not much of a festival for the poor.

Now in this world must come a time when lights are lit up in every heart. Every *Bharatiya,* every Indian, must vow to live a life of *dharma* and shine in knowledge. What kind of knowledge? The knowledge of the soul. When does he shine in that knowledge? In all the stages of waking, dreaming, and deep sleep—at all times. What is his responsibility? To light the lamp of knowledge in every heart in the whole world.

Embodiments of blissful Souls! Sacred Souls! In India humans were addressed as embodiments of *Brahman*, embodiments of soul, embodiments of divine knowledge and embodiments of Divine Consciousness. They were not called by any one name, they were not seen as male or female, young or old. No matter what their age, they were addressed as infinite consciousness. The ancient sages saw in man not humanity but divinity, godliness, and the essence of *Brahman*. As your birth mother for millions of births, it is Amma's sincere wish that you should all shine in the glory of that supreme state.

A mother never sees the faults of her children. You may come to Amma for knowledge and say, "Amma, I have committed a lot of mistakes." However, I will never focus on your faults. I will always love you even though you have committed, and are still committing a million mistakes. A mother always wishes her child to be well educated, wise, and full of true knowledge—shining with the knowledge of the Self. The *vina* of the soul should play melodiously. The mind should be entranced with bliss. Every nerve in the body should vibrate with the sound of *Omkara*. Every heart should be established in the unique knowledge of the *atma*. In every state, whether awake or asleep, one should be fully aware of the consciousness of the Self. As your birth mother, it is my wish that you should progress in this kind of love for God.

I have not come to you as a *Guru* or as *Devi*. The feeling of motherly love is very dear to me. In Indian culture, it has been taught that every female should be viewed in the light of motherhood. In southern India, even a small girl is not addressed by her name alone; we add "*amma*" at the end of the name. If her name is "Rajyam" we call her "Rajyamamma," because there is an indescribable sweetness in the word "*amma*" that stirs the heart. There are many problems in the world today. So let us try to make everyone's life good. Our culture teaches that everyone in this world should be happy:

Lokāḥ samastāḥ sukhino bhavantu

See how many *mantras* of universal prayers we have. *Vasudhaika kutumbam* means, "the whole world is one small family." We pray not for ourselves alone, but for everyone. These feelings are to be found in all universal scriptures. The *Vedas* and the *Bhagavad Gita* are universal scriptures, and so are the *Koran* and the *Bible*. These feelings are common to everybody. Does the sun belong to only one person? Does the moon belong to only one person? Take Amma as an example: If you were to say, "Amma belongs to us and only we will offer Her our salutations," what about everybody in the world who came and called Her Amma? It would be foolish to say Amma would only respond to Her own people and not to the rest—it would be utterly wrong. Everything belongs to God; therefore, Amma wishes that you should all elevate and be firmly established in the highest state. You are all very spiritual and devoted and it is Amma's sincere wish that you should all gain even more brilliance within and become aware of that indivisible and infinite oneness. Amma desires that you all shine brilliantly every moment in that experience of oneness.

Hari Om Tat Sat

Los Angeles *24 April 1997*

ॐ

DIVINE MOTHER LIVES IN YOUR HEART

Jaya jaya jaya Mā Jananī Mā
Janana maraṇa bhaya hariṇī Mā
Sundara vadanī suhāsinī Mā
Mangala karaṇī Maheśwarī Mā
Mahādeva mana mohinī Mā
Māyā nāṭaka dhāriṇī Mā (2x)
Jaya jaya jaya Mā Jananī Mā

Embodiments of Divine Soul,

Amma bestows Her unconditional motherly love and blessings on you. It is impossible to give a description of the *Lalita Sahasranama.* It is *advaitamrita varshana,* a shower of the nectar of *advaita.* All of you know about the chanting of the *Lalita Sahasranama.* Only one name of Divine Mother is enough to destroy the sins of millions of births. The divine names of the *Sahasranama* are very powerful because they contain many seed letters. When a small stone is thrown into a lake, it creates ripples which reach the outermost edges of the lake. In the same way, when we sit here and chant *Om,* the vibrations reach the very source of *Omkara.*

Your prayer reaches the Divine Mother to whom you are praying and on whom you are meditating, because She is Hridaya vasini, One who dwells in the heart. When you pray from the heart, Mother receives your prayers instantly. She destroys the bondages of ego, body and mind, and fills you with the illumination and effulgence of supreme bliss and eternal God Consciousness. That is why Mother is called Shabda mayi (the embodiment of Nada Brahman),

Charachara mayi (pervading all sentient and non-sentient things), Jyotir mayi (filled with light), Chin mayi (the form of consciousness), Vagatita mayi (beyond speech), Nitya mayi (eternal), Niranjana mayi (without blemishes), and Tattvatita mayi (beyond the subtle essences). Mother is *Para Brahman* (the Supreme Consciousness), Sri Chakra mayi (pervading the *Sri Chakra*), Uhatita mayi (beyond imagination), Veda mayi (embodiment of the *Vedas*), Jnana mayi (the very form of *jnana*), Brahma mayi or *Satchidananda* (Truth, Consciousness and Bliss)—even so many of these names fail to describe Her.

Many people think that the *Lalita Sahasranama* is a description of the Divine Mother. The *Lalita Sahasranama* is the essence of the *Upanishads*, the essence of the *Vedas*, the essence of *advaita*. The *Vishnu Sahasranama* is from Kurukshetra in India, from *Bhishma pitama,* but the *Lalita Sahasranama* is from Mother Divine, from the cosmos. It is like a divine jewel, and it elevates humanity to divinity. Every *mantra* is beyond *advaita*.

Try to learn the *Lalita Sahasranama*, children. On the East Coast, so many children recite the *Lalita Sahasranama* with a hundred percent correct pronunciation—very beautiful: Nirakara (formless), Nirbheda (without differences), Bheda nashini (One who destroys differences)—Divinity is formless and nameless. If we have differences, Mother removes them all completely from our heart. Bheda nashini means "Destroyer of differences." This means that you and your Mother are only one. So many *mantras* in the *Lalita Sahasranama* are beyond beauty. We cannot express their meaning—we have to experience them. So try to chant the *Lalita Sahasranama* every Friday. If you are not able to chant it once a week, then try to chant it at least on *pournami,* the full moon day. What is the connection between the full moon day and the *Lalita Sahasranama?* The full moon is *purna*, full, round and complete. On *pournami* day, there is a special lighting called *nitya. Nitya* means eternal, everlasting. So on the full moon day, your mind is in *vishuddha sattva.* When you are in that supremely pure *sattvic* energy, your words will spontaneously be a hundred percent truthful. You will have humility and you will experience that God is one. You will be like Anjaneya, full of humility, inner beauty and wisdom. Humility is the greatest enemy of egoism, so cultivate humility.

One of the most beautiful names of Divine Mother is Siva Shaktyaikya rupini. This *nama* is the very essence of the *Lalita Sahasranama.* It means that the *jiva*, the limited individual soul, merges with the eternal Soul. Oneness is the message of the *Lalita Sahasranama* and its very beautiful names.

There are many books that explain the literal meaning of all the names of Divine Mother. But books are very limited, children, so do not keep searching in books. Search in your heart, and experience the names in meditation. Even the knowledge contained in the *Vedas* is very limited. It is like a small pen flashlight in total darkness. However, the self-illumination of *samadhi* is like millions and billions of rays of bright sunlight that illuminate the Self. There are no words to describe this; you can only feel it.

You must experience that blissful state yourself, babies. That is the only expectation Amma has of you, children. She never expects anything else from you. You are so sweet and good, you have devotion and you have all the beautiful moral qualities in your life. Develop your devotion more and more and merge with your eternal Mother, who is Nirakara (formless), Nirbheda (without differences), Bheda nashini (One who destroys differences), Nirnasha (eternal), Mrityu mathani (Destroyer of death). There is no death for the soul. You are immortal, children!

The spiritual meanings of the *mantras* in the *Lalita Sahasranama* are very different from the literal meanings, which are limited due to our intellect. When you open your heart, the little ego is destroyed, and you gain wisdom. The entrance gate to spirituality is wisdom. It is a very beautiful entrance. Open the entrance gate of wisdom in your life and attain Realization, Self-illumination, your true destiny.

When we chant the *Lalita Sahasranama*, we develop a tender heart. Sometimes our heart is like a stone. We are very stubborn and think, "I must never do this, I must always be like this." Chanting one name of Mother Divine burns away all this stubbornness, because the tenderness in *Lalita Sahasranama* is beyond description.

When a child is hungry, to whom does he call? He calls his mother. He says, "Amma, give me food." He feels free with his mother. It is not possible to obtain motherly love and tender affection from anybody else. When a child makes a mistake, she tells only the mother, not the father. She confesses her wrongdoing to her birth mother and asks for forgiveness. It is the mother who gives the child spending money, so she can go to picnics or other places—these games are only possible with a mother. It is also said in the *Vedas*—there can be a bad son, but there can never be a bad mother. No matter what wrong the child has committed, the mother's love is always unconditional.

The *Lalita Sahasranama* is divided into sixteen divisions. The first division contains the description of Sri Mata. It is the description of the lovely form of the Mother, from Her beautiful crown to Her sacred lotus feet. The great Bhishma Pitamah at Kurukshetra blessed humanity with the *Vishnu Sahasranama*. The *Lalita Sahasranama* is the *prasadam,* blessing, bestowed on us from Manidwipa. When Mother Sita was being abducted by the demon king Ravana, She threw down Her jewels among the *vanaras* from the *pushpaka vimana.* The gems of *Sri Lalita Sahasranama* are showered on Earth from Manidwipa. The sages, kings, Gods, and even Brahma, all meditate on the *Lalita Sahasranama.* It is declared in this great hymn to Devi, that except for people in their last birth, that is, except for those who are at the end of the cycle of birth and death, no others can meditate on the *Lalita Sahasranama.*

This profound scripture is *vagatita,* beyond speech, and it is a great *shastra.* In fact it is the scripture of all scriptures, the Knowledge of all knowledge, and the *Veda* of all *Vedas.* The *Lalita Sahasranama* gives *atma jnana.* The profound knowledge of the Self is contained in the *Lalita Sahasranama*—the marvelous Atma vidya (knowledge of the soul), Maha vidya (the greatest knowledge), Sri vidya (knowledge of Divine Mother), Kama sevita. Kama sevita means She is worshipped by Parameshwara Himself. Mother is Kameshwara prana nadi; that is, even Kameshwara's life force or vital energies are in Mother's hands. Without Mother, even Shankara (Siva) is incapable of movement. Bereft of *chaitanya,* consciousness, all creation becomes still—the oceans, winds, mountains, all become motionless. With Mother's consciousness, when we gaze at the mountains, it appears that the mountains, drenched with sun, rain, wind, and providing minerals and precious stones for the world, are sitting in silent meditation.

When we look at the trees, we see them giving cool shade and providing so many nutrients selflessly to humanity. Nature gives constantly, without expecting anything in return. Man receives so much abundance from nature but gives nothing in return. We do not even water a plant selflessly—we do it with the expectation of flowers and fruit. When we water a plant with love, the plant is so delighted with our love, it trembles with joy. We are so moved when we feel unconditional love in a person's heart. Now we have lost that unconditional love and human beings have fallen to a very low level. People have lost their true worth. It has come to the sad state where people are aimlessly wasting time in the pursuit of acquiring too many meaningless material things. Through the words of the *Lalita Sahasranama,* Divine Mother calls sweetly to the child: "Come to me! Wherever you wander in the day, by evening you have to return to me. In whatever religion, path, or work you may be, ultimately you have to obtain *Brahma svarupam,* become one with *Brahman.*"

There is a wonderful *shloka* regarding this:

Girāmāhur Devīm Druhiṇa gṛhiṇīm Āgamavido
Hareḥ patnīm Padmām Hara sahacarīm Adri tanayām
Turīyā kāpi tvam duradhigama niḥ sīma mahimā
Mahā māyā viśwam bhramayasi Parabrahma mahiṣīm

This *shloka* means: "Even if You are limited to names and forms by ignorant people, You are Brahma mayi, the embodiment of *Brahman;* Akhanda jyoti svarupini, the very form of eternal light); Sat chit ananda Brahma mayi, *Brahman* as Truth, Consciousness and Bliss; Koti surya prakasini, the effulgence of millions and millions of suns, the energy of the great, all-pervading consciousness, Gayatri, Lalita Parameshwari; Para bhattarika, the great Empress!" Even the *Vedas* cannot adequately extol You, therefore You are known as Vedatita, beyond the *Vedas.* O Mother, as Your Consciousness cannot be known, You are called Jnanatita, beyond knowledge. You are Shabda Brahma mayi, the eternal *Omkara.* You are also Ayimkara, Srimkara, and Hrimkara—You are the embodiment of all the seed letters. You are verily the form of all *aksharas,* the letters of the alphabet. You are worshipped in the form of divine music. You are the *atma* of *mula chaitanya prakriti.* You are Maha vidya, Atma vidya, Brahma vidya, the embodiment of Sri Vidya, O Mother!

You are supremely marvelous! The *aishvarya,* true wealth, granted by the Divine Mother is the eternal wealth; it is the treasure of wisdom and salvation. The Mother of the universe bestows on humans *Atma vidya,* knowledge of the Self, and *Brahma vidya,* knowledge of Supreme Consciousness.

The following *mantra* declares that Mother is Svatmananda lavibhuta Brahma dhyananda santatih. Divine Mother, Brahma mayi, Herself meditates and distributes the bliss of that meditation to Her children. The Mother bestows the bliss of Her meditation on *rishis*, on Brahma, and all the other Gods. Divine Mother is the form of eternal, *Brahmic* effulgence.

You read in the *Lalita Sahasranama* that except for those who are devoid of ego and dispassionate, having conquered their passions such as anger and attachments, it is impossible to comprehend the Prajnana ghana svarupa Brahma mayi, the Mother who is the embodiment of supreme wisdom. Just as rock candy tastes sweet on all sides, inside and out, Brahma mayi is the same everywhere. That is why She is called Duradhi gama nissima mahima, of limitless glory.

"O Mother, Your *tattva,* or subtle essence, is known only to You—it cannot be understood by anyone else. You are incomprehensible, O Maha maya, Para Brahma mayi, Purna Brahmananda mayi, the Supreme Bliss of *Brahman!* You reside in and illumine the hearts of *yogis* with the delightful tinkling of Your anklets. A million *Omkaras* ever resonate from the sweet tinkling of those divine anklets."

Every atom of the *yogi's* heart vibrates with *Omkara,* and is filled with the bliss of Supreme Consciousness. The body is radiant with *Nada Brahman,* the bliss of the *Brahmic* sound of *Om.* Then these *yogis* are established in Supreme Consciousness in all the states of waking, dreaming and deep sleep.

Just as after tasting nectar one does not relish rice gruel, these *yogis* established in *Brahman* cannot relate to mundane matters. They are totally disinterested in worldly life and become either childlike or appear to be mad. They are not able to enjoy any worldly pleasures. Once *Brahmic* bliss is relished, can anything else taste sweet? After visiting Naga loka, the kingdom of snakes, is it momentous to spot an ordinary garden snake? After riding an elephant, would anybody want to ride a fox? The latter appear to be very insignificant. Similarly, after experiencing *Brahmic* bliss within, what other worldly enjoyments could possibly be desired? There is nothing left in this world to be relished after tasting the nectar of supreme bliss within. There is no book to be read, no pilgrimage to be undertaken, no need to go anywhere. It is wonderful! Supremely wonderful! It is transcendental bliss, not transient happiness; it is eternal joy. Meditation on the Self leads to the bliss of the Absolute.

The *Lalita Sahasranama* deals with *Atma Vidya,* knowledge of the Self. It is called *rahasya,* secret. The secret is within us. It has to be discovered and investigated.

Mother is Para mantra vibhedini. When we sow a seed in the soil, after a few days, without any effort on our part, it sprouts from the ground bearing two small leaves, and then grows into a tall tree. The Self that is verily the form of Supreme Truth is very subtle; the eye cannot detect it. When we create a small dot with a pen, we can only see it if our vision is good. How can we see the Self, which is a million or billion times more subtle, with the naked eye?

That which cannot be cut with a sword, or burned by fire, that which is truly amazing and gives radiance to everything, is *sarvajna,* omniscient. That which gives effulgence to the sun, luminosity to the moon and brilliance to fire is the *Atma,* the root cause of everything. The divine Self gives the infinite energy of consciousness to Brahma, the Creator and to all creation. That is why Amma calls you "embodiments of Divine Soul." It gives great joy to be addressed not just as a human being but as the embodiment of divinity.

Blessed souls, life is very short, we have come here to this world-stage for a few days. Why should we give pain to another? How can we be the cause of another person's sorrow and distress? Did someone cry because of our actions? How can we live with that? What is the purpose of our life? We should never at any time be the cause of another's pain. Our words should never hurt anybody. We should monitor our behavior and check whether we are creating problems for others. We should develop a very loving and giving attitude.

By meditating again and again on the Divine Mother's names, the *jivatma,* the individual soul, becomes blessed. The sins are destroyed, and the heart becomes soft—more tender than fresh butter, cooler than moonlight, more ambrosial than honey, whiter than milk. Nothing is more luminous than the Truth which is beyond the three *gunas.*

The *Lalita Sahasranama* talks about this *Shuddhatma,* pure consciousness, that gives effulgence to the sun, moon and *agni,* fire. That is why it is said that the inner eye should be opened to behold this *Shuddha Brahman,* the pure, supreme Self. When the inner eye is opened, the whole cosmos can be seen. With normal eyes you can see only around this room; with the inner eye, the seeker discovers who he is, who Divine Mother is, and what this universe is. He experiences infinite *Brahmic* bliss, and drenched in this remarkable bliss of the Self, he is always at peace. He becomes *Brahma svarupa,* the embodiment of *Brahman,* and shines radiantly as a *Brahma jnani.* Amma, as your own mother, wishes that all of you should become *Brahma jnanis.*

Amma has not come to you as a *Guru* or a *Devi.* Amma has come as your mother only. You have to become *Brahma jnanis.* You should not dwell in these lower planes, filled with untruth. You should remain in peaceful, elevated states. On those planes you will meet great sages. Here in the lower levels, you will see people of lower character. On the higher planes you will see great souls like Shankaracharya, Jesus, Mohammed and Buddha. In the lower planes you are among ignorant and confused people, wandering in this world in the pursuit of money. We are in a play. Mother wishes you to wake up from this dream. It is painful for Amma to see you in this confused state.

A wondrous, timeless, sacred Truth is shining in your heart. You should not put out that light and live in darkness. You should increase the intensity of that light and enlighten future generations. That is every human being's responsibility. You should give light and peace to all. If an ordinary flower dies we do not keep it in the house; but if it is fragrant like the jasmine, we preserve it even after it has withered. Similarly, without the knowledge of pure consciousness and the attainment of peace within, what is the use of our life? Life is definitely not just for eating and sleeping. It is not simply for earning a livelihood. There is a goal to be reached, to strive and search for—the wondrous knowledge of the *Atma,* to gain inner vision. There is a treasury of this marvelous knowledge buried deep in your inner world.

The word Kailasa means, "the place where all souls assemble." That Kailasa is here, in the *Brahma kupa,* in the *vishva kamalam,* the universal lotus of the *sahasrara.* Man has to obtain the infinite knowledge of pure consciousness and make his life an abode of peace.

The *Lalita Sahasranama* is the key to the secret path of enlightenment. Lalita means, "One with *lalityam,* One who plays." When the seeker turns inward and concentrates on the place between the eyebrows then his eye of wisdom is opened and this region becomes the playground for the charming sport of Lalita Devi.

When we watch that delightful play, we will be immersed in bliss. The seeker will be firmly established in the peace of *Brahma jnana,* and will not be disturbed by the turbulence of happiness and sorrow in life. Amma's desire is that everyone should attain that bliss. When a calf is tied to a rope, it wrenches at the rope, crying to go to its mother. When you gain the awareness that this world is not real, then all these attachments will not bind you. We have bound ourselves with all these iron chains, but none of them can bind us—this is the greatest truth. It may be bitter, but still it is the absolute truth.

So, divine souls, you should gain freedom and taste that inner bliss. It pains Amma deeply to watch you waste your lives, simply eating, sleeping and entangled in other useless, worldly activities. There is not much time left; forty, fifty, sixty years have gone by. When will we meditate? The body suffers with numerous aches and pains. We are not able to sit for meditation. So please do at least a little *sadhana.* Even if it is done with ego it is better than not trying at all.

Whether *sadhana* is done with ego or without devotion, Mother still grants knowledge. Mother thinks about Her children even if they do not call out to Her, just like the mother who will feed her child even if he does not ask for food. She grants *jnana aishwarya,* the true wealth of knowledge because She wants all Her children to be enlightened, to experience supreme bliss and to make this body a temple for Divine Mother. This is Amma's heartfelt desire.

Just before coming here, Amma gave talks every day in India on the *Lalita Sahasranama.* In each discourse, Amma discussed just one *mantra* for a couple of hours. Many thousands of people chant the *Lalita Sahasranama* in India. They are building a beautiful temple, a Universal Inspiration Center at Penusila. The *kumkum, sindura, turmeric* and bangles offered during sixty *crores* of *kumkum archanas* performed by devotees all over the world have been deposited in the foundation of the inner shrine. The structure around this shrine has been constructed with eighteen *lakh* bricks. Each brick is inscribed with the *mantra, Om Sri Lalitambikayai namah.* This has been done with great devotion and with the feeling that future generations should enjoy peace when they visit this temple. See how wonderful it is to feel that this whole universe belongs to all of us. Imagine how good it feels to have kinship with everyone in the universe. This should be experienced, not just talked about.

Children, do *sadhana.* You hearts should be illumined with the radiant qualities of forgiveness, love, peace and wisdom. Do not store negative qualities like anger, lust and greed in your heart—give them to Amma. She will burn them all before leaving this town. But Amma is always with you, where can She go? She is always with you. Meditation is for you to realize that Mother is always with you, to realize the truth that you and your Divine Mother are One. Whether this is stated in the *Bible,* the *Bhagavad*

Gita or the *Lalita Sahasranama*, the essence is the same—I and my Mother are One, I and my Father are One, it is all about oneness. The *Lalita Sahasranama* teaches this oneness, the knowledge of pure consciousness. Amma's heartfelt desire is that you should do regular *sadhana* and attain this oneness.

Hari Om Tat Sat

Los Angeles *25 April 1997*

ॐ

THE BHAGAVAD GITA—ALL PATHS LEAD TO THE SAME DESTINY

Om Trayambakam yajāmahe
Sugandhim puṣṭi vardhanam
Urvā rukamiva bandhanāt
Mṛityor mukśīya māmṛtāt

Embodiments of Divine Souls, Amma's Most Beloved Children,

Today is really very auspicious as we are in the divine presence of Lord Siva in all these temples. Over the years thousands of people have assembled here in the form of pure devotion.

The *Bhagavad Gita* speaks of four paths. The first path is *bhakti yoga*—not the ordinary *bhakti* but *ananya bhakti. Ananya* is pure devotion, one hundred percent devotion with discriminating faith. The second path is *karma yoga* or selfless service. In every spiritual faith, selfless service is mentioned as a form of love.

Sanatana Dharma can be visualized as a very big palace ground from which many paths, rituals and so forth emerge. Five thousand years ago, according to *Sanatana Dharma,* the divine incarnation of Lord Krishna unified all these rituals and spiritual paths and described them in the *Bhagavad Gita* as the four paths—*bhakti*, *nishkama karma* or selfless service, *dhyana,* and *jnana*.

The third path is *dhyana,* the path of meditation. Some people like Self-Realization through *jnana*, the path of knowledge. Every path leads to the same destiny, that is, the land of bliss. The land of bliss is Siva, auspicious. Really, bliss is only in our temple. This is the temple: Every human body, every being, is the greatest temple for the Self, the pure Self. The main aim of human life is Realization of the Self, the Truth.

Children, you are already on this great path. Continue with whatever beliefs you have in your life. Proceed, evolve, expand yourself and attain God-Realization. Have pure devotion, one hundred percent pure devotion. That is *bhakti yoga* in the *Bhagavad Gita*. *Bhakti* is very sweet. Without having *bhakti* some people talk about knowledge. Dry! They will have so many doubts—thousands and thousands of doubts. In *bhakti*, our heart melts like butter; it becomes softer than butter. *Bhakti* is so sweet. Ask God, *Ananyaschinta yanto mam:* "Grant me the true devotion—*ananya bhakti*." Ask God with tears from the bottom of your heart and not from the lips. Prayer must not come from our lips. Prayer must always come from the bottom of our hearts. Such a prayer purifies our entire life and melts this stony heart.

Because of the environmental forces in our lives, we are so stubborn, refusing to bend. We are filled with pride and problems. A hundred percent pure devotion melts our hearts and our hearts become pure like the Manasarovara. In the Mansarovara, the lotus of devotion blooms beautifully.

Children, offer your entire life to God with a hundred percent pure devotion and discriminating faith—not blind faith. Knowledge acquired from books or by listening to discourses is not enough. Have devotion—one hundred percent pure devotion. Ask Divine Mother, "O Mother, grant me a pure life. There are so many thorns in my heart—anger, lust, greed, jealousy, pride. Grant me liberation from all these immoral natures. Grant me pure devotion."

Just as described in the *Bhagavad Gita*, so many people practice *bhakti yoga* everyday. *Bhakti yoga* is very, very, very sweet. There are no adequate words to describe the devotional path. By means of *bhakti yoga*, *Bhakta* Meera and so many others attained God-Realization. They never thought of an idol as an idol or a picture as a picture. *Mrinmaya,* that which is transitory, subject to change, became *chinmaya,* changeless consciousness. This means that in India and in other places, when people worship God as embodied in the form of pictures, idols, *saligramas* and *Siva lingas,* etc., they perceive them to be the real form of God. Thus they feel surrounded with forms of divinity, which they relate to on all levels, because *mrinmaya,* that with form, becomes *chinmaya,* that without form.

So divinize your thoughts, purify each and every cell of your body with pure devotion. Have faith, one hundred percent faith toward God, and practice *sharanagati*—total surrender. Surrender, surrender and surrender to God! When we surrender there is no second question at all. A real surrendered soul has no doubts at all. He is so pure and has a hundred percent contentment in his life—in his entire life. He neither has greed nor craving. He doesn't cry for anything in his life. If he lives under a tree or in a hermitage or is even without a home, he has a hundred percent contentment in his life. This is because only in spirituality do we have that kind of contentment, not in materialistic life.

So, my dear children, understand the reality of the world. This world is nothing but the Divine. When we attain God-Realization we feel we understand that all this is pure consciousness, like a big ocean. Each age, such as the *Krita yuga*, *Dvapara yuga*, *Treta yuga* or *Kali yuga,* is a wave from this ocean. From that wave, innumerable droplets arise in the form of all the beings in creation. Once again the wave merges with the ocean. Now there is no wave. The entire thing is once again pure ocean—pure divine consciousness.

Children, we attain God-Realization, in four stages—waking, dreaming, sleeping and *turiya* states. The natural state which is only pure consciousness, is working every time. What are you not in this world? You yourself are time, you yourself are wisdom, you yourself are attribute-less, you yourself are divine, you yourself are Siva, you are Krishna, you are purity, righteousness, *dharma*. You are everything in this world—past, present and future. That is the highest level of pure consciousness.

So, my dear children, the essence of the *Bhagavad Gita* is to attain God-Realization, *samata* or equal vision. It is not possible when we are intoxicated by this world. But when we go beyond the level of this body, mind and intellect, which are the three cages, then we are in a pure blissful state, that is, *turiya*. In that *turiya* state, the state of pure consciousness, you yourself are divine. Pure consciousness is infinite, children. Merge in that infinite joy. Always be in that pure consciousness. That is the main aim of our human life.

Have *dharma* in your life. Cultivate *dharma* and truthfulness. Cultivate compassion and contentment. Without contentment there is no happiness in our lives. So cultivate all these qualities, purify each and every cell of the body with pure cosmic love and attain pure consciousness by practicing *dharma*. *Dharma* is so beautiful, and so is righteousness. The latter word is a close meaning for *dharma,* but does not define it entirely. *Dharma* is beyond everything. So, children, be always in *dharma*. Be always in truthfulness. Only one who has this inner vision is able to understand the reality in his life. In addition, *dharma* gives direction to your entire life. Give *dharma* the opportunity to lead your entire life.

My dear children, embodiments of *dharma*, embodiments of Truth, embodiments of Divine Soul, be always in your natural state of pure consciousness. We are not in our natural state because we have this unhappiness. When we attain our natural state through the path of devotion, or of selfless service, or of *dhyana yoga* or any other path, we are always in pure consciousness. How does a man behave in that state? There is no anger, lust, greed, or jealousy. These main immoral natures are at the human level. When you attain the highest peak of divinity, there all these mean natures do not exist. Desirelessness is the highest peak of *dharma*.

Our problems in innumerable births are only due to egoism. Do not kill even an ant, insect, bird or any being in this world. First kill your egoism. Egoism is the first problem in our life. We have so many problems in our lives. We always focus our minds on the physical problems, but the main problem is inside our body. Our first enemy is egoism. This is also mentioned in the *Bhagavad Gita* as *shatru,* or enemy. This *shatru* has always been haunting our life, for innumerable births. So at this moment, permanently send egoism away from your heart and cultivate humility. Humility is the main enemy of our egoism. So have humility. Humility beautifies our entire life. With humility we have honesty, truthfulness, inner silence, inner beauty, inner vision, and inner consciousness, pure consciousness.

Your self is pure consciousness, children. So elevate yourself to the highest peak and expand yourself. Be always in Truth. Some say, "Amma, it is very difficult in this *Kali yuga* to attain *dharma*, to practice truth." For instance, we have certain rules on the road. If we throw some garbage, such as banana leaves, paper, etc., we are punished by being charged a fine. Gradually as we begin to follow the rules, all the roads become so clean. But in the beginning it is very difficult as nobody wants to listen or follow the rules. Why do we need these rules? Initially the rule is very bitter and not sweet, but when we follow it, it gradually becomes commonplace. Similarly in the beginning, righteousness, truthfulness, honesty, nobility are all really very bitter. They are not tasty. But in the end, patience becomes elixir. In the beginning, patience seems to be very cheap and useless. At the end of our life we realize that because of patience we learned so many things: "My patience was my cover. It covered my entire life just like a safety valve." Patience is a big pillar in our life. It gives courage, compassion, and real righteousness in our life. Without patience and contentment there is no real meaning for our spiritual life.

So children, first practice *dharma*. Five thousand years ago the *Bhagavad Gita* began with *dharma—dharma kshetra*. Your whole body is a *dharma kshetra,* a place for *dharma*. In this *dharma kshetra* we must cultivate all of the divine attributes and also go beyond these attributes and attain Self-Realization. That is the main aim of our human life, the Realization of our Self. Here, "Self" does not mean our egoistic self but the Supreme Self, the land of bliss.

Kailasa means the beautiful mountain where all souls are assembled in one place—all the planets and all the worlds, even the ant and Brahma. It is the place where the sun, moon, and galaxies rest. That is Kailasa. Kailasa is not the physical mountain. It is *mangala*, very auspicious, pure, attributeless, only oneness and indestructible power—which is pure consciousness. Therefore, children, attain Kailasa at least in this birth. For innumerable births we have been just walking, talking, eating unnecessarily and thus immersed in this worldly intoxication. This is *maya*. *Maya* is very subtle. So open your third eye and understand the reality, pray to God for pure devotion and attain *yoga* in your life.

Yoga means to combine. All of you know about the *Triveni sangam* in Allahabad—the confluence of the three rivers Ganga, Yamuna and Maha Saraswati is called *yoga*. In *ayurveda* so many herbal combinations are called *yoga*. In the same way in spirituality, *manushyatvam*, being born as a human being, inwardness, *mumukshatvam,* having the desire to achieve Liberation, and *maha purusha samshayaha,* being in the presence of an elevated, realized Soul are together *yoga*. These four conditions must be combined to attain God-Realization. So whatever work we do in this world, if we have the heart and if we understand the reality, everything is *yoga* only. For example, if we just perform some activity, if we arrange the flowers in a vase, we can do the same work in a spirit of *yoga*. If we give anything to anyone, this is also *yoga*. Everything in our life, every minute in our life is really a *yoga* and a *yajna*. So have this feeling of dedication and self-discipline in your life.

Wake up early in the morning and start the day with prayer. You *must* start the day with prayer from the bottom of your heart. Pray for Realization and not for small materialistic benefits. Again, we are so blind. There is a story where a blind man along with some ordinary people enters a diamond mine. One is so compassionate that he gives diamonds to this blind man. However, the blind man gets so angry and throws away all the diamonds saying, "Are you teasing me?" The man replies, "No. I am not teasing you. These are diamonds. Take these diamonds." The blind man says, "No, these are stones." This is how he feels. So, do not ask God for material benefits. Ask God for true knowledge. That is the real diamond. Have only one noble request:

Rāvammā rāvammā
Rāja Rājeshwarī rāvammā

Rāvammā Ammā rāvammā
Rāja Rājeshwarī
Nirmala jīvana sudhālu tonakagā
Shānti tīramuna mannu cherpagā
Rāvammā..........

In so many births, Divine Mother has given us such beautiful clothes. This body is a beautiful dress for our soul. All these innumerable births are like dresses. *Nirmala jivana sudha* means a very pure life, and all the divine attributes in our hearts—Mother gives us so many jewels. We have lost all these attributes during these innumerable births. We are just like a little child who soils her clothes with mud, juice or ink after her mother dresses her up and sends her out to play. The child then comes to her mother and cries, "Give me another dress. This one is spoiled." Over and over again, Mother provides not one or two, but millions and billions of dresses. This human body has so many dresses! This human birth is also one dress.

O my immortal babies! Do not spoil this dress again. Have contentment. Have pure love in your life and pray for true devotion, not false devotion. Do not make a show of your knowledge. Just have a hundred percent pure devotion and pure consciousness in your life, and you must understand what is the reality. That is enough for our life. So ask God for this during the early morning of *Brahmi muhurta* between 3:30 and 4:30 a.m. Over here in America, the time is different. Here it is not possible. In India, thousands of people wake up between 3:30 and 4:30 a.m. They have a bath and meditate with the *Gayatri mantra* and chant the *Bhagavad Gita*. They do their spiritual practices until 6 a.m. So my babies, at least pray to God for ten minutes early in the morning before sunrise. We have twenty-four hours in a day. Spend at least one hour early in the morning for spiritual practice.

When you meditate, pray or chant divine names in the morning, continue in your faith, whatever faith you may have. Have faith in your *Guru* and in your spiritual practice and do not injure anyone else's feelings under any circumstances. That is very much important for a spiritual aspirant.

A real spiritual aspirant has these beautiful ornaments in his heart. The first is true devotion, and the second one is discriminating faith along with detachment, dedication, inner beauty, purity in word and deed, equal vision towards all beings in the world, truth, wisdom, nobility and all the divine attributes which, along with desirelessness, beautify his whole life. The sweet fragrance throughout his life also beautifies and gives fragrance to society.

This is the expectation from the *Bhagavad Gita.* In a society where all children have these noble and divine attributes, the society is fragrant. There are no words to explain this state. If anyone has greed, lust, anger or any of these limited immoral natures, the harmony in society goes out of balance.

So children, because you have devotion, you have so many *gurus* who have given so much to you. Some of you say, "Amma, you gave us so much." No, no, Amma has given you very little! So many great sages who are not visible to you are in caves or hermitages, never coming out into this world or being exposed to it. Yet, wherever they may be, they send their love and blessings to the entire universe. So amazing is their love! There are no words to explain their love. Amma and other holy persons come to you because you need them to come. So many people are in their own places and they send their love in silence.

Have respect for every belief. All paths lead to only one—to bliss only. There is only one Spirit. So, children, never injure anyone's belief under any circumstances. That is a very low state. Do not come down to that lowest level. Be always on the highest peak of wisdom. Where there is *dharma*, there only is wisdom. Where there is wisdom, there only is dedication. Where there is dedication, there only is divine bliss. So have divine bliss in your life. Attain pure spiritual consciousness at least in this birth. This is Amma's wish. You already know all these things. Amma has just summarized these points.

We are always in pure consciousness. That is *turiya,* the fourth state. When you open your third eye you understand, "O, I am the soul. I am not this body. I am not this mind." You have no expectations in this world. You have forgiveness in your heart and cosmic love, not ordinary love. We have no ordinary love in our hearts. Today we love our friends, but what about tomorrow? This is because we follow our mind. Mind is not a constant friend. *Buddhi*, intellect, also is very limited.

When we follow the pure consciousness, it is always constant because consciousness is Truth. Truth alone can stand without any support in this world. So follow Truth only. Meditate on the Truth only. Give your selfless service to Truth only. Truth is changeless; Truth is *Brahman*, *atman*, *maha purusha*, Devi, Krishna, Siva, Jesus, or whatever name it may be. All paths lead only to *satya,* Truth. This is so pure. Have Truth, one hundred percent Truth in your life, children. Do not tell lies under any circumstances. We have committed so many mistakes with our tongue only. So much pollution exists because our mind is not pure; our words are also impure. We injure others' feelings for very little reason. This unnecessary hurting of others is due to our ego and illusion.

There are so many dark forces in our lives. Children, keep a beautiful light in your heart, the light of Self-illumination. There is a big light in our heart—*Sivagni*.

There are so many *agnis,* fires. There are five types of fire, including lust and anger. Our anger, *krodhagni,* is more powerful than fire. But only one fire is auspicious and that is *Sivagni.*

Attain God-Realization through meditation. From this mortal frame meditation leads you to immortality. In that state you attain infinite joy. There are no words to describe that state. Experience that state. The *Bhagavad Gita* is not just a book in which you can read *shlokas* to keep and worship with flowers. You must follow its precepts of total surrender, pure devotion, knowledge and selfless service.

Our life is a beautiful temple for the divine soul. In this beautiful temple, Self-illumination is the main idol. There are four pillars in this temple. They are compassion, Truth, wisdom and righteousness. In this beautiful temple of the soul, there is an entrance gate, and that is selfless service. Selfless service towards all beings is the greatest *yoga* with which to merge with the Eternal. Children, merge with the Eternal. Give your selfless service. Where the self is one hundred percent *less*, there only is real service—one hundred percent service. So always remain behind the curtain and give your service to this universe. This world is your Self only. Love this world. Love all beings in the world. Have cosmic love in your heart. Develop, evolve and elevate yourself to the highest peak of Realization, that is, pure consciousness.

So, my dear children, my immortal babies, meditate! Have inner vision. Beautify your inner life with pure devotion, with wisdom. Where there is wisdom, there only is *dharma*. Have *dharma* in your life, children. Let *dharma* only lead your entire life. Be always in Truth and meditate on the Truth. Truth only is the real salvation. So, children, practice truth. Under no circumstances should you lose Truth. Whoever loses Truth loses everything, everything in his life. On the other hand, he who has Truth in his life has everything.

Children, meditate and elevate yourselves to the highest peak of *turiya,* which is the land of bliss. The main entrance to this land of bliss is wisdom. Have pure wisdom. Read the *Bhagavad Gita* daily and practice it in your life. Practice—rather than just learning and talking about divine messages—is very important. What value do words contain, children? Be a practical person in your life. Without practice these words are merely wasteful. There is no taste at all. If we practice, we attain silence, because the language of Lord Siva is silence. There are innumerable languages. God is not partial toward any country or any language. But God's language is absolute silence. So attain the absolute highest spirit. That is Amma's only wish for Her children.

Hari Om Tat Sat

Los Angeles *26 April 1997*

ॐ

MOTHER HELPS YOU UP THE LADDER OF DHARMA

Sindhūrāruna vigrahām trinayanām
Mañikya mauli sphurat...

Amma's Discourse [translated from Telugu]:

Embodiments of Divine Bliss,

Amma conveys her sincere motherly love to you all. Yesterday we talked about the superficial meanings of some of the *mantras* in *Lalita Sahasranama.* Divinity is not something to be talked about. Many times when I talk like this I find it meaningless and wonder why we are talking about it at all. The reason being that to verbalize feelings that are beyond expression seems unnatural. Its true nature or its reality diminishes. However, since such a marvelous and infinite state is unattainable, that very form of Brahma (*Brahma svarupa*) descends in the form of Rama, Krishna and Buddha *avataras* and elevates humans to that level.

Let us consider an example in this connection. A mother is watching her child play in the playground below. After a while, the child falls and cries. The mother who is watching does not ask the child to get up but comes running herself to pick up the child. The child who was playing, fell to the ground and hurt himself, lost blood, and cried. Looking at this scene, Mother took pity on him and that is why, in order to save him, She came all the way. She had to come.

Amma [sings a poetic line in Telugu] :

Veda sikharamula nilabadi bhaktulu
piluvaga davvuna parigedi

Mother is somewhere beyond the *Vedas* and yet She has to come down from that peak for the child can never climb up to that level. It is impossible. She takes him up the ladder of *dharma* step by step. In ancient India, many knowledgeable *rishis* stumbled on their path with regards to the matter of *dharma* and *adharma*. This is not a matter to be taken lightly. The point here is that when the great *rishis* themselves fell down the ladder by a step or two, what can one say about the humans in this *Kali yuga?*

When there is intense devotion in the heart one becomes like Hanumana and remains in absolute silence. That is sweet devotion or *madhura bhakti*. Even *madhuram* is not a befitting word to describe its sweetness. If you think it is as sweet as honey, then one can say it is sweeter than even honey. It is sweeter than *amrita,* ambrosia, for there is death for *devatas* even after they have taken *amrita*. For one who has consumed the superbly excellent *amrita* of *bhakti*, there is no death. His heart shines unabatedly with the splendor of *atma bhakti*. The Self gives him a sort of inner freedom. The radiant devotion illumines that unique light of knowledge in the whole heart and sets one on that shining *sumarga*, that good path.

It is said in the *Lalita Sahasranama* that Mother Divine is Krodhakar ankushojjvala. It is also said in the *Bhagavad Gita* that anger is the gateway to hell. So are infatuation and greed. These are the three doors to hell. In order to close these doors, it is said in the *Lalita Sahasranama* that Divine Mother removes the worldly attachments by drawing the child with the noose of love. Like beams of moonlight she showers rays of compassion from her eyes. Being completely drenched in that rain of compassion, the devotee forgets himself. A *yogi* forgets himself in *samadhi*. However, devotees like the *gopikas* in this condition forget themselves even while awake. That is to say they forget themselves even in the *jagrat avastha,* the waking state. They are always in a state of pure consciousness.

I hope you now understand that the *yogi* forgets himself during the experience of *samadhi*. However, when devotion wells up within a devotee who has *ujjvala bhakti*, radiant devotion, *ananya bhakti* as spoken of in the *Bhagavad Gita*—not ordinary *bhakti* mind you but *ananya bhakti*—tears of joy overflow from such a devotee.

Rama went to Shabari; Shabari did not go to Rama. Krishna went to Kubja and others; they did not go to Krishna. Jesus also went to his devotees even when mud was being hurled at him. Likewise, many great saints from the East have come here and sanctified this land. Did they come because you called them? Why did they come? They bore all the hardships of traveling through all the airports in the world out of their love and responsibility toward all beings in this part of the world.

The *Lalita Sahasranama* is a composition of love that depicts that unique responsibility of a Mother. Just as you know the effect of collecting all the honey at one place, it makes clear to us the responsibility of God toward the world and how God descended in many forms. No faults are visible in that love. It is only when that love decreases that one finds faults. When do you find fault? I don't find faults in you. However, the day my love for you decreases I will say, "you did this wrong and you did that wrong." Even when millions of mistakes have been committed, the *Vedas* say, there may be an evil son but there cannot be an evil mother. A child is constantly making mistakes, but a mother's heart is full of forgiveness.

What is forgiveness? Forgiveness is *tapas*, forgiveness is Truth, forgiveness is Knowledge, forgiveness is infinite love, forgiveness is infinite freedom of the soul (*akhanda atma svatantryam*). Those who have this freedom, have forgiveness. Forgiveness is said to be divine. When there is no forgiveness, then the heart becomes dry and one becomes a *rakshasa*, a demon.

When in the mother's womb, you take the flesh and blood of the mother and you are born. But once you have been born into this world, it is said that if you shed blood on this earth, you will become a demon. Your birth mother has transformed her blood into milk (*ksheeram*) and made it like ambrosia and given it to you. She has carried you in her womb for nine months. Similarly, Bhudevi, the Goddess Mother Earth carries you for ninety years. However, we are polluting this earth with our thoughts.

One of the *mantras* in the *Lalita Sahasranama* is Manonmani. Make your mind *unmani,* detached. When the mind becomes inward and goes beyond the stages of *dhyana,* meditation, *dhyatri*, meditator and *dhyeya*, the object of meditation, when it goes beyond the limits of *dharma* and *adharma* and unites Siva and Shakti, one attains the freeing knowledge of the soul. One experiences the divine feeling that one's self is everything in the universe. Therefore, the ancient divine *dharma* of India is like a great fertile land of millions of acres. If there was only one narrow path leading to that field, then there would be a traffic jam. That is why many pathways to the field have been kept open wherever possible so that everyone can enter the field via their desired pathway. Many have traveled this path by performing *yajnas*, while some have done *vratas* (fasts) and others have treaded the paths of *bhakti*, *jnana* and *dhyana,* among many others.

Five thousand years ago, divinity descended in the form of *Krishna avatara,* the incarnation of Lord Krishna, from the infinite womb of the cosmic lotus (*akhanda mainatuvanti sarasija garbhandam*) because the tree of *dharma* was wilting. He came to revive that tree of *dharma*.

When two children of Mother are hitting each other, what does Mother do? She comes and scolds the child who is hurting the other, and asks, "Why are you beating your brother?" All children in this world are equal in the eyes of God. Even if you do not love divinity, divinity has love for you.

God is not concerned with how many songs of devotion you are singing in praise of Him, but whether or not you are living in righteousness. God is not concerned with whether you are doing a lot of *puja* but He is waiting to see with what kind of inner heart you are praying. You may say you have been praying five hours or meditating ten hours but if you have not had even five seconds of concentration then all that is a waste. However, if you have concentration for even a fraction of a second and prayed to God with true devotion, then He will receive your prayers. We should practice that kind of devotion.

If you chant the *Lalita Sahasranama* everyday, then your heart will become softer than butter. I have peeped into the hearts of millions of people in India and am surprised to see their extraordinary devotion. They have such sweet sublime devotion. Then I wonder where they got such beautiful devotion. The *rishis* led *dharmic* lives in those ancient times. But even today in this age of *Kali yuga*, there are people in India with so much humility who are at the same time leading ordinary lives with glorious righteousness. They are radiating a beautiful shining inner heart with tender devotion. They are willing to sacrifice their lives but will not budge even a step from their moral character. They are willing to give up food and their lives for *dharma.* Many an Indian is ready to kill himself rather than live without *dharma*.

Blissful souls! May you conduct your lives with such *dharma!* You may live for only a short time and may die tomorrow and leave this body. It does not matter. However, perform at least one good action in your life. There is no meaning in living for ten years, just expanding your stomach and not doing even a single useful deed. A life without *dharma* is of no use. We have not come into this world just for these worldly pleasures pertaining to the body. We have come to serve the lotus feet of the Lord and to make this body His temple. We have come to sanctify every atom in our body with His sacred divine name, *Omkara*.

Prati roma kupam shabda Brahmam kavali

"The whole body should resound with the sound of Brahman." We have to practice devotion to that extent.

We should have a clear perception of knowledge. When our spirituality is raw and without maturity, then the feelings are dry and not good. No matter what it may be, when there is anger, nothing shines. There is a big fat ego behind it which is like a huge fearful lion. Sometimes when one frolics with a lion for a while, it could suddenly get enraged. Similarly, we could be practicing *bhakti* but the lion called the ego can surface enraged at any time. The better thing to do would be to send away this ego permanently. Therefore, when anger is gone, everything else is gone. When ego leaves our heart, everything will be auspicious. When you have the feeling of "I," "me,"and "my," then there is no hope. This is clearly stated in the *Lalita Sahasranama*. The *Lalita Sahasranama* is *Advaitamrita varshini*. It showers us with the bliss of *advaita*, nonduality. It is not something composed by anyone on this earth.

The eight powers or *shaktis* of *Devi* have sung this *Lalita Sahasranama*. Brahma and other Gods have also extolled it. That is why he for whom this is the last birth, is illumined by the gems within the *Sahasranama* and the meaning of the *mantras* contained therein. He attains the knowledge of nonduality and experiences this infinite consciousness as an ocean. This *akhanda chaitanya* is an infinite ocean. In this ocean of infinite consciousness, Jagat Janani, the galaxies are like small atoms. The millions of galaxies in this ocean are like mere atoms!

Just as you watch pictures on the television screen, consider an example of a picture on a screen where the screen is black on one side and white on the other. There are a few images on this screen or curtain. Those images represent the millions of beings in this world. All these images may look very big to you but in the play of the infinite consciousness of God, they are very small—they play a very small part—so small and insignificant that they are hardly visible to the naked eye. Therefore, why have this ego? Let us not have this ego for it is harmful. Let us pray for this ego to leave us permanently even before we pray for Knowledge or Self-Realization: "We are so puffed up with pride at the thought of our qualifications and the few dollars we have. We think we know a lot about the *Vedas*. What do we know Amma? We are behaving so unintelligently and foolishly. Forgive us Amma. Give us Knowledge and rescue us. We have been with You for so many lifetimes. However, we are unable to recognize the Truth and who You actually are." To know the Truth you have to open your third eye and only then can you witness the Truth.

What is Truth? I was born even before Truth. It is the sole and root support for everything in this world. I am of the form of time in its three aspects, (*kalatraya svarupa*). I am the *atma* and *Brahmamayi*. I am *mangala karamaina chaitanyanni nenu,* the consciousness that is all auspiciousness and the support for all that is existent. Thus this life is a total waste when we are unable to witness the Truth of

Brahma that is *vedatita, jnatita* and *sarvatita* (beyond the *Vedas*, knowledge and everything).

Just eating, sleeping, speaking useless words and enacting the same roles in the same old play, you are constantly roaming here and there. Only when you illumine the light of Truth in your heart that you will witness that infinite resplendent one and only Brahma in the whole creation everywhere. You will realize that splendid state wherein you will feel "I am Brahma present in everything. There is nothing different from me in this whole world."

Ekamevadvitīyam Brahma Nanyad asti akincanaḥ

You must have already realized that this statement of *Sanatana Dharma* from the *Vedas* was spoken in India many billions of years ago!

Blissful souls! It is a boon to be able to live your life even for a second in the best possible way. It is useless to live a life of a thousand years if it is not of service to others, without the knowledge of the Self and freedom of the self. Even if you live for only a second, it is Amma's heartfelt wish that you should live your life in the best way with a heart that is beautiful, without ego. Lead a life full of Knowledge and with the aroma of peace enhancing the fragrance of the society in this world.

Hari Om Tat Sat

Los Angeles — *26 April 1997*

ॐ

BE ALWAYS IN ETERNAL DHARMA

Swamiji: *Jai Karunamayi!* On this pleasant evening, I welcome all of Amma's most beloved children for Amma's final discourse in Los Angeles. Amma always says that this is not the end but the beginning, because Amma is always with you. Amma always tells us, "Wherever I may be, I am always with you." We can be with Amma only in meditation.

Today is a memorable day. From early morning, from 7 a.m. until now, we have been having many beautiful programs. We were able to spend most of this time in Amma's divine presence. We had two rounds of meditation and then Amma talked to us about the *chakras* in the body. Later we had the *homa*, a fire ceremony. Many of those who attended have been telling me that it was a wonderful experience.

Whether it is meditation, a discourse, a *homa,* or any other form of worship, the energy and vibrations that flow from Amma's sacred feet are unexplainable. Many devotees have experienced this in meditation. Many people come to Amma with their problems, the main one being that they cannot sit in meditation for long periods. With Amma's blessings, however, today they were able to sit in meditation for several hours! Amma was saying this morning that we need a lot of practice in meditation, we need regular *sadhana*. *Sadhana* is extremely important. Amma often asks the question, "Who is your real friend?" The answer is: "*Sadhana* or regular practice is your true friend."

The *Saraswati mantra* meditation that we have learned from Amma is Her greatest blessing, but we need to practice it regularly. For example, sitting in a room full of medical textbooks will not make us doctors; we have to study the books. Some people may think, "Why must we do *sadhana?* Can't we get *jnana* just by listening to discourses and reading books?" That is why Amma gave an example and said that no one can become a physician just by looking at medical books. You have to study them, go to schools, attend colleges, practice on patients, and then only will you become a doctor.

Similarly, you cannot become a singer just by thinking about music or reading some books. You have to practice singing. The same thing applies to dance. No one can become a dancer simply by looking at pictures of dance poses or by watching dancers. For any art we need both study and practice.

Amma not only teaches us meditation, She makes us sit in front of Her and practice meditation. It is very important to meditate in Amma's presence. Amma designs meditation retreats in such a way that we are made to meditate for ten, twelve or even fourteen hours in one day. There are different kinds of retreats for aspirants depending on their ability. The rounds of meditation will be for one hour, one-and-a-half hours or two hours duration.

Every Sunday there is a meditation retreat in Amma's *ashram* in Bangalore and people meditate for twelve hours, starting at 3.30 a.m., the auspicious *Brahmi muhurta.* However, in this country it is difficult for you to do this because of the climatic conditions and other circumstances. The best time for meditation is during the *Brahmi muhurta,* between 3.30 and 4.30 a.m., but here in the western countries, Amma is giving an exemption. She is saying that you can meditate before sunrise, between 5 and 6 a.m.

However, it is important to meditate during the *Brahmi muhurta* on auspicious days such as the full moon day or on festivals like Christmas, *Ugadi*, *Dipavali*, Easter, New Year's day or your own birthday—any day that you feel is auspicious.

Amma is saying that one hour of meditation during the *Brahmi muhurta* is equivalent to one year of meditation—one whole long year. One full year! Amma has given an explanation for this: Our bodies are made of the *pancha maha bhutas,* the five elements. The vibrations of the rays from all the planets fall on our bodies and exert a strong influence on our thoughts and actions. However, during the *Brahmi muhurta* these rays do not affect us, because the *Brahmi muhurta* is cosmic time and only cosmic rays are flowing at this time. That is why it is the ideal time for meditation. We need to meditate daily for hours at a time and then only will we be connected to Godly consciousness. *Jai Karunamayi!*

Amma's Discourse:

Ātmā tvam Girijā matiḥ sahacarāḥ
Prāṇāḥ śarīram gṛham...

Om Śri Rāma Rāmeti Rāmeti...

Om śaraṇāgata dīnārta paritrāṇa parāyaṇe
Sarvasyārti hare Devī Nārāyaṇī namōstute

Om praṇatānāma prasīdasya
Devī viśvārti hārinī
Trailokya vāsinām
iti lokānām varadā bhavām

Embodiments of Divine Souls, Amma's Most Beloved Children,

This morning we had two hours of meditation. A day will come when we will meditate for twenty hours per day, forgetting our body, mind and everything in this world. Go beyond this world and sit in meditation for even twenty-four hours every day—that day must come in your life. Children, pray for that great day.

To meditate is to be in our real Self. Meditation purifies our inner self, it purifies the body and mind. Deeds performed in innumerable past births form our *samskaras* and *vasanas*. Some of these are good, others bad. Due to our negative *samskaras* we poison our lives with our own hands—we have so much anger, so much jealousy towards others and so many negative attitudes in our life.

Trividham narakasyedam dvāram nāśanam ātmanaḥ

There are three gates to hell. The first is anger, lust is the second, and desire the third. Righteousness is the entrance gate to bliss, purity and wisdom. So children, do not walk that path of lust, anger and desire. We have innumerable exits on the roads in this country. If you miss your exit, you go in the wrong direction and have to come all the way back. If we take wrong exits, we miss our programs and appointments, and we get so angry and frustrated because so much time is wasted. So do not miss your exits at any time, children. Be careful and stay on the right path. Righteousness, truth and wisdom are your exits. If there is anger, lust, jealousy, greed, know immediately that this is not your exit. If you take these exits, you will undoubtedly miss your path.

Trividham narakasyedam dvāram....

Narakam means hell. Anger is very bad. Because of anger we have *aham*, ego; because of egotism, selfishness; because of selfishness, inner darkness. We have so much darkness, so much ignorance in our life. There is no light, no richness, and no inner happiness in our life. So be always in righteousness, *dharma*; be always in real *dharma*. Let *dharma* rule your entire life.

What is *dharma?* When a teacher gives his knowledge in full to all his students without any partiality, that is *dharma.* When we travel on roads, we have to follow traffic rules—that is *dharma. Dharma* in the family, in the office, in our worldly life, in our inner life—there must be *dharma* everywhere. Let *dharma* only rule your entire life. If you have *dharma*, you have no fear; if you deviate from *dharma*, you are always in fear—you are afraid of your own shadow. So, my dear children, be always in that true *dharma*, be always in Truth only, be always in real spirituality. Do not miss your exits under any circumstances, be very careful in life. You have already lost forty years, fifty years, you have only limited time now, so try to understand the value of time, meditate and continue your spiritual practices.

Be in your own belief—Amma never wants to erase your notes. Keep your notes, proceed in your path, but Amma expects you to elevate from your present level. Expand, elevate, and if you love someone, develop that love more and more and have divine love. From that divine love elevate to cosmic love.

Love is the nature of the soul, and we have *akshaya,* inexhaustible and imperishable love in our heart. Our heart is more vast than the sky. The sky is very limited. Our heart is more pervasive than the sky, it is deeper than the ocean. Our heart is sweeter than honey, more tender than butter, whiter than milk and more fragrant than jasmine—it is impossible to describe the sweetness of the heart. The heart is divinity, spirit. So children, be always in *dharma*, meditate, meditate, and purify each and every cell of your body with pure, one hundred percent devotion.

Devotion is the main foundation of a spiritual life. Without devotion knowledge is not sweet. Ordinary knowledge about the world, talking about unimportant, mundane matters may feel good to listen to but a feeling of emptiness remains within. We ourselves have doubts whether our actions are right or wrong. If we have devotion there are no doubts at all, we know we are right because devotion is so pure, devotion is so sweet, devotion beautifies our entire life. In one hundred percent devotion, we have contentment. Without contentment there is no devotion at all. So, children, have contentment, one hundred percent contentment, and be mentally detached.

Physical renunciation is not important; mental renunciation is very important. If we love God deeply, we renounce everything in this world and have attachment only to divinity. We love everything in this world because we see divinity in everything. That becomes our vision. So develop pure devotion in your heart, develop an attachment to God in your heart. Then you will have *jnana,* divine knowledge, and *vairagya,* detachment.

Children, be real spiritual aspirants and wear the beautiful ornaments of kindness and compassion. Go beyond compassion also, and have forgiveness in your life. Forgiveness is *tapas*, forgiveness is divine, forgiveness is spirit, so have forgiveness and love everyone—not only your family members, not only the people of your own country. Love the entire universe, not only mankind—love the bird kingdom, the animal kingdom—love every creature in this world. That is your responsibility—to see divinity in everything in this world, even in mud particles. In India, when we lie down on Mother Earth in the forests or some holy places, we can hear the beautiful vibrations of the *Vedas* in every particle! In Tanjore, in Thiruvayyur, Thyagaraja Swami sang so many divine *kirtanas.* Even the dust particles of that holy land still sing that music. We can hear it if we have the heart to listen.

The entire universe is filled with divine vibrations. Open your hearts, children, and listen to the music of God, that is silence. When we go to the seashore, we can hear the music of the ocean. Even in deserts, there is music—the wind blows with the sound of *Om*.

Once when we were in Kashmir, where there are many beautiful mountains—such as Perinaga, Shesha naga, and Antara naga, all named after snakes—when we were near the Sesha naga, which has been named after Adi Sesha, the thousand-headed serpent, we sang some songs in *Desha raga*. *Desha* is a very beautiful *raga*. When we opened our eyes the entire mountain seemed to tremble—while listening to the *Desha raga* the whole mountain moved like a snake!

Children, if we have a sensitive and true heart, we are able to listen to the music of the stars, the oceans, the deserts, even the tiniest particles of mud. When we see the mountains, they appear to be in meditation, deep meditation. All the planets rotate continuously and give light to this world, and they are in absolute silence. The oceans are in silence and Mother Earth is in silence. They all seem to be in meditation. Only mankind is talking too much. We commit so many mistakes with our tongue.

That is why we need the *Saraswati mantra*. The *Bible* and the *Bhagavad Gita* are universal holy scriptures. In the same way, the *Saraswati mantra* is also universal. When we repeat it, our negative words are controlled. Some people have a lot of contentment and their words are very powerful. They sparkle like jewels and touch our hearts. Other people have no contentment and are always criticizing others. When we talk to them, we also become restless and commit mistakes with our tongue. So, babies, never behave like that. Chant the *Saraswati mantra*. It immediately removes all the negativity from our hearts, our minds and our tongues. We get a balanced state of mind, because it removes all our unnecessary emotions.

It is not good to be too emotional. If you are too emotional, your friendships are not constant. Be very careful with your friends. When you are balanced, your friendship is constant and lasts to the end of your life. The *Saraswati mantra* gives great balance in our life, in our thoughts, in our words and in our deeds. Saraswati is divine knowledge, elixir. Saraswati reveals Herself in our words as one hundred percent contentment, purity, wisdom and truth. Then the words you speak are not really your words—they all come from Truth, from Saraswati only.

Even if you have no knowledge of the *Vedas*, *Upanishads*, *Bible* or other sacred scriptures, you receive that knowledge when you meditate on Saraswati. You get a connection with divinity. The *Saraswati mantra* is like a telephone operator. When you meditate correctly with this *mantra,* you immediately get a connection with, and receive messages from, Divine Mother Saraswati, no doubt.

Never commit mistakes with the tongue. Purify your heart and thoughts, divinize your thoughts, have contentment in your mind and heart. Meditate for at least five to ten minutes daily. If you do not have even five minutes, just repeat the *mantra* with pure and true devotion for a few minutes while driving.

The *Maha Mrityunjaya mantra,* the healing *mantra*, is also universal. There are innumerable healing *mantras* in the *Vedas*, particularly *Rudra parayana.* An American girl, a seeker, is really amazing. She chants the *Namakam, Chamakam,* the whole *Rudram* daily, as well as the *Khadga mala* and the *Lalita Sahasranama.* So many children worship Divine Mother, and many others chant the *Gayatri mantra.* All these are boons not from this birth but from the good deeds of innumerable past births. These children were born in India in the highest spiritual families in previous lives. That is why in this birth they are able to chant the

Saraswati mantra, the *Maha Mrityunjaya mantra* and the *Lalita Sahasranama.* This is God's grace. So my babies, beautify your inner life with true devotion, meditate on the Truth and attain Self-illumination.

Saraswati is Truth; Saraswati is very powerful. Truth is very, very powerful, no doubt. So follow only the truth. Let *dharma* alone rule your entire life. Be a good wife, be a good husband, be a good father, be a good child, be a good teacher, be a good doctor, be a good citizen—be good in every aspect of life. Honesty is true wisdom—where there is honesty there only is real wisdom. So children, be always in honesty. Meditate for purification.

Devotion purifies our negative thoughts and words, controls our tendency to criticize, and removes all low thinking and feelings. In devotion we elevate ourselves, feel great contentment, and have pure love towards all beings. If you do not have the heart to give love to your neighbors, how can you give your love to the entire world like Jesus or Buddha? They embraced this whole world not with their arms, not physically, but with their divine love. Unseen divine hands embrace the entire cosmos. Open your eyes and see how divinity beautifies this vast universe.

When we open our third eye, we see how much service all the planets give to this universe. They are in absolute silence and seem to be in meditation. The oceans, mountains, the two thousand year-old redwood trees of California—all nature is in meditation. When we observe nature, when we love nature, our heart becomes so wise. Mother Nature gives you so much. You never give Mother anything in return. It is your responsibility to love Mother Nature and give something to the world in the form of service. The essence of human life is selfless service. Spirituality and meditation are for personal purification, but the essence of human life is to give selfless service to all beings in this universe and to merge with the Eternal.

So children, embodiments of *dharma,* embodiments of eternal souls, you are not the physical body, you are eternal, you are the Soul! Be always in eternal *dharma. Dharma* is very, very powerful—the very sound of the word *dharma* is so sweet! Be always in *dharma*, be always in Truth, be always in wisdom—that is your Amma's only wish—be always in wisdom.

Cultivate mental renunciation, for without mental renunciation we are very childish—even if we are ninety years old, we are very childish, we have no knowledge. So let *dharma* alone rule each and every minute of your entire life and purify your inner self with the the fire of divinity. Attain the eternal *dharma*, attain the *Atman,* the real Spirit, and touch the bliss, taste the bliss!

Children, practice meditation every morning for at least ten to fifteen minutes. Walk your own path, proceed in your own belief. If you have no *mantra*, meditate with the *Saraswati mantra.* If you have another *mantra,* meditate with your own *mantra*, and if you have belief in the *Saraswati mantra*, meditate with the *Saraswati mantra* also. If you want to meditate with your own *mantra* as well as the *Saraswati mantra,* there is no problem. First meditate with your *Guru mantra*, your main *mantra,* do all your spiritual practices, and add the *Saraswati mantra*.

How many times you repeat this *mantra* depends on your interest. If you have time repeat it a hundred and eight times. There is a reason for this: There are seventy two thousand nerves in our body, and there are a hundred and eight important junctions in these nerves which are connected to the seven *chakras.* The main hundred and eight junction points are in the nervous system of the brain. When we repeat any *mantra,* we say the *Om mantra* before it. The *Om mantra* is the main fuse *mantra.* For instance, if we say, *"Sri Rama"* without the *Om mantra,* there is some power; but if we say, "*Om Sri Rama,*" there is a hundred percent power. So when we add *Om* at the beginning of a *mantra*, it becomes very powerful.

Saraswati is *nada*, sound. She is all sounds—bird sounds, animal sounds, the ocean sound, planet sounds, and all musical sounds, both vocal and instrumental. Saraswati is all the languages, and She is also absolute silence. Maha Lakshmi is *kala*, light. "*Maha*" means "great," "Sri" means "lighting," so "Maha Lakshmi" means "the greatest lighting, Self-illumination." Maha Lakshmi has so many forms—She is in grains and edibles such as vegetables, fruits and seeds as Dhanya Lakshmi, and She is Santana Lakshmi, the wealth of children. As Dhana Lakshmi, She is money, as Saubhagya Lakshmi, auspiciousness, as Shanti Lakshmi, peace, as Arogya Lakshmi, health—good health is also wealth.

There are so many forms of Lakshmi in our life: Your wife is your Lakshmi without a crown. She is your energy. Great souls like Shankaracharya, Vivekananda and other holy persons were able to walk alone in life. However, you do not have the capacity to be alone in this world, so God has given you the boon of a husband or wife. Each is the energy of the other, so do not criticize each other. Both of you should always be in *sattva.* If you are in *rajas* and *tamas,* there will be criticisms and quarrels. If both are in *sattva*, both are in *dharma* and both are in truth, there will be no quarrels or misunderstandings at all. If your family life is peaceful and happy, if you have a hundred percent contentment and peace, it is easy to walk very smoothly on the path of *dharma* and attain God-Realization.

Family life is necessary for you because you are not able to live alone in this world, you need so much mental support. You need each other, so do not criticize each other and do not quarrel. The vibrations in the home are disturbed by quarrels and harsh words. But if we always play some beautiful divine songs, chant *mantras* and perform worship, the vibrations in our home become very pure, powerful and peaceful. Here in this church, the vibrations are very, very powerful, very peaceful. When we enter the church we get into a peaceful, silent mood because so many holy persons have prayed here, and the atmosphere has been purified and beautified by spiritual practices.

In the home the vibrations are different. Try to keep good vibrations in the home always. In a music room full of instruments such as *vinas* and *sitars,* with images of Saraswati and Nataraja, the walls, windows, ceiling, and even the floor—every part of the room—seem to sing! This is because there are only musical vibrations in the room—the vibrations of melodious *ragas* such as the *Revati raga*, *Kalyani raga*, *Mohana Kalyani*—beautiful *ragas*. Divine Mother loves all these *ragas*.

When we criticize others using harsh and mean words, the negative vibrations are recorded in the atmosphere. The room may have beautiful decorations, but there is no peace in the atmosphere. No matter how you arrange it, there will be no peace. In a small and simple hermitage, however, we have so much contentment. This is because the *Lalita Sahasranama,* or the *Mritunjaya mantra,* or the *Saraswati mantra,* or the *Om mantra,* or the *Narayana mantra*, or the *Vishnu Sahasranama*, or some spiritual book such as the *Bhagavad Gita* or the *Bible* are always being chanted there, and the whole atmosphere is full of sacred vibrations.

Keep a small room for your meditation, and whenever you are very tired, go to that room, sit in the lap of God in silence, and pray to God for peace: "O Lord, give me peace, I am so tired. I am so tired in this life. For a little happiness, I am working, working, working. I want some happiness, but I get so tired working continuously. What is my ambition, just earning money?" Money is important in this world, but *dharma* is different, it is much more important. Money can never give us contentment, but *dharma*, spirit, wisdom and truth will give us lasting contentment and peace. Cultivate contentment in your life.

My dear children, we must have some values, for without values life is meaningless. If I tell you in words, "I love you so much," I limit my love. There are no words to express my feelings towards you; and the same applies to you. How can you express your love for Amma in words? It is not possible. We have a soul connection—it is not a worldly friendship or a blood relationship, it is beyond this world. There are no words to express this feeling in any language in this world. So children, we need good values in life. We need devotional values, spiritual values, family values, societal values—so many different kinds of values.

If we all have one *sankalpa*, one firm resolve, that there should be no wars in this world, our combined *sankalpa* will destroy the thoughts of all those people who thirst for war. If you reinforce the power of your combined *sankalpa* with the *Gayatri mantra* or the *Saraswati mantra*, it becomes extremely powerful. Negative thoughts are powerful, no doubt, but the power of your combined *sankalpa* will go directly to the negative thoughts and destroy them. We should chant "*Lokah samastah sukhino bhavantu*" every day for the peace in the world, because wars are not good. Thousands and thousands of people are killed, leaving countless families in tears. How many mothers, wives and children are left helpless—it is very sad. Never allow wars. Stop wars by the power of your meditation.

In the olden days, people had beautiful feelings. In ancient *vedic* times, the *rishis* collected *darbha* grass for fire sacrifices according to *Sanatana Dharma,* and performed *yajnas* for universal welfare. These *rishis* had young disciples whom they loved more than their own children. They gave food to the children under their care first and then to their own children. We do the same thing even now in our *ashram.* The people who help in the *ashram* eat only after all visitors have been fed; and Amma eats last of all. We wait for everyone to finish, that is our culture, and sometimes we get to eat only at five or six in the evening. This is not a good time for taking one's first meal, so sometimes we do not eat at all. Only when we ourselves have experienced hunger can we understand another's hunger.

So children, these are very, very beautiful feelings—I cannot express them in words. We must maintain these values in every moment of our life: Give first preference to society, and second to the family. Without society and family values, our life has no value—it is a hundred percent empty. If we live only in selfishness, really we are in death, for selfishness is death.

Selflessness is one hundred percent elixir. One who has selflessness in his heart has so much inner beauty; he does not need any spiritual practice. Spiritual practices are for those who are selfish and egotistic and want to elevate to the selfless state. If we already have selflessness in our heart there is no need to study the *Vedas*, perform *yajnas* or chant *mantras.* We chant *mantras* and meditate to remove the pollution in our heart.

It is very easy to talk about *advaita,* but very difficult to practice it. Be a real *advaitin*, have *Brahmic* awareness in your life and attain God-Realization.

Many children ask Amma, "How is it possible to sit in meditation for a long time?" *Pranayama* is the key to meditation; without *pranayama* there is no meditation. *Pranayama* is regulation of the breath, and it helps us concentrate. We are able to sit in meditation for a long duration, for even one to two hours. *Pranayama* gives our body one hundred percent oxygen, one hundred percent concentration in meditation, balance of mind, self-confidence, willpower and self-respect. We need self-respect because we live in society. Without self-respect, life has no meaning. So have self-respect and give respect to others also—that is your responsibility. Do not talk in a low manner even to a small child. To give respect and take respect from others is a very beautiful and cultured way to behave.

Children, culture and civilization do not mean wearing beautiful clothes. Civilization means having contentment in our heart, living in truth, liberation from the six inner natures, and elevation to the highest peak of wisdom. So be truly civilized in your inner self. Have a rich inner life. Now there is so much poverty in our inner life, so many unnecessary things weigh heavy on the heart. Give up all your burdens and pains to Amma and be free. When you have only one suitcase, it is easy to carry, but if I were to put a hundred suitcases on your head, you would be overburdened. At present you are carrying the *karma* load of innumerable births. In the U.S.A. you have very big trucks, but even these are not large enough for this *karma* load. So give your entire *karma* load to Amma and She will crush it into ash.

Children, do not carry that *karma* load any longer, give all the negativity to Amma, and take love and peace from Amma. Elevate to true wisdom, babies, that is Amma's wish. When I am here, why do you fear? Give me all the negative *karma* load of innumerable births. Even if you have committed thousands and thousands of murders and bad deeds, Amma can take away all your pain and problems. She will remove the load from your head. You are bent over by the heavy load of *karma*. If your mental body is in wisdom and happiness, your entire life blooms with the fragrance of peace. If your mental body is in pain due to *karma* load, you are depressed, and have no mental or physical happiness in your life.

Your social life and birthday parties are very superficial, just saying, "Hello, hello," to each other without any real friendship. Seek a real friendship with the Divine, have a real connection with divinity. In worldly friendships, today we have friends, tomorrow we have none. The only permanent relationship is with God. So be always in peace and in *dharma*, love each and every being in this world, have forgiveness in your heart, and develop purity more and more. Cultivate inner wisdom and inner beauty and share your spiritual feelings with your friends also.

Wake up early everyday and pray. Prayer purifies the inner life. Meditate on the *Saraswati mantra,* your own *mantra* and chant the *Maha Mrityunjaya mantra*, the healing *mantra,* for mental strength and willpower. All the negative energies are controlled by the power of the *Maha Mrityunjaya* healing *mantra,* and you attain immense willpower—you get the strength of hundreds of elephants in your heart.

A *sadhu* who lived in our hills was jealous of Amma. He took a huge rock and threw it from a hill 4,800 feet high. I was sitting in a beautiful place under a *banyan* tree, surrounded by all the deer, birds, monkeys and wild buffalo who were my friends. The jealous *sadhu* threw the big rock from the hill. It was coming down very fast towards Amma, so Amma told it to stop. The stone stopped. It had to stop. If you have willpower you can stop even the planets in their orbits!

[Amma laughs, someone in the audience says "*Jai* Ma!"]

If you say, "Stop, stop! Do not come!" it will stop, it must stop, no doubt. So children, have that kind of willpower, stop all wars—stop wars in the home, wars in the family, wars in society, wars between friends, the wars inside, egotistic wars, world wars, stop all the wars in life. Develop strong willpower and give your selfless service to this universe. Love everyone, have a great heart, a big heart, open your heart and welcome divinity into your life. Beautify your life with the fragrance of divinity and be always in true righteousness.

Hé Ghanaśyāmā Govindā Nanda Mukundā Govindā
Ghana ghana nilā Govindā Tirumala vāsā Govindā
Hṛdaya nivāsā Govindā Sankaṭa haraṇā Govindā
Venkaṭa ramaṇā Govindā

Embodiments of Divine Souls, Amma bestows on all of you Her unconditional motherly love. In the divine *Sanatana Dharma* of ancient India, in some past birth, all of you must have worshipped the lotus feet of Bharata Mata, Mother India, with the golden flowers that bloom in Kubera's garden. You must have worshipped the Divine Mother's lotus feet with precious gems and pearls with unparalleled devotion—that is why you were born in that sacred land. It is said:

Manuṣyatvam mumukṣatvam
Mahā puruṣa samśrayam

"Human birth, intense desire for Self-Realization and proximity to a great soul are very difficult to attain." Human birth is very difficult to attain. There are eighty four *lakh,* that is, eight million four hundred thousand species of living creatures in this world. You have to evolve through all these and have the merit of innumerable births, otherwise it is not possible to attain this human birth; it is so sacred. In addition, in this birth you have had the privilege of being born into an ancient and pure culture, a holy *samskriti*. Your father, mother and grandparents have had devotion to God through many births, and you have inherited some of that devotion. Along with that devotion and culture, you have also been blessed with a good education and good values. Your physical body is given to you by your mother:

Jananī janma bhūmiśca svargādapi garīyasī

"Your Motherland is more glorious than Heaven." You have read in the scriptures that there is nothing holier than the land of your birth or the mother who gave you birth. We have unknowingly preserved caves filled with darkness in our lives—the darkness of anger and other negative qualities.

I have seen many amazing incidents in the forest. In the early days when we went there some of the villagers would get drunk, hide out in the dark and throw stones and dirt on us. However, no matter what they did there was no response from Amma. For example, if I give you a flower and you do not take it, the flower stays with me. Similarly, if anyone scolds you and you do not accept that anger, then it will remain with that person. Do not accept anger. So even when they threw dirt at Amma, Amma did not react and they did not understand this, because people are at different levels.

If a person says angry and harsh words, we must not respond in the same manner, we must not stoop to that level. Speech is Saraswati—She resides in the *vag bijas,* or seed letters. Sometimes when we speak, our words are not well received even by our own people. When our words contain no selfishness and Divine Mother resides in them, then we will be able to do good to all beings. This is the supreme truth.

I used to meditate in a canyon called the Lakshmi Gayatri Gundam. This place is very dear to me. This canyon is like a huge canal in the shape of a serpent. It is very beautiful. The area is a lovely wilderness but people are afraid to go near it because many bears and tigers roam there. These animals do not harm anyone. I used to live there for long periods, and when anyone came to visit me they would bring some cashew nuts and raisins and other food as offerings. Usually I did not eat all of them, so the squirrels, birds, monkeys and other animals used to freely partake of the offerings.

When I did not eat for long periods, the squirrels would notice and, filled with compassion, they would gather some grains and feed me. See how beautiful that is! Where did those squirrels get education? Did they study at Cambridge or Boston University, or in Varanasi? The illiterate squirrels gathered some grains and fed me. When some of the grains fell down, the squirrels picked them up again and put them in my mouth, so that I would have to eat. The squirrel's heart is filled with compassion and unconditional love and it feels, "How can you go without food for so many days?" It wants to give so much in return for a few nuts!

We humans gain all this higher education, we attach some degrees to our names and put on airs of grandeur, but there is no worthiness inside. Our heart is always filled with discontent, our behavior reveals low culture and our words are poor in refinement. We speak impulsively; we do not think before we speak. We do not stop to reflect how our words will affect others.

It is said that the ancient Indian did not believe in the next instant. The future cannot be foreseen by anybody; no one knows what will happen in the next minute. Mother Sita did not know She would have to go the forest, but She had to go there twice. Nobody can escape the path of destiny—even Mother Sita had to follow it. There can be no plan for tomorrow in life. Ignorant people may make plans but they can die prematurely and never reach their goals. So the people of ancient India did not live in the future, they lived in the present moment.

In Gayatri Gundam, I used to feed the colorful birds with some seeds and they would be so happy. They would bathe in the lake in the canyon and sprinkle me with the water. I used to sit among the rocks in the hot sun, meditating, and these birds used to keep me cool by sprinkling water from the lake on me with their wings. Where did this compassion in the birds' hearts come from?

O humanity, what has happened to the compassion in your heart? The *Vedas* declare that you are the embodiment of divinity, purity and immortality, and with all your credentials why have you lost the compassion and humane behavior that even the birds and animals display? Where has this discontentment come from? Why are you burning in this relentless fire of discontent?

It is because of lack of *tyaga*, self-sacrifice. Only *tyaga* will give us *amritatvam,* immortality. When there is no self-sacrifice we are really dead, though still living. When we have self-sacrifice, even after we die we are immortal.

There was a wild buffalo in the forest. You all know, even a tiger is afraid of the wild buffalo. It is so dangerous. I would sit for meditation in the early morning under the shade of a tree, but by noon the hot sun would be shining on me. This buffalo used to stand beside me and keep me in his shadow for hours together. Where did this kindness in this wild animal's heart come from? When you love and respect nature, nature becomes your servant. The love should be real; the vibrations should be pure, not superficial like lip service. When we have true love towards all the birds and animals, all nature, even the *pancha maha bhutas,* the five elements, serve us.

The *sadhu* I talked about earlier became very jealous of Amma, and hurled a huge stone at Her. Amma asked the stone to stop, and it stopped. There was no kindness in the *sadhu's* heart but the stone had compassion, it did not hurt Mother. Man, you drink milk and eat many sweets and good food, why are you making your heart poisonous? Even though they eat seeds and grass, birds and animals have tender affection in their hearts. Where has this compassion come from? Why is only man's heart so hard and full of poison?

You are chanting the *Narayana* and *Rama mantras* with devotion. You are reciting the *Vishnu Sahasranama* which destroys all the five great crimes such as the killing of cows, women, and *brahmins,* as well as adultery, thievery and other horrible sins. You are chanting the *Lalita Sahasranama* and the *Maha Mrityunjaya mantra*, and chanting the divine name of God—why is there no kindness and compassion in your heart? Where has all this discontentment come from? This happens because your prayer comes only from the lips, not from your heart. Prayer is not simply a collection of *mantras.* The *Bhagavad Gita* is not just a scripture for chanting. It is a sacred book which teaches you how to live your life. We have to practice the selfless *karma yoga* of the *Bhagavad Gita* in our daily life. We have to practice selfless service. A little devotion is necessary:

Svalpamasya dharmasya trāyate mahato bhayāt

A tiny spark of fire can cause an immense conflagration. In the same way, kindling even a small fire of *dharma* illuminates our entire life. *Dharma* should be present in all aspects of our life. We have a *dharma* as a wife, a husband, a child, a doctor and a citizen. For example, if a sick patient calls the doctor in the middle of night, it is the *dharma* of the doctor to serve that patient without any irritation or resentment.

There are so many *dharmas* and we have to practice them all. While practicing these *dharmas* man has to make sacrifices. Human birth is divine. It means sacrifice and service to all. Today in our world the value of self-sacrifice has been lost, but in *Sanatana Dharma* sacrifice was given the most important place. To sacrifice all for another's happiness was given the highest status. From this ideal of selfless service only, the great tree of *Sanatana Dharma* took root. Those who maintain this *Sanatana Dharma* in their hearts have wondrous *atma shakti*—fire cannot burn them; the sun cannot wither them; none of the five elements can harm them; a sword cannot cut them; nothing can injure them. If fire touches them, the fire may burn but they will not be burned.

Divine Mother Herself is fire; She can turn anything into ashes. Those who are devoted to Her attain divine, radiant energy. Mother Sita entered the fire to establish Her purity. We should make even our clothes holy by using them to wipe another's tears. If we dry only our own tears we become selfish; if we can share other's pain we will become pure, we will be greatly enlightened. A person who loves all becomes more radiant by sharing his love.

Embodiments of Divine Souls, your *Sanatana Dharma* is very great. Always live in *Sanatana Dharma.*

I cannot describe in words the compassion of the birds and animals in the forest. Even hissing snakes danced to the chanting of God's names. There is a *tapovanam*, a meditation forest called Shivaranjani very deep in the forest—you have to walk twelve or fifteen kilometers to reach it. There is no trail, the path is full of thorns. You get many cuts and bruises walking in that jungle. Nobody ventures there—it is full of snake pits and surrounded by hills. Once I went there and sang very softly, and the hills echoed with the sweet sound of the chants of the *Sivananda Lahari* and the *Saundarya Lahari.* Children, we should not sing only Devi chants, we should always sing Siva and Shakti chants together. So I was singing one verse from the *Sivananda Lahari* and one from the *Saundarya Lahari* alternately, and when I opened my eyes I saw hundreds of snakes dancing in the early dawn!

All birds, animals and reptiles are attuned to music—this is a great truth. Only our hearts are not softened by anything. This hardening of the heart must be due to the effect of *Kali yuga.* Everyone is good, but it is due to the influence of *Kali yuga* that the heart is encased in a hard shell, like the hard unbreakable shell of a tortoise. Our hearts used to melt easily; there was a lot of kindness in our hearts—if a person was in trouble, we would run and help him. Now we are apathetic, we just look the other way—what does it matter to us? If we have to give a *rupee* to anyone we feel resentful; we are not able to give even a little food to anyone.

Why is there so much selfishness? This should never happen to us. It has happened because of the effect of the present *yuga,* otherwise it could never happen, because we are the embodiments of the Divine, we are pure *atma.* We can die tomorrow, so what have we done today? Have we done any good to anyone with our hands? We have used our hands just to eat or to clothe ourselves, or to go shopping for ourselves. We have not given food to a poor child or helped a poor child get an education. If you help a person who is in trouble, I cannot describe in words how much illumination this small service will bring to your heart. As your dearest Mother I am asking you to preserve this wondrous *dharma* in your heart like a precious pearl.

Your mother sometimes nags you by saying, "Son, why are you behaving like this? Why are you roaming aimlessly in life?" When you come home in the evening, sometimes your mother nags you like this and you get irritated with her. In the same way, Amma is feeling disappointed in you and says "Son, what is this? Are you going to be concerned about this contemptible body all the time?"

There is a song in Kannada—those of you who speak Telugu can understand it. It means:

"O mind, how long will you waste your time immersed in this physical body? You are being deceived. Pray to the lotus feet of the Divine Mother with your whole heart. There are millions of galaxies under Divine Mother's lotus feet. Under Her sacred lotus feet are the heavens, and liberation, and everything else. Her lotus feet illuminate all the worlds below."

Śaraṇye lokānām tavahi caraṇaveva nipuṇau

"Your divine feet are the refuge for all the worlds." The *Vedas* declare that one who has taken refuge at the lotus feet of Divine Mother can never be destroyed.

Brahmādiścapi kinkarī kurute

"Even Lord Brahma and all the Gods serve and worship those divine feet." So when you meditate on those sacred lotus feet you cannot be destroyed.

You are unable to meditate because your heart is closed due to the influence of *Kali yuga*. We are suffering because of the ego. Only when our egotism decreases will we be able to meditate. But will you agree if you are told that you are egotistic? You will not listen. Mother tells you gently, yet Her words are not acceptable to you. However, Mother has a responsibility, so She asks,

"Son, are you going to waste this life also? Try to cultivate devotion at least in this birth."

You answer, "But I have devotion!"

"Son, this is not the devotion you need. It is only one percent devotion, you need to develop a thousand percent devotion."

If you have only one *rupee* in your hand and want to travel on a plane, you will not even be allowed to enter the airport. You need a lot more money and the necessary documents to travel on a plane. Similarly, to enter the land of bliss, this one *rupee*-devotion will not suffice; a lot of inner purity is required. Yet you get angry when you are questioned about your inner state. Instead of developing inner purity, you will not even agree that you lack it. You are agreeing now only because Amma Herself is questioning you, because Amma is your Divine Mother. She is nagging you, "What is this my child? Why are you sitting in the darkness of selfishness and ignorance? Open the eyes of selflessness."

Amma [sings in Kannada]**:**

Mosahoda beda manave, manave
Inna daru olliya deya dehamelu āsi iṭtu
Kshaṇa mātra manasāra
Devi pāda smarasida varige
Ashta siddhi nava nidhi gala koduva
sura kāmadhenu nallave
Sundareshana priya Rānī
Lambodara Kumāra Jananī
Harikesha priya vāsinī Nārāyaṇa sodarī

If you meditate on Divine Mother's lotus feet for just one second even without knowledge and devotion, She bestows on you the eight *siddhis* and nine *nidhis*. But do not ask Mother for those things; ask only for one thing—the state of Liberation. This song declares with great clarity that you have been deceived by your mind for innumerable births—do not get deceived this time. The decision is in your hands.

Amma has come to Los Angeles and very gently She has nagged you a lot. She has scolded you a lot—scolded in a tender and loving voice: "What is this my son? Why are you still in the darkness of ignorance? Wake up from this deep sleep! You have to wake up! Throw away all unnecessary baggage, proceed on your eternal journey to the Divine. If you cannot travel alone I will carry you. Come!"

With Her million hands Amma wants to take every one of Her children to the destination of salvation—this is Her heartfelt desire. She is telling you: "O my Child, I will always be with you!"

When you get awareness, you will know that Amma is always with you. She is always behind you. You will hear the beautiful melodious sounds of Her tinkling anklets, you will feel Amma's inhalations and exhalations. She will be involved in your smallest activity. You must attain *Brahmic* awareness in which you will experience the Divine Presence. You cannot understand this now because you are not in that awareness. Meditation leads you to *Brahmic* awareness. That is why you must meditate regularly.

Hari Om Tat Sat

Los Angeles *27 April 1997*

APPENDICES

PRONUNCIATION KEY

All Sanskrit and Non-English words other than Devi's names, proper names and places are in italics throughout the text. Only the words in the shlokas, stotras and kirtanas (i.e., Sanskrit quotations) have been spelled using the International Standard of Sanskrit Transliteration.

KEY TO TRANSLITERATION & PRONUNCIATION

Letter	Sounds Like
a	o in son
ā	a in father
au	ow in now
e	ay in play
i	i in fill or ee in feel
ī	ee in feel
o	o in oh
u	u in full
ū	oo in moon
bh	bh as in scrub hard
c, ch	ch (not k) in chant
ch	ch+h in catch her
cch	ch+ch in watch child
çch	ch in achoo
d, ḍ	th in the, or d in dusk
dh, ḍh	the in breathe, or dh in Godhead
g	g in go (not gel)
gh	gh in big heart
h	h in aha
j	geh in large house
kh	kh in silk hat
n	n in under
ph	ph in up-hill
r	between r and ri
s	s in sun
sh, ś, ṣ	sh in wish
t	between t and d
ṭ	t in ten
th, ṭh	th in light house, th in ant hill
y	y in yard

Stotra, Shloka and Kirtana

The following are listed alphabetically by the first word. Unless indicated otherwise, all verses are in Sanskrit. The International Standard of Sanskrit Transliteration has been used. Please refer to the key on page 361.

Annapūrṇāyai namaḥ *Sadā pūrṇayai namaḥ*	Salutations to the Divine Mother who nourishes all; salutations to Her who is eternally complete.
Anyathā śaraṇam nāsti tvameka śaraṇam mama *Tasmāt kāruṇya bhāvena rakṣya rakṣya Janārdanī*	You are my sole refuge, I have no other. So protect me, protect me, O Janārdani, for Your heart overflows with compassion.
Ātmā tvam Girijā matiḥ sahacarāḥ prāṇāḥ śarīram gṛham *Pūjā te viṣayopa bhoga racanā nidrā samādhi sthitiḥ* *Sañcāraḥ padayoḥ pradakṣiṇā vidhiḥ stotrāṇi sarvā giro* *Yadyat karma karōmi tat tad akhilam* *Śambho tavārādhanam*	In this body, which is Your temple, You dwell as the Self. Divine Mother Girija, Sri Parvati Devi, is the intellect, and the *pranas*, the five forms of vital life breath, my companions. Please consider all my worldly actions to be Your worship, my sleep the state of *samadhi*. With every step I take, I walk reverently around You; every word I say is a hymn in Your praise; all that I do is Your adoration, O benevolent Lord Siva.
Bhadram karṇebhiḥ śruṇuyāma Devāḥ *Bhadram paśyemākṣabhir yajatrāḥ* *Sthirair angaistuṣṭu vāgam sastanūbhir* *Vyaśema Deva hitam yadāyuḥ*	O lord! May we always hear auspicious words with our ears; may we see only good everywhere with our eyes; may we be still and control our speech and speak only good words. May we enjoy a life that is beneficial to the Gods, performing only good actions as long as we live.

Bhavānī tvam dāse mayi vitara driṣtim sakaruṇām *Iti stotum vāncan kathayati Bhavānī tvam iti yaḥ* *Tadaiva tvam tasmai diśasi nija sāyujya padvī* *Mukunda Brahmendra sphuṭa makuṭa nīrājita padām* —*Saundarya Laharī: v.22 Adi Shankaracharya*	Even before Your devotee can utter the word "Bhavani," when he wants to call out to You and beg You for one compassionate glance, You bestow on him the status of oneness with Your divine feet. Your sacred lotus feet are eternally adored by Vishnu, Brahma and Indra, king of all the gods, by placing their dazzling, jeweled diadems on them as they bow down before You.
Brahmānanda maya Maṇidwīpa vāsinī *Bindu trikoṇa Śrī Cakra sanchāriṇī* *Brahma dhyāna sukham dehi Manonmanī*	O Mother, who dwell in Manidwipa, the land of supreme bliss, and in the center of the innermost triangle of the *Sri Chakra*, pervading it, bless me with *Brahmananda*, the supreme bliss of meditation.
Caturbhiḥ Śrī kaṇṭhaiḥ Śiva yuvatibhiḥ pancabhir api *Prabhinnābhiḥ Śambhor navabhir api Mūla Prakṛtibhiḥ* *Catuś catvārimśad vasudala kalāśca tri valaya* *Tri rekhābhiḥ sārdham tava śaraṇa koṇāḥ pariṇatāḥ* —*Saundarya Lahari: v.11 Adi Shakaracharya*	There are four *Sri kanthas*, Siva triangles, and five Siva *yuvatis*, Shakti triangles, which represent the nine manifestations of Mula Prakriti, the basic foundation of the created universe. The *bindu* is in the center. There are two lotuses, one of eight petals, the other of sixteen. There are also three surrounding circles and three lines.This is the form of Your abode, the *Sri Chakra*.
Devī viśva vigrahā bhāvanā mātra santuṣta hṛdayā	Devi, who is embodied in the universe, is satisfied simply by the devotee's desire to offer Her something, even if he is physically unable to do so.

Dharmaḥ rakṣati rakṣatiḥ	Dharma protects, it verily protects.
Dhyānam nirviṣayam manaḥ *Satyam jnānam anantam*	Freeing the mind from thoughts is true meditation. Meditation is Truth and Knowledge, it is eternal.
Dhyāyet padmāsanasthām vikasita vadanām *padma patrāyatākṣīm* *Hemābhām pītavastrām karakalita lasad* *hema padmām varāngīm* *Sarvālankāra yuktām satatam abhayadām* *bhaktanamrām Bhavānīm* *—Dhyāna śloka: Sri Lalitā Sahasranāma.*	O Bhavani, I meditate upon Your beautiful form seated in the lotus, a gentle smile on Your face, and lovely soft eyes, large as lotus petals. Radiating a golden hue, dressed in yellow silk, You hold a golden lotus in one hand. Decorated with jewelled ornaments, Your heart overflowing with compassion, You eternally protect Your devotees.
Ekamevadvitīyam Brahma nanyad asti akincanaḥ *Satyam jnānam anantam*	Brahman is the only One, without a second. Nothing else exists. Brahman is verily Truth, eternal true Knowledge,.
Etat te vadanam saumyam locana traya bhūṣitam *Pātu naḥ sarva bhūtebhyo Kātyāyanī namostute*	O Katyayani Devi, Your calm and peaceful countenance, lovely as the moon, is further beautified by Your three divine eyes. Protect us from all fear and affliction, O Mother, we bow and surrender to You.
Girāmāhur Devīm Druhiṇa gṛhiṇīm *Āgamavido Hareḥ patnīm Padmām* *Hara sahacarīm Adri tanayām*	O Supreme Consort of Para Brahman! Those well-versed in the *Vedas* say that You are the Goddess of Speech, Saraswati Devi, wife of Brahma. Others say that You are the lotus-born Padma,

Turīyā kāpi tvam duradhigama niḥ sīma mahimā *Mahā Māyā viśvam bhramayasi Para Brahma mahiṣī* *—Saundarya Lahari: v.98. Adi Shankaracharya*	Lakshmi Devi, consort of Hari (Vishnu). Still others proclaim You to be the Daughter of the Mountain, Parvati Devi, consort Of Lord Siva. However, You are beyond these three, You are Maha Maya, of boundless glory, who revolves the wheel of the universe.
Gurur Brahmā Gurur Viṣṇu Gurur Devo Maheśwaraḥ *Gurū sākṣāt Parabrahma tasmai Śrī Gurave namaḥ*	Salutations to the glorious *Guru* who is Brahma, Vishnu and Maheshwara (Siva)—the embodiment of Supreme Brahman.
Hé Ghanaśyāmā Govindā *Nanda Mukundā Govindā* *Ghana ghana nīlā Govindā* *Tirumala vāsā Govindā* *Hṛdaya nivāsā Govindā* *Sankaṭa haraṇā Govindā* *Venkaṭa Ramaṇā Govindā*	Salutations to Lord Krishna, whose body is dark as dense clouds heavy with rain. He is known as "Govinda," "the Master of the senses," "the One who tends and loves cows." The beloved son of Nanda, who dwells in my heart, is a beautiful blue. He is also called Venkata Ramana of Tirumala, the Remover of all suffering and afflictions
Hé Iśwarī brahmāṇḍa bhāndodarī kānti dhūta japāvalī *Akhilanḍa koṭi brahmāṇḍa nāyakī koṭi koṭi yoginī gaṇa sevitā*	O Supreme Sovereign of the whole universe! All the myriad planets are contained in Your womb. Countless millions of Energies ever serve Your sacred feet.
Jaya jaya jaya Mā, Jananī Mā	Salutations to You again and again O Mother, Remover of the

Janana maraṇa bhaya hāriṇī Mā *Sundara vadanī suhāsinī Mā* *Mangala karaṇī Maheshwarī Mā* *Mahādeva mana mohinī Mā* *Māyā nāṭaka dhāriṇī Mā*	fear of birth and death. With a charming smile on Your lovely face, You bless all beings with every kind of auspiciousness. O Supreme Sovereign of all creation, You enchant and captivate Lord Siva's heart. You are the stage on which this world play is enacted.
Kshana mātra manasāra Devi pāda smarasida varigen *Ashta siddhi nava nidhi gala koduva sura kāmati nallavem* —*Telugu song.*	If you pray to Mother for even one second, and surrender at Her lotus feet with deep devotion, She will bless you with the eight supernatural powers and all the nine kinds of wealth. She will fulfill your every desire.
Kṣamā tapas kṣamā yogam *Kṣamā jnānam kṣamā sarvam*	Forgiveness is the greatest austerity. It is the *yoga* of meditation—the royal road to union with God. It is true Knowledge, it is verily everything! Forgiveness leads the seeker to the attainment of the ultimate goal—Liberation
Lokāḥ samastāḥ sukhino bhavantu	May the entire universe be happy and prosperous.
Mahādeva Śiva Śambho *Māra koṭi sundara Prabho* *Sarveśwara Karuṇākara mūrtim* *Sāma gāna priya Veda mūrtim* *Parameśwara Gangādhara mūrtim*	Salutations to the great Lord Siva, Bestower of peace on all. His beauty surpasses a million Kamadevas, (Gods of Love). The Supreme Ruler of all creation is the embodiment of compassion. He is the personification of the *Vedas*, and loves the chants of

Patita pāvanā Paśupate *Mahādeva Śiva Śambho*	the Sama Veda. The Lord of all beings, who wears the holy Ganga in His matted locks, washes away all impurity.
Mokṣa dvāra kavāṭa pāṭana karī	Divine Mother alone can open for us the doors to Liberation.
Mosahoda beda manave, manave *Inna daru olliya deya dehamelu āsi iṭtu* *Kshaṇa mātra manasāra Devi pāda smarasida varige* *Ashṭa siddhi nava nidhi gala koduva* *sura kāmadhenu nallave* *Sundareshana priya rānī Lambodara Kumāra jananī* *Harikesha priya vāsinī Nārāyaṇa sodarī* *—Kannada song*	O my mind, do not be deceived, do not be so deeply immersed in the body. Is not the Divine Mother the wish-fulfilling cow, Kamadhenu, for those who meditate on Her lotus feet? She bestows on them the eight supernatural powers, and the nine great treasures. O Mother, bless me, that from now on I may meditate for at least a moment on Your divine feet. You are the beloved Queen who reigns over the heart of the beautiful Lord Siva, the Mother of Lord Ganesha and Lord Kartikeya. You dwell in Harikesh and are the sister of Lord Vishnu.
Muktā vidruma hema nīla dhavalā	Pearl, coral gold, sapphire and pure white.
Nāma sahasra pāṭhaśca yathā carama janmani *Tathaiva viralo loke Sri Vidyācāra vedinah* *—Lalita Sahasranama Phalashruti, Shl. 75*	Only a rare one, for whom this is the last birth, will be able to recite the Thousand Names, and know how to worship the Divine Mother.
Ninne madi nammiti Amma.....Amma.... *Ninne madi nammiti nikanna mākevarammā* *Akhilāṇḍa koti brahmāṇḍa nāyakī Amma....Amma....*	O Mother, my heart trusts only You, I have no one else. O Supreme Sovereign of millions of universes!

Ninne madi nammiti Amma.....Amma....

—Telugu song.

Om Ayīm Śrīm Hrīm Saraswatī Devyai namaḥ	*Om!* Salutations to Saraswati Devi, who is embodied in the seed letters *Ayim*, *Srim* and *Hrim* as Sound, Light and Energy.
Om namaḥ Śambhave ca Mayobhave ca *Namaḥ Śankarāya ca Mayaskarāya ca* *Namaḥ Śivāya ca Śivatarāya ca* *Sriman Mahādevāya namaḥ* *—Sri Rudram: 8th Anuvāk: verses 9 to 11*	Salutations to the Source of happiness and all that is auspicious. Salutations to the Lord, who bestows earthly welfare and divine bliss. Salutations to Siva, the very embodiment of the auspiciousness, more auspicious than anything.
Om namaste astu Bhagavan Viśveśvarāya *Mahādevāya Trayambakāya Tripurāntakāya* *Trikāgni Kālāya Kālāgni Rudrāya* *Nilakanthāya Mṛtyunjayāya Sarveśvarāya* *Sadāśivāya Śriman Mahādevāya namaḥ* *—Sri Rudram: End of First Anuvāk.*	*Om!* Salutations to You, O Lord of the Universe, the Supreme Lord, the three-eyed One, Destroyer of the demon Triipurasura and the three cities. You are the fire known as *Trikagni*; You are the fierce and terrible Rudra, who consumes creation at the end of a *kalpa* (time cycle) as the *kalagni* fire. O blue-throated One who has conquered death, ruler of all, eternally auspicious, O luminous and glorious Supreme Lord, salutations once again!
Om namo Bhagavate Rudrāya	Salutations to the luminous Supreme Lord, Rudra the fierce One.
Om praṇatānāma prasīdasya Devī viśvārti hāriṇī *Trailokya vāsinām iti lokānām varadā bhavām*	*Om*! O Devi, remover of the afflictions of everyone, be pleased with us, who bow at Your lotus feet. You pervade the three worlds, so bless us all.

Om śānti śānti śāntiḥ	*Om!* Peace, peace, peace to all everywhere.
Om Śaraṇāgata dīnārta paritrāṇa parāyaṇe *Sarvasyārti hare Devī Nārāyaṇī namōstute*	O Mother, Your heart melts at the sight of suffering. It is Your nature to relieve the pain of those who take refuge in You. You remove all afflictions, O great Goddess Narayani, Lakshmi Devi, consort of Lord Vishnu, I surrender to You.
Om sarva mangala māngalye Śive sarvārtha sādhike *Śaraṇye Trayambike Devī Nārāyaṇī namostute*	O Consort of Lord Siva, O auspicious Mother with three divine eyes, You are the very essence of everything auspicious! You fulfill all desires, both material and spiritual. I take refuge at Your lotus feet Mother, for You alone are Lakshmi Devi known as Narayani. Please accept my humble salutations.
Om Śri Cakra vāsinyai namaḥ *Om Śri Lalitāmbikāyai namaḥ*	Salutations to Divine Mother Sri Lalita Devi, who resides in the *Sri Chakra*.
Om taccham yorāvṛṇī mahe *Ghātum yajnāya ghātum yajnapataye* *Daivī svastir astu naḥ svastir mānuśebhyah* *Ūrdhvam jigātu bheṣajam* *Śam no astu dvipade śam catuṣpade*	We worship and pray to the Supreme Lord for the welfare of all beings. May all miseries and shortcomings leave us forever so that we may always sing for the Lord during the holy fire ceremonies. May the Gods rain peace on us. May all medicinal herbs grow in potency so that all diseases may be cured. May all men and animals be happy and at peace.
Om Trayambakaṃ yajāmahe sugandhim puṣṭi vardhanam	I worship the three-eyed Lord Siva who is fragrant and nourishes all beings. Like a ripe cucumber ever clinging to the creeper,

Urvārukamiva bandhanāt mṛtyor mukṣīya māmṛtāt *Om āpo jyotir rasomṛtam Brahma bhūr bhuvasvar* *Om*	may I become one with You—freed from death in the attainment of Immortality. *Om!* Brahman is the waters, the immortal essence of light, earth, ether and the celestial realms.
Rāvammā Ammā Rāvammā *Rāja Rājeshwari Rāvammā* *Nirmala jīvana sudhālu tonakagā* *Shānti tīramuna mammu cherpagā* *Rāvammā Ammā Rāvammā* —*Telugu song.*	O Mother Raja Rajeshwari! Please come to us. Make our life pure and sweet as nectar. Lead us to the shores of peace. Come, come O Mother!
Rogān aśeṣān apahamsi tuṣṭām *Ruṣṭātu kāmān sakalān abhīṣṭān* *Tvām āṣṛtānām na vipannarāṇām* *Tvām āṣṛtā hyāśrayatām prayānti*	When You are pleased, O Mother, You remove all ailments and sorrow, and fulfill every desire of Your devotee, even when angry. No harm can befall those who take refuge at Your lotus feet. In fact, they themselves become the refuge for others.
Sanātanī Ārya Ārādhya Devī *Akhaṇḍa Caitanya Brahma svarūpiṇī* *Koṭi koṭi yoginī gaṇa sevitā* *Akhilāṇḍa koṭi brahmaṇḍa nāyakī* *Ādī madhyānta rahitā* *Kānti dhūta japāvalī*	O ancient, eternal, most reverently adored Devi! You are the manifestation of indivisible Supreme Consciousness. Countless millions of pure energies ever serve You as Your attendants. You have created and are the Supreme Sovereign of the whole cosmos. You are without beginning, middle or end. Your complexion rivals the delicate loveliness of the hibiscus blossom.

Sanakādi munīdrulu ni charaṇāmbuja dāsalu *Dīnulagu anadhalu ni divya kripā pātrulu* *Amma ani piluvagane kshaṇamu niluvajālavu* *Karuṇā rasa drishtito vodini cherchu konduvu* *Neevu kāni demi kaladu bhuvinī dayā sāgarī* *Neevu candamāmā vagunu velugu bratuku reyī* —*Telugu song.*	Sanaka and other great sages are servants of Your lotus feet. Even helpless orphans receive Your love and grace. If we call, "Amma!" just once, You cannot delay even for a second! With a compassionate look You will take us on Your lap. O Ocean of Compassion, what is there in this world except You? You are the moonlight that illumines this dark life.
Sarva mantrātmike sarva yantrātmike sarva tantrātmike *Sarva yogātmike sarva jnānātmike sarva sarvātmike* *Sarva rūpātmike sarva nāmātmike sarva śaktyātmike* *Sarva mokṣātmike sarva svarūpe hé Jagan Matṛke* *Pāhimām Devī namo tubhyām namo namaḥ*	O Mother of the entire Universe! You alone are embodied in all *mantras*, *yantras* and *tantras*. You are everything that exists—You are True Knowledge and Liberation, as well as the path that leads to *moksha*. You are the Supreme Divine Energy that pervades all names and forms. Protect me and lead me to Salvation, O luminous Divine Mother! I offer my humble salutations at Your lotus feet again and again
Sindūrāruṇa vigrahām trinayanām *Māṇikya maulī sphurat* *Tārānāyaka śekharām smita mukhīm* *Āpīna vakṣoruhām* *Pāṇibhyām alipūrṇa ratna caṣakam* *Raktotpalam bibhratīm* *Saumyām ratna ghaṭastha rakta caraṇām*	O Mother with three divine eyes, I meditate upon Your radiant red form. You who, sweetly smiling, have adorned the crescent moon like a jewel in Your crown of rubies. Your full-figured beauty is enhanced by Your hands—one of which holds a crimson lotus, and the other, a jewel-encrusted bowl thronged by bees. I visualize Your peaceful face and painted feet, red upon a golden footrest inlaid with precious gems.

Dhyāyet Parām Ambikām
—Dhyāna śloka: Śri Lalitā Sahasranāma.

Śivaḥ Śaktyā yukto yadi bhavati śaktaḥ prabhavitum *Na ca Devam Devo na khalu kuśalaḥ spanditumapi* *Atas tvāmārādhyām Hari Hara Virincādibhir api* *Praṇantu stotum kathamakṛta punyaḥ prabhavati* *—Saundarya Lahari v.1 Ādi Shankarāchārya*	Siva, the Lord of Gods, has no expansion or power unless He is connected with Shakti. Without Her, He is incapable of any movement whatsoever. Therefore who except those with great merits accumulated in past births can adore and sing Your praises, O Mother Divine? Even the great Gods Brahma, Vishnu and Siva worship You.
Śivāyai namaḥ *Śiva Śaktyaikya rūpiṇyai namaḥ*	Salutations to the consort of Siva. Salutations to the One who is of the indivisible, eternally united form of Siva and Shakti.
Sṛṣti kartrī Brahma rūpā Goptrī Govinda rūpiṇī *Samhāriṇī Rudra rūpā Tirodhāna karīśwarī*	O Mother, when You create the universe, You are Brahma. When You nourish and sustain it, You are Govinda, incarnation of Lord Vishnu. At the time of dissolution, when You reabsorb all creation into Yourself, You are Rudra, the fierce form of Siva.
Sudhā samudrāntara hṛdayan *Maṇidwīpa samrūḍha bilvāṭavi madhya* *Kalpadruma kalpa kādamba Kāntāra vāsa priye* *Kṛtti vāsa priye Sarvaloka priye* *Sādarārabdha sangīta sambhāvanā sambhramā lola*	O beautiful and luminous Goddess, You dwell in the heart of Manidwipa, the jeweled isle, which is surrounded by the ocean of nectar, in the midst of flourishing forests of *bilva*, *kadamba* and wish-fulfilling trees. O Beloved of Siva, the Lord who wears skins, You are the Beloved of the whole world. We praise the Goddess who is worshipped as song that rises as sound from the

Nīpasragā baddha cūli sanā dhatrike sānumat putrike *Viśva digmaṇḍala vyāpi māṇikya tejaḥ sphurat* *Devī Vāmādibhiḥ śaktibhiḥ sevite* *Dhātṛ Lakṣmyādi śaktyaṣṭakai samyute* *Mahākavi Kālidāsa.*	base of the throat. Your hair is fastened together with strings of *nipa* blossoms. Brilliant rays of light blaze from Your jeweled anklets and illumine all the universes. You are eternally adored and served by Vama and other *shaktis*, including the eight forms of Lakshmi Devi.
Sudhā sindhor madhye sura viṭapi vāṭī parivṛte *Maṇidwīpe nīpopavana vati cintāmaṇi gṛhe* *Śivākāre mance Parama Śiva paryanka nilayām* *Bhajanti tvām dhanyāḥ, katicana Cidānanda laharīm* *—Saundarya Laharī: v.8. Ādi Śankarācharya*	Blessed indeed are the few who adore You, O Supreme Wave of Divine Bliss and Splendor! Siva, the supremely Auspicious One, forms the triangular couch on which You recline in the chamber of *chintāmani*, wish-fulfilling gems. You are there amidst a pleasure garden of *nīpa*, or *kadamba* trees, on the jeweled isle Maṇidwīpa, in the Ambrosial Ocean, Sudha Sindhu, fringed by rows of wish-bestowing trees
Yā Devī sarva bhūteṣu matṛ rūpeṇa samsthitā *Namas tasyai namas tasyai namas tasyai namo namaḥ* *Yā Devī sarva bhūteṣu śakti rūpeṇa samsthitā* *Namas tasyai namas tasyai namas tasyai namo namaḥ* *Yā Devī sarva bhūteṣu dayā rūpeṇa samsthitā* *Namas tasyai namas tasyai namas tasyai namo namaḥ*	Salutations again and again to the Divine Mother who resides eternally in all beings in the form of Supreme Energy. She alone lives in all beings as energy, compassion, forgiveness, class and Consciousness. We bow again and again in loving adoration at the lotus feet of that radiant Devi who is the Supreme Sovereign of all the countless universes, and who removes all obstacles from the path of Her devotees.

Yā Devī sarva bhūteṣu kṣamā rūpeṇa samsthitā
Namas tasyai namas tasyai namas tasyai namo namaḥ
Yā Devī sarva bhūteṣu jāti rūpeṇa samsthitā
Namas tasyai namas tasyai namas tasyai namo namaḥmaḥ
Ya Devi sarva bhūteṣu Cetanyetabhidhīyate
Namas tasyai namas tasyai namas tasyai namo namaḥ
Sarva bādhā praśamanīm trailokyam Cākhilāṇḍeśwarīm
Namas tasyai namas tasyai namas tasyai namo namaḥ

Yeshteshtu nodidaru sāladammā
Ishtārdha gala kuduva drishtānta rahitayā
Yeshteshtu pogādidaru sāladammā
Yeshteshtu nodidaru yeshteshtu pādidaru
yeshteshtu pogādidaru sāladammā
Nishtayol bhajisuvā sishta janarigalla
Parama nishtayola bhajisuvā sishta janārigalla
Drishti gochara satata srishtiyola kānadā
Ashtaishvarya galā drishtike hari suvā

There is no place without You. No matter how many times I look at You, or whenever or wherever I look at You, it is not enough. No matter how much I sing about You or praise You, it is not enough! You are always visible to those good and disciplined people who pray to You with supreme faith and deep devotion. O Meenakshi Devi, Supreme ruler of all, Sovereign Ruler and Daughter of Vijaya Nagari, the city of victory, You bless Your devotees with the eight kinds of wealth, *bhukti*, and

Vijaya nagarī Meenākshi sutā Swāminiyā	also with that which is not visible in this creation, the highest state of *mukti*, Liberation.
Yogaḥ citta vṛtti nirodhaḥ	*Yoga* means control of the modifications of the mind, i.e., controlling thoughts.